Gender and Physical Education

Gender and Physical Education offers a critical and comprehensive commentary on issues relating to gender in the context of physical education in schools and in teacher training. The book challenges our understandings of gender, equity and identity in physical education, establishing a conceptual and historical foundation for the issue, as well as presenting a wealth of original research material.

The book delivers a critical analysis of the progress and shortcomings of contemporary policies and practice in physical education as they relate to gender, and reflects on the similarities and differences between developments in the UK, US and Australia. It also offers new frameworks for research, policy and practice with a view to advancing gender equity, and addresses the roles that teachers, educators and policy-makers can play in challenging existing inequalities.

Gender and Physical Education is an important text for students and lecturers in education, teacher educators and providers of continuing professional development in physical education, and anybody concerned with gender issues in education, physical education or sport.

Dawn Penney is Senior Research Fellow at the Department of Physical Education, Sports Science and Recreation Management at the University of Loughborough. She is co-author of *Politics, Policy and Practice in Physical Education* (also published by Routledge).

Gender and Physical Education

Contemporary issues and
future directions

Edited by Dawn Penney

London and New York

First published 2002 by Routledge
11 New Fetter Lane, London EC4P 3EE

Simultaneously published in the USA and Canada
by Routledge
29 West 35th Street, New York, NY 10001

Routledge is an imprint of the Taylor & Francis Group

Typeset in Times by Steven Gardiner Ltd, Cambridge
Printed and bound in Great Britain by Biddles Ltd,
Guildford and King's Lynn

British Library Cataloguing in Publication Data
A catalogue record for this book is available from the British Library

Library of Congress Cataloging in Publication Data
Gender and physical education: contemporary issues and future
directions / edited by Dawn Penney.
     p.   cm.
   Includes bibliographical references and index.
   1. Physical education and training – Social aspects. 2. Sexism in
   education. 3. Gender identity in education. I. Penney, Dawn, 1966–
   GV342.27 .G46 2002
   613.7'071 – dc21   2001048673

ISBN 0-415-23576-6 (pbk)
ISBN 0-415-23575-8 (hbk)

Contents

vi *Contents*

Contributors

Julie Bedward is a qualitative researcher who has conducted several major studies as a Research Fellow at the University of Birmingham since 1987. She is currently working on a number of projects in the School of Education, including a study of gender differences in learning.

Tansin Benn is a Senior Lecturer at the University of Birmingham. She is head of the Physical Education, Sports Studies and Dance Department. Her teaching and research interests cross arts, sport and teaching boundaries.

David Brown was formerly a teacher of physical education and French. David then became a lecturer in physical education with the Department of Physical Education, Sports Science and Recreation Management of Loughborough University. He is currently a lecturer in the School of Postgraduate Medicine and Health Sciences in the Department of Exercise and Sports Sciences at Exeter University.

Kim Bush is a doctoral candidate in sport pedagogy at Ohio State University. She is a former collegiate field hockey player and coach. Her research interests relate to feminist approaches to understanding urban adolescent girls and empowering them in relation to issues surrounding physical activity, sport and their bodies.

Gill Clarke is a Senior Lecturer in physical education and autobiographical studies in the Research and Graduate School of Education at the University of Southampton. Gill is also deputy director of the Centre for Biography and Education at the University of Southampton. Gill has published widely on issues around sexuality, physical education and sport.

John Evans is Professor of Physical Education in the Department of Physical Education, Sports Science and Recreation Management at Loughborough University. He is author of *Teaching in Transition: the Challenge of Mixed Ability Grouping* and editor of *PE, Sport and Schooling: Studies in the Sociology of PE*; *Teachers, Teaching and Control*; and *Equality, Education and Physical Education* (all by Falmer Press). John is editor of the international journal, *Sport Education and Society*. His research interests centre on the study of policy, teaching and equity issues in the secondary school curriculum.

Margaret Gehring is a faculty member at Ohio Weslyean College and a doctoral candidate in sport pedagogy at Ohio State University. She is a former collegiate cross country runner and coach. Her research interests are in using feminist perspectives to study female coaches in American collegiate ranks.

Jo Harris is currently Director of the Physical Education teacher education programmes at Loughborough University, where she also contributes to masters degree programmes in physical education. Jo taught for twelve years in state secondary schools and has twelve years' experience of teacher education. Jo gained her PhD in 1997 and has published articles in academic and professional journals, produced numerous teaching resources and directed many in-service training courses for both primary and secondary school teachers. Jo has a particular interest in physical education's contribution to health and associated issues relating to personal and social education, citizenship, inclusion and lifelong learning.

David Kirk joined Loughborough University in November 1998. He is currently Professor of Physical Education and Sport. His research interests include young people in sport, curriculum change in physical education, the body, schooling and culture, and situated learning in physical education and sport. His most recent book is *Schooling Bodies*, published in 1998 by Leicester University Press.

Doune Macdonald is a Reader in the School of Human Movement Studies, the University of Queensland. She coordinates the health and physical education teacher education programme and her current research interests include HPE curriculum construction and change, teachers' work, and young people and physical activity.

Mary O'Sullivan is an Associate Dean in the College of Education at Ohio State University. Her research interests are in teaching and teacher education reform. She teaches graduate classes in supervision, educational reform, curriculum and instruction in secondary physical education and an undergraduate class in social issues in physical education and sport. She is a former collegiate field hockey player and likes to travel, read and play golf.

Dawn Penney is a Senior Research Fellow at the Department of Physical Education, Sports Science and Recreation Management at Loughborough University. Dawn has previously held research positions at the University of Southampton, the University of Queensland and De Montfort University, and is the reviews editor for *Sport, Education and Society*. Since 1990 Dawn has been researching contemporary policy and curriculum developments in physical education and has published widely in academic and professional journals. She is co-author with John Evans of *Politics, Policy and Practice in Physical Education* (1999, E&FN Spon, an imprint of Routledge).

Emma Rich graduated from the Department of Physical Education, Sports Science and Recreation Management at Loughborough University with a first class Honours in Recreation Management in 1998. She was awarded a research scholarship at Loughborough where she is investigating the social (re)construction of gender in teaching physical education. Emma is also a member of Women in Sport Regional Advisory committee for the Sports Council. Emma is now a lecturer in Gender, Identity, Health and Physical Education in the Department of Physical Education, Sports Science and Recreation Management, Loughborough University.

Anne Williams is Professor and Head of the School of Education at King Alfred's College Winchester and Honorary Senior Lecturer at the University of Birmingham. Her research interests include teacher education and physical education. She has published widely on primary school physical education, gender issues in physical education and on teacher education.

Jan Wright is an Associate Professor and Research Director of the Graduate School of Education, University of Wollongong. She has taught in the areas of curriculum and pedagogy and socio-cultural perspectives of physical education to undergraduates for the last twenty years. She played a key role in the development of the new NSW Senior Syllabus in Personal Development, Health and Physical Education (PDHPE) and has been employed by the NSW Dept of Education and Training to provide professional development on the socio-cultural perspective that underpins this syllabus. Jan has published widely on gender and physical education and is co-author of *Becoming a Physical Education Teacher* (Addison-Wesley, 2000) with Richard Tinning, Doune Macdonald and Chris Hickey.

Preface

Why a book focusing upon gender and physical education? Gender has not been the major focus of my research or writing on contemporary physical education. I certainly do not consider myself an expert on gender issues and nor do I have the background of years of engagement with literature focusing upon issues of gender, sexuality and identity in education, physical education and sport that others (including contributors to this collection) can claim. In embarking upon this project, I was therefore acutely aware that my qualification to lead it could be questioned. However, I undertook the project in the hope that with the support and encouragement of colleagues, we could help to extend the accessibility of, and engagement with, literature and research focusing on gender. This book confirms (if we need any confirmation) that all of us, not only an 'expert few', need to be extending our understandings of the issues and pursuing ways in which we can better respond to them in policies and in practice in physical education teaching and teacher education.

The process of editing this collection and contributing to several chapters has greatly advanced my own understanding of gender and equity in physical education and I am therefore very grateful to have had the opportunity to work with the talented and remarkably understanding colleagues who are the contributors. It has been an opportunity that has enabled me to bring to the fore issues that I have often been aware have been present in my research and data, but that have remained marginal in my writing. It has been a challenging and rewarding experience, demanding that I not only ask new questions of data, but also of myself, my own experiences and attitudes. I hope that those reading the book will be encouraged to be similarly reflective and be inspired to continue to pursue the issues in their daily lives.

In producing the book I have also become aware of the limitations of any single text, and of the scope of current research in physical education. We certainly do not claim to have filled all the gaps in research or writing on gender, equity and identity in physical education. Rather, the hope has to be that we have highlighted the need for sustained and extended research and commentary on those issues. There is much that each of us can do individually, but also much to be achieved collectively. I hope that readers will see the benefits of bringing together people from different backgrounds, with knowledge of different literature, to speak on issues of shared interest and concern. The interchanges which I have had with the authors and which I have tried to facilitate between them, have demonstrated that by working together we can challenge each other in very positive and productive ways. My thanks therefore go to all involved in the production of the book and in the various research projects upon which I and the other contributors have drawn.

Part I
Setting the agenda

1 Introduction

John Evans and Dawn Penney

This chapter outlines our rationale for a focus upon gender and equity in contemporary physical education and draws attention to the breadth and complexity of the issues that this text seeks to address. It considers why professionals in all walks of physical education should be concerned with gender issues at the beginning of the twenty-first century, a period of rapidly changing lifestyles, life chances and expectations. We draw attention to long-standing inequities in the policies and practices of physical education in schools, and address the roles that teachers, teacher educators and researchers can play in either reinforcing or challenging sexism and inequity in physical education and sport.

Why do we need a gender agenda?

Gender has long been 'an issue' for physical educationalists in schools and in initial teacher education in the UK and elsewhere. As David Kirk illustrates in chapter 3, both as a school subject and as a 'profession', historically physical education in the UK has developed in explicitly gendered ways. While we cannot change that history, nor simply judge it comparatively against the standards of propriety and expectation of our now so-called (post) 'modern' world, neither can we overlook its contemporary relevance for the practices and policies of education and physical education. Several of the contributions within this collection show that physical educationalists have seemed slow to respond to debate and research that has highlighted sexism and sex differentiation in physical education and to confront inequitable gender relations in schools and the subject, sometimes despite their stated best intentions to entertain curriculum change. Why is this so? Why has there been so little surface level, let alone deep structural, change? The paucity of 'gender related' innovation evident in physical education over the last twenty years may have had as much, if not more, to do with the absence of a positive encouragement and steer on gender matters from central governments in the UK as any shortfall in the attitudes and interests of physical educationalists in schools and training institutions. The result is that many schools in the UK today entertain practices comparable to those that would have featured in physical education many decades ago. A tad more 'health related exercise' perhaps, a few more women 'heads of PE', but many single sex departments, dominated by male heads of PE, offering a thoroughly unreconstructed sex differentiated curriculum and pedagogy of sport and physical education. Current advertisements for jobs for teachers of boys', or alternatively girls' physical education are testimony to the fact that in many schools, organisational concerns continue to co-mingle with deep-seated stereotypical, ideological and cultural values to produce sex-differentiated curricula and single sex grouping, particularly in games. The experiences that girls and boys receive in physical education are likely to reinforce stereotypical images, attitudes and behaviours relating, amongst other things, to how they should feel about their own and other's bodies, who can legitimately participate in what physical activities, when and why.

Yet members of the physical education profession still frequently claim a commitment to ensuring that there is a place in physical education curriculum for *all* children irrespective of background; a place that they value and enjoy, not one in which they feel uncomfortable, unwelcome and marginalised. As we will see in the chapters that follow, we still have a long way to go in order to achieve these ideals – in arenas of policy making nationally, in schools and in training institutions. However, this book aims to go beyond critique. It seeks to not only demonstrate an undeniable need for a 'gender agenda' in contemporary policy, curriculum development and everyday pedagogical practice in physical education, but also to inform the development of that agenda and in particular, extend it beyond what we regard as longstanding and now outdated 'discursive boundaries', ways of thinking and acting in physical education and sport. We emphasise that what is needed in physical education is not *a* gender agenda but gender *agendas* – that engage with social and cultural diversity, are capable of providing for the needs of individual girls and individual boys, and that celebrate individuality. The contributions in this collection demonstrate the difficulties and challenges that arise in seeking to establish these agendas in policy and practice in physical education, but importantly, also point to the potential to do just that. Readers will see that there are pressures in contemporary society, often reflected in Government policies on education, that press the profession to maintain, rather than eradicate, inequities in the status quo. While acknowledging the desire for stability and the ongoing resistance from many sources to discourses and practices that seriously challenge inequities, we also celebrate the progress that has been made towards more equitable, innovative and inclusive practices in sport and physical education. It is talk of 'the possible' and evidence of progress and ideas for further advances that will enthuse and inspire yet more widespread innovative action. In these respects we highlight the value in looking beyond national boundaries and gaining insights and ideas from developments in other countries, where there may be greater support for and opportunities to develop 'new agendas' in and for physical education.

We are all players in this gender game

There are dangers inherent in talking abstractly about the 'subject' and 'the profession'. It incorrectly suggests that Physical Education is a unified and homogenous phenomenon, when it patently is not; and when understanding its diversity of cultures, of knowledge, values attitudes and practices needs to be acknowledged as a precursor to knowing better how it may change. It may also lead us to feel that we are somehow positioned outside of, or apart from, its 'discursive regimes'; its stereotypes, values, assumptions, ways of thinking and acting about its subject matter and those who are touched by it. The problems of sexism and inequity in physical education, and equally, the potential to address them, are easy to identify as someone else's concern. Thus, part of our emphasis here is to stress the need for each of us to position ourselves firmly within, rather than as somehow removed from, the gendered discourses of physical education. This may help us assess more adequately how, individually, departmentally and institutionally, we may be implicated in processes of social reproduction or change. The chapters that follow document the ways in which pupils, student teachers, teachers, teacher trainers, policy makers, politicians and researchers all variously play an active part in the production, reproduction and potential transformation of these discourses. Many readers will identify with one or more of these identities. In accepting those identities we may be able to more readily accept some of the roles and responsibilities that are inherent in them. In several chapters we also reflect on the power-relations in education and physical education. Once again, the temptation is to point to the constraints that we variously feel inhibit our attempts to 'do things differently'. But it must be acknowledged that a better understanding of the nature of these constraints is a precursor to moving beyond them. There is a critical need to counterbalance talk of constraint and restriction with that of opportunity, and to therefore acknowledge that education and physical education remain arenas in which we *are powerfully positioned* to influence children's and young people's attitudes, experiences and behaviours, for the better or worse.

None of this is neutral: we have an agenda

To talk in terms of 'better or worse' directs us to a further important characteristic of the work of all individuals' variously engaged in physical education; namely that it is inevitably, inescapably value laden and never 'interest free'. For our own part, we make no apologies for vigorously taking sides against those forms of oppression, including racism, sexism, homophobia and elitism, that debilitate, damage and ruin people's lives, alienating them not only from their own and other's bodies but from involvement in physical activity and sport. Elsewhere we have detailed the contested nature of physical education in schools, the struggles within and beyond the profession to determine how the subject should be defined, what form it should take, and what and whose values it should promote (see for example Evans and Penney, 1995; Penney and Evans, 1999). Throughout this book we will see further evidence of such contestation, highlighting that we cannot and should not expect agreement upon these issues, and that for those who do choose to challenge inequities in education, it will not be a comfortable ride. We all have particular visions of what the subject, the pupils or students that we may be engaged with, are and ought to be. We can, therefore, safely anticipate diversity in opinions about the ways in which (particular) gender identities can and should be expressed in physical education. Exploring that diversity may prompt us to either position, or potentially, *re*position ourselves in the debates and practices surrounding the issues of gender and physical education. Acknowledging that no one can claim value neutrality on this issue may be a first but critical step towards understanding it better. Identifying our position(s) and being honest about our agendas may take time and be uncomfortable. It is therefore appropriate at this point that we shed light on the personal agendas and values that have shaped our thinking on these issues, and for us to position ourselves in relation to the debates that follow.

'Futures have to be made, they do not just happen' (Young, 1998: 79). We have already alluded to the need for creativity and innovation in teaching and teacher training, that goes beyond the PE classroom and schools and relates fundamentally to the communities they serve. As Young (1998) has stated 'curriculum debates, implicitly or explicitly, are always debates about alternative views of society and its future' (ibid.: 9). Perhaps all too rarely do curriculum debates extend to these levels. Instead they remain conveniently confined to the detail and nuances of the curriculum, either overlooking or deliberately ignoring the implications of those intricacies in relation to whether they will serve 'a future society that we can endorse or a past society that we want to change' (ibid.: 21).

'In changing times *is it* time for change?' (Penney, 1999, our emphasis). Fashions change in social and educational theory with all the regularity of a manikin's poise and when they do it is all too easy to forget how the ideas, understandings and agendas of the 'old' have helped, and can help fashion the thinking and practices of the 'new'. Rarely are discursive developments, discrete, unrelated or ideologically pure. Fifteen years ago we may have approached the introduction to this book with the interests of 'equal opportunities' uppermost in mind. The concepts and language of Marxism and of interpretative sociology may usefully have shaped our thinking on gender and physical education. The former would have directed our attention to structural issues, in particular, to the relationships between education and the economy and how social class values, interests and hierarchies are reflected in schooling and physical education (Evans, 1984; 1986). Our attention may have centred on the organisation of schooling, on processes of selection, differentiation and socialisation (usually finding in favour of middle class, white, male values) and the structuring of work and leisure opportunities in and outside schools. The latter, would have drawn our attention to the processes of schooling. In particular, to the ways in which meanings and values are attributed to physical and social objects of the social world and how structures of convention, action and identity are created and reproduced in schooling and physical education. Together, these perspectives, especially when later integrated with the more liberating perspectives of feminism forced us to ask; who gets access to what forms of schooling, curriculum, knowledge, experience and opportunity in education and physical education? Whose values and interests are benefited and privileged in this process, and why? Before the advent of rampant neo-liberalism in the UK (reflected most obviously in the Governments of the Thatcher years), a variety of policy legislation in the UK and elsewhere broadly reflected these democratic concerns (Wright, 1999).

Although there were limits to the agendas of theoretical perspectives of this kind, they did help make more complex our view of schooling and physical education. And, to a degree, they pressed us to avoid thinking in crude generalisations about 'children', 'pupils', 'men', women', 'masculinity' and 'femininity' in education and physical education. They forced us to consider that 'individuals' and social groups may be positioned differently in the social order by virtue of their relationship to the means of production and the benefits (or otherwise) derived from their social class position as well as their culture, gender, ethnicity and physical ability. They illustrated that these factors co-mingle in education to belie crude claims about the way in which boys and girls, men and women differently experience the opportunities putatively available to them in education, physical education and wider society. They prompted acknowledgement that categories of identity, for example, of masculinity and femininity, are social realities that not only change historically but also are experienced differently according to specific economic, ideological, political and social structures (Hargreaves, 1994; Colwell, 1999). Sadly, the merits of this way of thinking all too rarely found expression either in research on physical education, or in the practices of teachers in physical education and sport in schools.

This remains the case today. For example, it is not uncommon to hear the over-generalised and undifferentiated wisdom, peddled by proponents of health in physical education, that 'individuals' should exercise for thirty (or so) minutes a day if cardiovascular health is to be achieved. Girls and women, of different class, culture and ethnicity, are likely to receive this news rather differently. The single woman raising a child and the person engaged in physical labour for the majority of their out-of-school waking hours, is not likely to treat this information in the same way as the child of middle-class parents enjoying time and opportunity to exercise at will. Neither are the concomitant feelings of inadequacy, guilt and pathology likely to be evenly shared. To talk of girls' or boys' interests in physical education as if each is a homogenous cultural category is, therefore, as unhelpful to the cause of theoretical progress in physical education as it is to the task of curriculum development in schools. Ethnicity, culture, ability and social class codetermine how an individual is likely to receive and respond to the experiences of physical education. As we emphasise in the following chapter, that the focus of this text is on 'gender issues' should not then lead us to either reduce the complexity of identity to sexism or gender alone, or fail to explore the interaction of these elements with the range of other identities that prevail on the sociocultural terrain. The historical paucity of research on ethnicity and disability in physical education, for example, is now matched only by the more contemporary deafening silence on social class as an 'object' of study and analysis in education and physical education. We share Skeggs' (1997) view that a retreat from class analyses whether in the corridors of academia, in the corridors of power or in schools and classrooms is distinctly disturbing, and we add, unhelpful to social progress in education and physical education. As Skeggs points out, 'retreatists' either ignore class or argue that it is an increasingly redundant issue. There have been plenty of politicians adopting this blinkered stance in recent years. She reminds us that when

> a retreat is being mounted we need to ask whose experiences are being silenced, whose lives are being ignored and whose lives are considered worthy of study . . . to ignore or make a class invisible is to abdicate responsibility (through privilege) from the effects it produces. To think that class does not matter is only a prerogative of those unaffected by the deprivations and exclusions it produces. Making class invisible represents a historical stage in which the identity of the middle classes is assumed.
>
> (Skeggs, 1997: 7)

It helps us avoid difficult and unpalatable questions relating to the material consequences of capitalism and inequalities in wealth and opportunity in education and wider society. It also reminds us that issues of class, ethnicity, disability, sexuality and gender have to be considered both independently and together, if we are to begin to appreciate the decisions and actions of teachers and pupils in education and physical education. The performance and educational achievements of girls and boys, of all classes, cultures and abilities in the curriculum should, then, occupy the attention of teachers, parents and politicians alike.

A decade ago educational researchers were revealing the social inequalities in both access to and success in physical education in schools. The curriculum in schools and furthermore, training institutions, was clearly gender differentiated. Boys and girls experienced a differentiated curriculum – sometimes rationalised with the powerful rhetorical logic of 'different but equal' – boys and girls having access to different forms of educational experience. Boys were shown to also enjoy more opportunities to engage in physical recreation, particularly out of school hours. It took researchers to point out that the games encouraged for girls – netball, hockey and dance not only carried less prestige than soccer, rugby and cricket but were also less readily pursued into adult life. A host of practices which seemed trivial on the surface, from the habit of calling girls and only girls by their first names, to the teasing remarks which teachers sometimes directed at their female pupils, transmitted messages concerning the appropriateness of gender as a differentiating principle. These contributed to the conceptions that pupils hold of masculinity and femininity and their place and their position in different forms of physical education, sport and recreation.

The task of generating and sustaining interest in seriously addressing these practices and their inherent inequities has been and remains far from easy. Twenty years of a Conservative government in the UK did very little to help teachers of physical education address these concerns. At a time when the profession was just beginning to think creatively about the curriculum content and teaching of physical education, a series of retrogressive educational policies brought them to a halt. As Penney discusses further in chapter 7, the educational agenda shifted perversely from issues of social inclusion and equity to how to manage the implementation of a profoundly conservative and retrospective national curriculum, including one for physical education. All attempts to embed a firm commitment to equal opportunities in the teaching of physical education via the new 'official texts' were progressively and often very obviously resisted by government ministers.

A decade on and one could be forgiven for presuming that the issue of 'access' no longer has relevance in discussions of the curriculum of physical education, particularly as the issue of social inclusion has, with the return in 1997 of a New Labour government, returned to the foreground of educational policy developments. However, we need to keep in mind that while the obvious common feature of the experience of migrants to the UK has been the prejudice that they have encountered during successive policies of assimilation and multiculturalism, they constitute an extraordinarily diverse set of communities. Gender differences in responses to school, and physical education within it, have been a salient feature amongst these groups and the under-use and under-representation of 'their' physical cultures in school physical education and sport, and in higher education, remains evident (Davies and Evans, 2001).

Meanwhile the position of women and men in Britain's mainstream cultures has shifted on a number of fronts (Davies and Evans, 2001). Statistics are now showing that girls are outperforming boys in just about every aspect of the curriculum at all levels (from schools to university), and that boys are badly underachieving in schools and have real problems ahead of them in coming to terms with the demands of a post-modern age. As we emphasise in the following chapter, such statistics and generalisations continue to hide important differences within the gender groups. But at the same time, differences between men and women remain very much an issue, not least because for all their achievements at school and university, many women continue to face real barriers in translating those achievements into leisure and work opportunities that are comparable with those enjoyed by their male counterparts. In physical education specifically, boys and girls may now enjoy equal access, albeit to a differentiated curricular, but not to extra curricular sport and physical education. As later chapters vividly illustrate, it is folly to assume that the goal of providing equal opportunities, either to the same range of curricular experiences or to a range diverse enough to capture the range of interests that children bring to school, has been achieved. Physical education still has some way to go before it can claim to be providing the skills, aptitudes and motivations for all pupils to enjoy involvement in physical recreation as a form of leisure. Furthermore, it still ensures that, having engaged with the subject, the majority of boys and girls will leave schools with their (perhaps stereotypical and prejudicial) conceptions of femininity and masculinity and their application in contexts of physical activity and sport, essentially intact and unchallenged. In the processes of schooling they will have learnt that for their particular gender there are appropriate forms of employment and leisure, and appropriate attitudes towards their own and others' bodies and sexuality in relation to physical activity and health.

Any serious consideration of the relationship between gender and education is, therefore, likely to generate questions that go to the heart of our teaching and curriculum in physical education. These concern how the curriculum is organised and selected; how teachers teach, how pupils are grouped for teaching purposes, how they are evaluated and assessed; how teacher and pupils are defined as competent or otherwise by their peers and how aims are formulated and operationalised in practice. Given that each or all of these questions may touch on deep-seated interests and identities of physical education teachers it is highly unlikely that answers will be easily or quickly obtained. Answers in terms of curricular and pedagogical reform are certainly not simply to be seen as a matter of implementing either mixed sex or single sex grouping, or of giving girls football, or boys netball and lacrosse. The problems of formulating and effecting curriculum change in physical education as in other areas of the school curriculum are both varied and substantial. There is a clear need for further investigations into the processes and challenges of curriculum reform and in particular, investigations which focus upon the way in which pupils of different class, culture, ethnicity, ability and sexuality differently relate to and experience various forms of physical activity. Issues of identity, as well as those of access and opportunity, will need to be forced to the fore in all this. Investigations will need to be as appreciative of the perspectives and problems of both teachers and pupils as of the social, organisational and political contexts in which they are located. Innovation uninformed by this form of enquiry may be as insubstantial as it is short lived.

Progressing our agenda

The following chapter pursues at a conceptual level the implications of the changes in society, youth culture, sporting cultures, body cultures and gender relations in all of these, for our work as researchers, policymakers, teachers and teacher trainers in physical education. These concepts are necessary if we are to advance upon what we have identified as notably limited progress in recent years in the UK in extending understandings of gender equity and in developing policies and practices that express and promote understandings that will pose serious challenges to established practices in physical education and sport at all levels.

A chapter by David Kirk then completes the first part of the text. Kirk's historical perspective provides a crucial reference point for our readings of debates about contemporary and possible future developments in physical education, particularly where gender issues are concerned. The strength and depth of influence of the historical foundations of the subject and the profession in contemporary times is vividly apparent in the chapters that comprise the second and third parts of the book.

In part 2, our concern has been to draw upon contemporary research that is actively seeking to 'extend gender agendas' within physical education teaching and teacher education. The chapters by Clarke, Benn, and Brown and Rich each reflect important endeavours to adopt and further extend existing conceptualisations of gender in contexts of physical education, and in so doing, challenge and advance established policies and practices. These chapters highlight the need, undoubted difficulties, but also potential rewards of policies and practices in physical education being shaped by under-standings of gender that embrace the inter-relationships between various dimensions of equity and seek to provide for the multiple identities that children and their teachers bring to school.

Part 3 reports research that has specifically explored the representation and expression of gender issues in contemporary policy and practice in physical education in England. Penney, Harris, and Williams and Bedward variously present data that tells us much about the work yet to be done if physical education in schools is to be a forum in which the pursuit of gender equity is to go beyond conceptually limited, sporadic and sometimes tokenistic gestures. In many respects these chapters do not celebrate the progress that we may have hoped would have been forthcoming with the development of a national curriculum in England and Wales. However, that should not deflect our attention from some of the crucial messages that they provide for prospective future developments in policy and practice. Both explicitly and implicitly their analyses say much about what could be done better and differently where gender equity is concerned in physical education.

The book ends with a section that seeks to locate the UK-focused initiatives and developments within an international context, and draw researchers and teacher educators from overseas into the debates about the 'state of play', progress and remaining shortcomings in relation to gender equity in physical education. The chapters by O'Sullivan, Bush and Gehring, and Wright, point to there being both important similarities in experiences relating to the pursuit of gender equity in physical education across international boundaries, but also diversity and differences in those experiences. Both characteristics are important in terms of what we can all learn from each other in looking to progress thinking and practices in our respective countries.

The future and in particular, future research concerned with gender equity in physical education, is the focus of Macdonald's concluding chapter. Macdonald's critical reflection on the work that has preceded provides us with substantive and conceptual challenges to take forward in development of research, policy and practice in physical education settings.

These are exciting and also challenging times for physical educationalists. Never before has the subject been so prominent in the public eye, as issues of health, sport performance and physical literacy continue to occupy the attention of politicians and parents alike. If nothing else we hope that this book will convince readers that unless issues of identity, gender, equity and sexuality are placed centre stage in all forthcoming debates, then we can have little hope that the best interests of all young people in physical education and sport will be well served. A reading of this modest text may help press the profession towards the pursuit of more worthy progressive educational ideals.

References

Colwell, S. (1999) Feminism and figurational sociology: contributions to understandings of sport, physical education and sex/gender, *European Physical Education Review* 5(3): 219–41.

Davies, B. and Evans, J. (2001) Changing cultures and schools in England and Wales, in J. Cairns, D. Lawton and R. Gardner (eds) *World Handbook of Education 2001: Values, Culture and Education*, London: Kegan Paul, pp. 190–206.

Evans, J. (1984) Muscle, sweat and showers. Girls' conceptions of physical education and sport: a challenge for research and curriculum reform, *European Physical Education Review* 7(1): 12–19.

Evans, J. (1986) Introduction: personal troubles and public issues. Studies in the sociology of physical education, in J. Evans (ed.) *Physical Education, Sport and Schooling. Studies in the Sociology of Physical Education*, London: Falmer Press.

Evans, J. and Penney, D. (1995) The politics of pedagogy: making a National Curriculum physical education. *Journal of Education Policy* 10(1): 27–44.

Evans, J., Davies, B. and Penney, D. (1994) Whatever happened to the subject and the State in policy research in education?, *Discourse: Studies in the Cultural Politics of Education* 14(2): 57–64.

Hargreaves, J. (1994) *Sporting Females: Critical Issues in the History and Sociology of Women's Sport*, London: Routledge.

Penney, D. (1999) Physical education: in changing times is it time for a change?, *British Journal of Physical Education* 30(4): 4–6.

Penney, D. and Evans, J. (1999) *Politics, Policy and Practice in Physical Education*, London: Routledge.

Skeggs, B. (1997) *Formations of Class and Gender*, London: Sage.

Wright, J. (1999) Changing gendered practices in physical education: working with teachers, *European Physical Education Review* 5(3): 181–99.

Young, M.F.D. (1998) *The Curriculum of The Future: From The 'New Sociology of Education' to a Critical Theory of Learning*, London: Falmer Press.

2 Talking gender

Dawn Penney and John Evans

Introduction

In the previous chapter we discussed a number of issues that point towards the conceptual underpinnings of the analyses that we and others present in this book. In this chapter we focus explicitly on conceptual matters. This provides an important foundation for reading the chapters that follow. In the first part of the chapter we direct attention to concepts that are central to debates about and understandings of 'gender issues' and 'gender equity' in physical education. We then shift the focus to concepts that in our view enable a more complete and better understanding of the representation, expression and exclusion of gender in policy and practice in physical education. We deconstruct familiar and established ways of thinking and conceptualising 'policy' and 'practice' and re-position these concepts within a view of policy as a complex, ongoing, relational and contested process in which many people at many sites (including schools, teacher training institutions and government departments) have a part to play in advancing gender equity in physical education. We present the concepts of *text* and *discourse* as key tools for the analyses of gender in physical education, enabling us to explore and reveal the ways in which particular values and interests find expression in the policies and practices of physical education, while others are not given scope to emerge. In the final section of the chapter we comment upon the role that research and researchers may play in furthering understandings and expressions of gender equity in the subject.

Setting the agenda: gender and equity

In seeking to clear some conceptual ground, the starting point probably needs to be 'gender' itself. Typically, the key distinction that is made is between 'sex' and 'gender'. It is not uncommon in the literature on 'gender' for sex to be identified with biological differences between men and women and gender with social/non-biological issues that are typically associated with talk of 'masculine' and 'feminine' identities, personal characteristics and social behaviours. However, this nature/culture division/dualism is itself deeply problematic. As the seminal work of Shilling (1993) illustrates, 'it is important to recognise that the body is not simply constrained by or invested with social relations, but also actually forms a basis for *and contributes towards* these relations' (p. 13). The biological body helps shape relations, it is not independent of them; we are embodied; 'Social relations may take up and transform our embodied capacities in all manner of ways, but they still have a basis in human bodies' (ibid.: 13). Like Shilling, we think the body is profitably conceptualised

> as an unfinished biological and social phenomenon which is transformed, within certain limits, as a result of its entry into, and participation in, society. It is this biological and social quality that makes the body at once such an obvious, and yet such an elusive phenomenon.
>
> (Shilling, 1993: 13)

Below and throughout the book we also point to other inherent short-comings of traditional but still commonplace conceptualisations of gender which reduce what are, in effect, complex socio/biological processes, to simplistic and specifically, to singular characteristics or traits. Such conceptual-isations may well be 'based on unitary conceptions of sexual character' (Hargeaves, J., 1994: 147) with the result that 'There is widespread assumption that all girls and women have a set of characteristics which is constant and common to them as females, and which is distinctly different from the set of characteristics common to boys and men' (ibid.: 147). As we and others in this text highlight, unitary conceptions of gender are highly problematic. In particular they serve to deny or conceal commonalities in the characteristics and experiences of some men and some women, but also ignore the diversity in the characteristics and experiences of women and men. The diversity reflects that we are not 'only' women or men, but also 'many other things'; we have multiple identities. Thus, when we talk of 'gender equity' we are referring not only to whether boys and girls/men and women have *access* to particular forms of experience, for example, in the physical education curriculum, but also to whether they can express and develop attitudes and behaviours relating, for example, to their sexuality, shape and physical cultures, that help frame their identity, define who they are and what they want to be. In this vein, any analysis of equity in physical education will necessarily embrace both structural and existential issues. It will embrace multiple identities and multiple differences and in particular, be concerned to consider 'when and how differences become disadvantages that threaten to undermine oppor-tunities for all individuals to enjoy meaningful and equitable participation in social and civic life' (Collins *et al.*, 2000: 38).

As these brief comments have already indicated, in 'talking gender' we are not only concerned with the experiences of women or girls. Although some of the authors contributing to the book have chosen to research and write about the experiences of women or girls, our emphasis is that boys and men are not absent from our text. In a sense males and females are always present discursively, even if not materially so. Indeed, in this vein we might argue that the identities of men and women are always and inevitably inextricably bound or related; and that analyses are incomplete if the relational elements of masculinity and femininity are not recognised and brought to the fore. In more than one sense then this must mean that our concern remains the interests and experiences of *all* children, girls and boys. Many of the issues that are discussed in relation to policy and practice in physical education have clear relevance for both girls and boys, even if some past and current work has focused attention on the interests of the former. Our emphasis is that gender needs to be recognised as an issue for men and women, boys and girls in arenas of physical education and sport. We have endeavoured to reflect this in our writing, but are also acutely aware that there will be readers who may feel that we have not achieved the right balance of representation of issues, or of people. Some will see absences, for example of a chapter that focuses explicitly on boys and/or masculinities and/or other particular groups of men or women. We recognise the arguments for such foci but also stress the need for more research into the experiences of various groups of people in physical education. Gaps remain in our understanding of whose experiences are represented in physical education research and literature. However, we also see dangers that research and/or writing (including our own) with a focus on groups of individuals bounded in relation to gender can appear to express and reinforce exactly the binary thinking that we are seeking to move beyond. Thus, our approach has been to press towards greater integration rather than polarity in discussions. It is an approach that both some men and some women may see as diluting the strength of arguments that relate specifically to either the interests of men and boys, or alternatively, those of women and girls within and beyond arenas of physical education and sport. In advocating integration are we saying that differences within these groups are more important than those between them? Our stance could certainly be read in that way. Our response is to say that it should be seen to reflect a concern that both differences between and within are important, and that our conceptual-isations of gender and our writing about gender issues in physical education needs to engage with that complexity. There is no one way of doing this, nor one way that should be seen as 'the right way'. As the various chapters within this text demonstrate, different authors will, in their own ways, make different contributions to the debates. We hope that collectively, the chapters will be regarded as a worthwhile contribution to debates about gender and identity in physical education and be seen as useful to both men and women within the profession who are concerned to advance gender equity in our subject and in our societies.

So what is advancement of gender equity really about? Literature in physical education and policies established for the subject have variously used the language of, and have stated commitments to 'equal opportunities', 'equality', 'equity' and most recently in the United Kingdom, 'inclusion'.

These terms continue to be interchanged without the meanings of particular terms in particular contexts being adequately pursued. Hence our concern to clarify our own focus on equity and the way in which this embraces a commitment primarily to social justice. We establish equity as a reference point from which talk of 'equal opportunities', 'equality' and 'inclusion' can all be critically explored to assess whether, in the ways in which they are used and in the proposals that they are associated with, they embrace a commitment to equity. We suggest that in some instances, the answer will be 'yes', but as Talbot (1993) has previously highlighted, more often than not, policies and practices couched in these various terms will fall short of this commitment.

'Shifting thinking' to embrace equity is as much about redefining what we regard as problems in physical education as it is about identifying solutions. It demands that we reflect upon the value judgements inherent in our defining certain things (behaviours, attitudes, practices) as problematic. Invariably, this will reveal that problems are defined as such in relation to a dominant set of values or behaviours that it is assumed should 'naturally' be embraced and celebrated by all. Many claims to be addressing equality and/or equity in physical education and sport have failed at this first hurdle in terms of demonstrating a commitment to equity. They include many initiatives directed towards increasing participation amongst 'target groups'. All too often a lack of participation in specific forms of sport valued by dominant groups in society is defined as problematic. Rarely is the cultural specificity of the celebrated form of sport questioned. From an equity perspective, the lack of participation that has been identified may not be a problem at all. Rather, the relative absence of opportunities for people to participate in other more culturally relevant forms of physical activity and sport (that are central to 'other' (non-dominant) cultures and that embrace 'other' values) may be the 'real' problem to address.

Language is a useful and powerful tool in critical discussions concerned with issues of equality and equity. A commitment to equity prompts us to question our use of the term 'other' and the value judgements inherent in its use. Are we implying different but equal status, or deficit? A commitment to equity is not about denying difference, but neither is it merely about recognising or respecting difference. It is about valuing and celebrating difference as *a resource*, in our schools, in physical education and sport, and in our societies. Thus, as Evans and Davies (1993) explain 'the issue must not be whether differences can be dissolved . . . but how they can be celebrated in ways which negate prejudice and stereotyping and at the same time respect individual cultural identity' (p. 19). These are clearly difficult issues to deal with conceptually and empirically. Celebrating 'difference' does not mean that we should accept that anything goes, that all attitudes and behaviours are of equal value and equally 'good'. This would quickly lead us into a deep and relativistic quagmire in which everything must be considered important but nothing of value; racism, sexism, elitism, poverty and squalor enjoy the same authority and standing as all other more liberal attitudes or goals. The social fact is that moral and ethical codes inevitably have to be considered in our judgements of the 'difference' that we see. But all the while we need to bear in mind that that we cannot assume that our codes are superior to others, or worse still that others do not possess a moral code at all. Thus, from an equity perspective, no *one* set of values or behaviours should be regarded automatically or straightforwardly as superior to others, or as 'the norm' against which others are measured or judged. There is recognition that at different times, in different places and cultures, different behaviours and values will be regarded as normal, legitimate and desirable. Furthermore, this diversity may be regarded as a richness to celebrate and explore rather than deny. Celebrating difference and ensuring that all individuals feel that they have a legitimate place in physical education, in schools and in contemporary societies are matters that are pursued throughout the subsequent chapters. We see that although some advances have been made towards greater gender equity in physical education, in arenas of both policy and practice there is a clear case for gender to be 'on the agenda'.

Extending agendas: the complexities of 'gender issues' and 'gender equity'

In this section we draw attention to some key characteristics that in our view need to be central to our conceptualisations of gender. First, we consider the fundamental shortcomings of talking of 'masculinity' and 'femininity'. In our view, acknowledging multiple masculinities and femininities is a first but crucial step if we are to broaden thinking in relation to the behaviours that we regard as legitimate for men and women, the body shapes they may have, the physical activities which they may participate in. All too often, judgements are made in relation to a single and stereotypical image of masculinity or femininity that has come, over time and because of powerful vested interests, to be viewed as the norm. It may be the case that for many people, the singular and dominant is an unproblematic norm. The social, cultural and historical specificity of the norm is overlooked or denied, as is the way in which the specificity serves to marginalise or exclude some members of our schools and societies. Recognition of these issues is crucial if we are to enable alternative identities, masculinities and femininities to be legitimately expressed and pursued, and to encourage appreciation of their value. The history of the women's movement, of anti-racism, or of gay rights is evidence that stereotypes rarely go uncontested, and that values are rarely allowed to stand still.

Talk of multiple masculinities and femininities directs us to the fact that gender can never be viewed in isolation from the many other dimensions of sociocultural and economic life that shape our identities. Our analyses and understandings will always fall short if we do not engage with the dynamics between gender and issues of class, ethnicity, ability, sexuality, age, and religious and cultural values. Lists such as these always need to be presented with caution. There are always dangers of overlooking a crucial 'identity' for someone. However, it serves to make the point that we all have multiple identities, that masculinities and femininities reflect and express. It also draws attention to the inherent shortcomings of making generalised statements, or developing policies and practices in physical education, that are directed towards 'girls' and 'boys' as if these were discrete and homogeneous groups. As teachers are all too aware, children – both girls and boys – are individuals. In 'talking gender' we need to be able to accommodate their individuality and acknowledge the ways in which gendered identities are embedded with and mediated by, other identities. As we see in subsequent chapters, these 'other identities' can have an important bearing upon the masculinities and femininities that any individual will relate to, value, and regard as legitimate and accessible to them. Broadening thinking in relation to these issues is critical if we are to move towards greater gender equity in physical education.

It is appropriate to acknowledge that a focus upon multiple masculinities and femininities is not without potential pitfalls. Francis (2000) notably makes the point that hegemonic notions of masculinity and femininity may be positioned at the top of a hierarchy, with other forms located below them. Furthermore, she argues that to suggest that there are different categories of masculinity and femininity is to imply 'something more fixed than is the case' (p. 14). Francis' work thus prompts us to seek to avoid polarising debates and to stress the dynamic nature of gender and gender relations in physical education and sport.

In the chapters that follow we see both evidence of progress towards a greater level of sophistication in addressing gender in physical education, and clear failure on the part of policy-makers and practitioners to embrace such complexities. Issues of class, ethnicity, sexuality, ability, age, religion and culture have obvious bearings upon the ways in which both men and women will be positioned socially, culturally and in status and value in contexts of physical education and sport. The same issues also impact upon the ways in which we may position ourselves. We are all differently positioned, but also in different positions to (re-)position ourselves in contexts of physical education and sport, in arenas of policy and curriculum development in education, and in society. Following Rich (2001) we use the term 'positioning' as an active as well as a passive verb. As Rich's research on the life histories of women (in physical education and sport) consistently indicates, the activity of 'positioning genders' is an act of agency as well as of passivity and constraint. Differences between us in these respects arise not only by virtue of our being either male or female. Inherent in our multiple identities is the potential for us to be subject to 'multiple forms of oppression and discrimination' (Cole and Hill, 1999: 3). Marginalisation is a reality for many women but also for many men in physical education and sport as in many other forms of socio-economic life. It is something that will be experienced to varying degrees by different people in particular settings. As indicated above, people are judged in relation to prevailing norms that are not arbitrary and that are defined by dominant groups. Consequently, some people will be viewed as deficient and/or deviant, and subjected to prejudice in physical education, education, sport and society. Throughout this book we point to the need to pursue who – and more specifically, *which* women and *which* men – are being positioned 'at the margins' in and by the policies and practices of physical education. In parallel we consider the different scope that particular women and particular men have to be proactive in seeking to reposition themselves and their values and interests in educational arenas, in sport and in society. Analysis is therefore, directed to both the positions accorded to individuals and the positions that they may access and legitimately occupy.

As is apparent from the discussion above, power-relations are central to achieving more comprehensive conceptualisations of gender equity. The identities and positions that are occupied and can potentially be occupied by particular women and men always need to be understood and explored 'in context'; specifically in the political, social, cultural, historical and institutional contexts in which they are set. Characteristics of these contexts create both opportunities and barriers for the expression of particular identities, masculinities and femininities and serve to position them as either legitimate and to be celebrated – or equally, as undesirable. But perhaps the most important way in which these contexts are relevant to our concerns for greater gender equity is in the way in which they influence and in many instances constrain our potential to actively redefine the norms that underpin the exclusion and marginalisation that we seek to eradicate. We, along with the other contributors to this collection, have experienced the limits to our own scope to access and influence those who hold central positions in policy and curriculum development in physical education. As other educational policy researchers have similarly observed, agendas for social justice will not be shared by all and nor are they welcome in all arenas (see for example, Griffiths, 1998; Ozga, 2000). As we discuss in later chapters, this is also vividly reflected in the policies and practices of physical education, as much by what is missing from those policies and practices as what is present in them.

Policies, practice and the pursuit of gender equity

Having pointed to the limits of contemporary policies and practice in physical education and furthermore, our scope to influence them, it is appropriate to shift to a more positive orientation. We may be able to extend our ability to influence future developments in physical education by developing a better understanding of the ways in which policies and practices take particular forms (forms which can either reinforce or challenge inequities). We therefore direct attention to work within the field of 'education policy sociology' and the key concepts that this has provided for critical sociological inquiry. The starting point is to deconstruct the familiar conceptualisations of 'policy' and 'practice'; of policy 'making' and 'implementation'. Work such as that undertaken by Stephen Ball and his colleagues (see for example Ball,

1990; Bowe *et al.*, 1992) has led the field in advancing our thinking on 'policy matters'. In many respects we have seen that the language of description and analysis is inherently problematic. This is a point reflected in the use of textual markers ('. ...') to indicate the shortcomings of particular words, and their inability (because of the likelihood that they will be understood within dominant and established frames of reference) to accurately portray the intended meanings. For the same reasons we often extend talk of 'policy' to 'policy and curriculum development'. Our emphasis is that the two are inextricably linked. Policy is not an isolated, abstract 'thing' set apart from the individuals and practices that are found within schools. It is a complex, ongoing, contested and relational process, that encompasses both what we may have in the past viewed as 'policy' and that which we term 'practice', and in which the boundaries between 'making' and 'implementation' are blurred and complex, involving many sites and many individuals, both within and beyond education systems (see Penney and Evans, 1999). Policy viewed from this standpoint 'is more about "*process*" than "product"' (Ozga, 2000: 2); it is 'struggled over, not delivered, in tablets of stone, to a grateful or quiescent population' (ibid.: 1). Acknowledging that policy is a social process is at the same time to note that it is also likely to be an emotional process, inherent in which are issues of identity, gender and sexuality. In this sense the 'body' is fundamentally, inextricably implicated in the policy process and therefore has to be accommodated in any analysis of sociocultural and educational change.

The ongoing struggles and contestation over, and adaptation of, texts are also key characteristics of the policy process. As Bowe *et al.* (1992) emphasised, policy is about the creation and re-creation of texts in many sites and by many individuals. There is thus plenty of scope in this process for various interests to come into play, to be privileged or equally, marginalised or excluded, at various points in time. Who privileges or marginalises what interests, where and why, are important issues to consider in relation to gender equity in physical education. We point to the concept of discourse as probably our most potent tool in addressing these issues (Penney and Evans, 1999). In talking of discourses we are concerned with the interests and values that are reflected, legitimated, promoted, or equally subordinated or excluded via particular modes of communication (linguistic and corporeal) and the meanings attached to the form and content of that communication. Discourse is the concept that captures the way in which texts produced historically and contemporaneously within and beyond contexts of physical education shape thinking, particularly in this instance, about issues to do with gender. As we have identified in our previous explorations of policy, we can identify particular discourses with particular interests and values and, thus, the presence of various discourses in the texts of policy-makers, teachers and pupils. We have repeatedly emphasised that not all discourses are accorded equal status, or even a visible presence in those texts. Following Ball (1990) we note that in critically exploring texts, what is *not* said is as important as what is. Several chapters in this collection serve to demonstrate the 'power of silence' in subordinating or excluding particular interests, identities and individuals. In chapter 7 particularly we see that silence on issues should not be read as a signal of neutrality on gender issues. In that chapter and others we also see another important dimension to discourse, that identifies it as a concept that clearly engages with the notion of policy as 'process rather than product'. In Ball's (1990) words, discourses are also about 'who can speak where, when and with what authority' (p. 17). Anyone seeking to advance equity in physical education will be aware of these issues that turn our attention back once again to matters of 'position' and where we can locate ourselves in a policy process that is always and inevitably highly political (see for example, Ball, 1990; Graham with Tytler, 1993; Penney and Evans, 1999; Taylor *et al.*, 1997).

Understanding the form and content of particular texts (which may be policy documents issued by central government, curriculum materials produced by teachers or their 'act' of teaching itself, i.e. the pedagogical text), and our varying abilities to influence that form and content, demands that we locate texts 'in context'. More specifically, it demands that we explore the historical, political, economic, social, cultural and institutional contexts that locate, shape and are shaped by particular texts. Several points need to be considered here. First, the various dimensions of context always create both opportunities and set limits to the type of texts that can legitimately arise in a particular context. Second, those same dimensions also create both possibilities and set limits in relation to the ability of particular people to shape texts. Third, all texts are in a dynamic relationship with contexts and as such work to either legitimate, reinforce and reproduce the values, interests and inequities inherent in them, or serve to challenge and potentially re-shape contexts in these terms. Hence our emphasis that we are all actors in the policy process, albeit differently positioned and variously able to influence thinking and actions. We should never deny the importance of structural issues in the exploration of policy matters. Indeed, we have argued that the complexity and extent of these has placed a stranglehold upon teachers' work in contemporary England and Wales, if not internationally (see Evans, Davies and Penney, 1994; Hargreaves, 1994). However, this book is testimony to our continued belief in the significance of the 'spaces for action', the 'scope for slippage' (Bowe *et al.*, 1992); that is to say, in the capacity of teachers and teacher educators to reshape physical education in more equitable ways and to promote policies and practices that better respond to gender issues.

Finally, we should address the position of researchers in the policy process. In important respects both individually and collectively, the authors of the chapters in this book are speaking from the margins of policy and curriculum development in physical education. Neither they nor the agendas that they pursue enjoy central positions in that development. Many of us have seen and experienced that 'Policy influence is a struggle to be heard in an arena where only certain voices have legitimacy at any point in time' (Ball, 1994: 112), and that the voices of critical educational researchers rarely have this legitimacy. The term 'critical' refers to our underpinning interest in social change towards greater gender equity, in education, physical education and in society. Not surprisingly those whose interests serve an inequitable status quo, whose values currently dominate and are represented and promoted in the policies and practice of education and physical education, are unlikely to welcome the prospect of innovation and change. However, even if marginalised, research and researchers may play a key role in socio-educational change. Like Ozga (2000) we contend that inherent in research are 'opportunities for change' which 'contribute to its power as an *educational process*, and help to explain why policy-makers are so anxious to ensure that research is encountered by teachers only in predictable and limited ways' (p. 70). The change that is referred to here is change on the part of both 'the researched' and researchers themselves. Ozga explains that 'research may bring about further transformation of the researcher, as he or she is altered through the generation of new insights and attitudes' (ibid.: 70). Variously, those of us writing for this collection have experienced such transformation, both in the context of our respective fieldwork, but also in the act of writing. Our hope is that this book will further facilitate and promote new insights, extend discussions, and open up a dialogue between all parties committed to equity in physical education.

References

Ball, S.J. (1990) *Politics and Policy Making in Education: Explorations in Policy Sociology*, London: Routledge.

Ball, S.J. (1994) Researching inside the State: issues in the interpretation of elite interviews, in D. Halpin and B. Troyna (eds) *Researching Education Policy. Ethical and Methodological Issues*, London: The Falmer Press.

Bowe, R. and Ball, S.J. with Gold, A. (1992) *Reforming Education and Changing Schools: Case Studies in Policy Sociology*, London: Routledge.

Cole, M. and Hill, D. (1999) Equality and secondary education: what are the conceptual issues?, in D. Hill and M. Cole (eds) *Promoting Equality in Secondary Schools*, London: Cassell.

Collins, C., Kenway, J. and McLeod, J. (2000) Gender debates we still have to have, *The Australian Educational Researcher* 27(3): 37–48.

Evans, J. and Davies, B. (1993) Equality, equity and physical education, in J. Evans, (ed.) *Equality, Education and Physical Education*, London: Falmer Press.

Evans, J., Davies, B. and Penney, D. (1994) Whatever happened to the subject and the State in policy research in education?, *Discourse: Studies in the Cultural Politics of Education* 14(2): 57–64.

Francis, B. (2000) *Boys, Girls and Achievement: Addressing Classroom Issues*, London: Falmer Press.

Graham, D. with Tytler, D. (1993) *A Lesson for Us All. The Making of the National Curriculum*, London: Routledge.

Griffiths, M. (1998) *Educational Research for Social Justice: Getting Off the Fence*, Buckingham: Open University Press.

Hargreaves, A. (1994) *Changing Teachers, Changing Times: Teachers' Work and Culture in the Postmodern Age*, London: Cassell.

Hargreaves, J. (1994) *Sporting Females: Critical Issues in the History and Sociology of Women's Sport*, London: Routledge.

Ozga, J. (2000) *Policy Research in Educational Settings: Contested Terrain*, Buckingham: Open University Press.

Penney, D. and Evans, J. (1999) *Politics, Policy and Practice in Physical Education*, London: Routledge.

Rich, E. (2001) *Strong Words, Tough Minds, Trained Bodies. A Life History Narrative Analysis of Female Student Teachers of Physical Education*, unpublished Ph.D thesis, Loughborough University.

Shilling, C. (1993) *The Body and Social Theory*, London: Sage.

Talbot, M. (1993) Gender and physical education, in J. Evans (ed.) *Equality, Education and Physical Education*, London: Falmer Press.

Taylor, S., Rizvi, F., Lingard, B. and Henry, M. (1997) *Educational Policy and the Politics of Change*, London: Routledge.

3 Physical education: a gendered history

David Kirk

Introduction

Many people who grew to adulthood between the 1960s and 1990s in Britain will believe that British society has moved a long way to resolve gender issues in sport and physical education. They may point to women's participation in marathon running or rugby, or look to girls and boys playing together in co-educational physical education classes as proof that we now have equality between the sexes in sport and physical education. However, some less sanguine members of the public may remind us that girls remain more likely to drop out of sport than boys and that in some elite sport contexts women do not receive the same rewards as men for what are arguably as good or better performances. Others might suggest that in order to gain public recognition and acceptance of their participation, women have increasingly had to 'play like men' (Hargreaves, 1994), or rather, like certain men. As other authors in this collection emphasise, particular forms of masculinity remain dominant in many sporting contexts and this dominance serves to exclude both women and men from participation, enjoyment and/or achievement in sport.

Those people taking an optimistic view in these debates may argue that the barriers to girls' and women's full participation in physical education and sport have now been removed, and that whether and how to participate is now a matter of individual choice. They might concede that more could be done to motivate disaffected and inactive girls, but would still contend that the problem, if one still exists, is down to individual choice and enthusiasm rather than structural barriers. A historical perspective on this issue reveals that the optimists do have a point; there has indeed been some progress. However, history also shows that they may have underestimated the enormity and complexity of gender in physical education and overestimated what has been achieved (Mangan and Parks, 1987). In this chapter, I adopt an historical perspective, arguing that physical education as an activity in the school curriculum has been gendered since its first appearance in the modern era, which dates for our purposes here from the 1880s and the beginning of mass compulsory schooling in Britain. What this means is that for over one hundred years, the practices that make up physical education have been strongly associated with stereotypical views about the behaviours and activity that is appropriate for girls and boys respectively and with notably singular images of femininity and masculinity. I present three episodes from the history of physical education in Scotland between the 1950s and the 1970s to show that this gendering of the subject has been profound and far-reaching. I suggest that what we now regard as legitimate knowledge in physical education has been strongly influenced by this gendered history and that this influence is invariably overlooked. Many members of the general public and of the teaching profession do not recognise the gender dimensions of physical education and assume that the subject is unproblematically androgenous, or gender-neutral. The inability to recognise the lasting influence of the gendered history of physical education has serious consequences for children's experiences of and opportunities in physical education and sport. As other chapters in this book confirm, for many girls and more boys than is often acknowledged, these experiences and opportunities are limited because of the ongoing influence of the past.

The chapter begins by examining a 1954 conference debate between female and male physical educators in Scotland over the future of physical education and in particular, over which version of gymnastics should be taught to Scottish schoolboys. It then moves on to take a closer look at the debate through the writings of David Munrow (for the 'male perspective') and Marjorie Randall (for the 'female perspective'). These respective spokes-people for men and women demonstrate that the gendering of physical education was actually constitutive of the form the subject could take in schools and higher education institutions. Finally, the chapter turns to an investigation of the Munn Report of 1977 on the curriculum in Scottish schools (SED/CCC, 1977) and the separate submissions to the Committee from female and male physical educators. This episode in the history of physical education in Scotland represents the 'bottom line' in terms of the selection of versions of physical education for the official curriculum of government-funded schools. The debates that I report occurred in Scotland but serve to illustrate issues that have relevance well beyond this national context.

A debate in Scotland

From the 1880s up to the 1950s, gymnastics was the main content of physical education programmes in government schools. By the end of the Second World War, three distinct versions of gymnastics were competing for teaching time in school physical education programmes (Kirk, 1992); the Swedish (or Ling) gymnastics; educational gymnastics; and German or Olympic gymnastics. In November 1954, delegates from the Scottish Physical Education Association (SPEA) and the Scottish League of Physical Education (SLPE) met in Edinburgh to discuss 'Physical Education Today and in the Future' (The Leaflet, 1955: 6) and specifically to consider which of three versions of gymnastics should be taught to boys in Scottish schools. The SPEA represented male physical education teachers and the SLPE represented female teachers, with the conference being organised by the Scottish Joint Consultative Committee on Physical Education (SJCCPE).

At this 1954 conference delegates failed to reach an agreed position regarding the future provision of gymnastics in the physical education curriculum for boys in Scotland. The SJCCPE organised four further one day meetings to debate the issue. The outcome of these meetings was that boys would continue to be taught Swedish (or Ling) gymnastics on the grounds that the other contender for the 'top spot', educational gymnastics, would undermine the traditionally high standards of skill developed in Swedish gymnastics. This outcome was ironic given the title and focus of the conference, which was intended to make decisions about the future. Within a decade, the 'winner', Swedish gymnastics, had disappeared completely from the school curriculum, and the contender, educational gymnastics, had been embattled and bruised. The distant third placer in 1954, Olympic gymnastics, emerged to take pride of place in physical education programmes throughout Britain. How could this conference of physical educators have got things so badly wrong? To understand the issues debated and the decisions made we need to further explore the development of each of the three forms of gymnastics and the values and traditions that each was associated with in 1954.

Swedish (or Ling) gymnastics

Swedish (or Ling) gymnastics had been the hallmark of the professional female physical educator between the late 1890s to the 1940s, and the version of physical education officially approved by the then Board of Education (working in partnership with the Scottish Education Department[1]) for use in elementary schools in Scotland. The Swedish system was invented by Per Henrick Ling in the early decades of the nineteenth century and consolidated into a system of physical training at the Central Gymnastic Institute in Stockholm, which he founded. It involved mostly free-standing exercises that sought to systematically exercise each part of the body through increasingly intricate flexions and extensions. It also involved some apparatus work such as vaulting (see Board of Education, 1909). Teaching within the Ling system was highly formalised and particularly in the 1800s featured movements performed to militaristic commands such as 'at the double!' and 'fall in!' It was easily practised with large groups in confined spaces (Munrow, 1955). The Swedish system was boosted in Britain in the 1880s through the work of Swedish Gymnasts appointed by the Board of Education to organise physical education in its elementary schools. Swedish gymnastics formed the foundation of women's professional training and was supplemented by training in massage, remedial exercises and games.

Educational gymnastics

Educational gymnastics made a rapid and dramatic impact on female physical education from the first appearance of Rudolf Laban's ideas on movement and dance in Britain in the 1930s. Modern Dance was built on a radical critique of 'unnatural' movement patterns in industrial society that in Laban's opinion, had much to do with the presence of mental illness and personality disorders. Laban's philosophy argued for the release of dangerously pent up and inhibited energies through free, spontaneous movement. Although Laban's main concerns were focused on the theatre and industry, female physical educators quickly applied his ideas to gymnastics during the late 1930s and through the war years. Educational gymnastics borrowed from modern dance a concern for the qualitative dimensions of movement experience and selectively adopted some of the rhetoric and ideas of the fast growing and fashionable child-centred progressivism in British educational circles of the time. In particular, ideas associated with humanistic liberal individualism found expression in educational gymnastics (Ministry of Education, 1952).

German or Olympic gymnastics

The third form of gymnastics was witnessed in its modern form for the first time by British physical educators at the 1948 London Olympic Games. German gymnastics had been around at least as long as Ling's system and involved work on apparatus such as the rings, parallel bars and pummel horse. At the beginning of the twentieth century it had vied with the Swedish system for selection (by the Interdepartmental Committee set up by the Royal Commission on Physical Training (1903) to produce a Syllabus of Physical Exercises for British schools) as the official system of physical training. It lost that contest and suffered the stigma of its German origins after the First World War, being neglected by all but a handful of enthusiasts in Britain until the 1940s. However, following the 1948 Olympics, which presented gymnastics as a competitive sport made up of the six activities of floor-work, vaulting, rings, bars, beam and pommel horse, there was an increasing level of interest in this version of gymnastics and a growing number of advocacies for its inclusion in school programmes.

Gender and gymnastics

It is important to note that each of these three version of gymnastics had strong gender associations. Swedish gymnastics was the staple of women's physical education during the first half of the twentieth century, but it was also widely practised by men. When women performed Swedish gymnastics, their movements were required to be dainty, nimble and flexible. When men performed Swedish gymnastics, they were required to be strong and powerful.

Curiously, as it was practised in government schools with co-educational classes, Swedish gymnastics took on an androgynous form where the sex of the individual was made to appear irrelevant to the activity. I have speculated elsewhere that this may only have been possible when Swedish gymnastics was taught to pre-pubescent children and became problematic as older and physically more mature children were staying on at school (Kirk, 2000).

Educational gymnastics was invariably associated with women's and girls' physical education, and the education of young children in the infant school. The influence of Laban's philosophy and the ideology of child-centredness that was the orthodoxy of the 1950s and 1960s in primary schools added such depth and strength to the practice of educational gymnastics that it provoked both intense support and considerable hostility. While the hostility came mainly from men, there were also many women physical educators who regarded educational gymnastics with some suspicion. The focus of opposition from the men were the claims that it was possible to develop generalised movement competencies through gymnastics and that there was little or no place for competition in the gym. The men were also extremely uncomfortable with the women's interest in movement as an aesthetic activity. Meanwhile opposition from women can be associated mainly with those women who were members of the 'old school' of Swedish gymnastics, who decried the informality and apparent lack of discipline of educational gymnastics.

Olympic gymnastics was practised by both men and women, and practised differently according to dominant notions of femininity and masculinity. This was most obviously expressed in the different activities that comprised Olympic gymnastics for men and women respectively; namely rings, pommel and parallel bars for men, and asymmetric bars and the beam for women. In 1954 this form of gymnastics was too new to be a genuine contender in the deliberations over which form of gymnastics would dominate physical education. However, its ultimate victory in debates and developments signalled new gender associations in physical education, a matter that I return to later in the chapter. But first, let us return to the question posed earlier: how did the conference delegates in 1954 get it so wrong in their decision to support Swedish gymnastics for boys as the future of their subject? Quite clearly, even though educational gymnastics was the rising star of physical education in the early 1950s, its strong association with the education of girls and women probably ruled it out of contention for the men. However, we need to note that the decision required a conference and four one-day meetings, indicating that the result was far from a foregone conclusion and nor was it an uncontested decision. In the next section I pursue the gender issues involved in the choice between these forms of gymnastics and consider what it was about the activities themselves and the forms of movement that they required that meant that they were firmly aligned with dominant forms of femininity and masculinity.

Inside the debate

By the end of the 1950s, male physical educators were in the majority within the profession, something that had never happened before in Britain. Before long they began to champion two developments that up to this time were quite alien to physical education (Kirk, 1992). The first of these was the idea that physical education was not primarily about gymnastics at all or rather, should not be in Britain. Instead, they argued that physical education should be centred on the sports and games that first appeared in the mid- to late 1800s in the schools for social elites such as Eton, Harrow and Westminster. Hugh Brown, then Director of the Scottish School of Physical Education,[2] captured this important and dramatic shift in his comments on training programmes for male physical education teachers in the 1950s.

> The curriculum in the Colleges of PE is ever-widening. This is something that I rejoice to be able to report, and my only comment is 'high time, too!' We are British people – for which I can find no cause for apology – and we are a games-playing nation. It has always puzzled me, for instance, that gymnastics should be regarded as being synonymous with Physical Education. Gymnastics is a part – a very valuable part – of a vast subject, and in some countries it may have been looked on as being the main fraction of the whole. No longer is that so here. However good a system may be, the folly of adopting it in its entirety and foisting it upon people, unadapted to peculiar needs, is at last recognised. What may delight the Germans or the Danes, and what suits their national characteristics, does not necessarily make a similar appeal here. Now we are recognising this!
>
> (Brown, 1958: 92)

The second development that the male physical educators championed was the use of science in the service of physical performance. This work began in earnest after the Second World War in university departments of physical education, at Leeds and Birmingham in particular. The first and most prominent achievement of this scientific approach was the development of work in the areas of strength and endurance, two dimensions of physical performance closely associated with the sports that were then clearly identified as 'male' (primarily rugby, athletics and weight-lifting). The application of a scientific perspective also generated new developments in the area of skill acquisition and motor learning.

During this period, female physical educators had also been involved in debate about the desirable content of their subject. For them the issue was not the place of gymnastics, but the relative place of which form, and specifically, the respective merits of Swedish versus educational gymnastics. By the end of the 1950s the 'new school' of the educational gymnasts were in the ascendancy. As male antagonism to educational gymnastics began to become increasingly more vocal through the 1950s, two major issues focused the debate between the 'female' and 'male' perspectives that became very evident in physical education. The first issue was the controversy surrounding the level of specificity required for skill development and the matter of transfer of training. The second concerned the application of objective standards to gymnastic performance and the place of competition in the gym.

The specificity of skill development

In his book *Pure and Applied Gymnastics* first published in 1955, Munrow suggested that in moving away from the Swedish system after the Second World War, male and female physical educators had reacted in different ways to the question of skill specificity.

> The men have made overt acknowledgement that other skills are as important and have 'diluted' the gymnastic skill content of gymnasium work so that now boys may be seen practising basket-ball shots and manoeuvres, carrying out heading practices or practising sprint starting. . . . The women, in the main, have . . . 'diluted' the traditional gymnastic skills by a quite different device. They have ceased both to name and to teach them. Instead, a description is given, in general terms, of a task involving apparatus and individual solutions are encouraged. A much wider range of solutions is thus possible; some may include traditional skills but many will not.
>
> (Munrow, 1955: 276)

The problem with the female alternative to the Swedish system, as Munrow saw it, was that pupils rarely had the chance to consolidate their skills because no specific skill teaching took place.

The educational gymnasts' reply to Munrow's challenge came from Marjorie Randall in 1961 in her book, *Basic Movement*. In the opening chapter of the book, Randall contested Munrow's functional definition of gymnastics, suggesting that 'the masculine approach . . . has become largely outmoded so far as women's work is concerned' (Randall, 1961: 12). She claimed that 'Women's gymnastics . . . have been emancipated from the restricted practices of stereotyped patterns of movements based upon anatomical classification. The physiological and anatomical ends . . . are incidentally served' (ibid.: 12).

The major aim identified by Randall was the achievement of what she termed body awareness, which included neural control combined with a higher level kinesthetic awareness, that could be developed through experience into an intuitive control of movement. Also in contrast to the male approach she added to this the need to engage the child cognitively. She accused the men of stressing only the physical effects of exercise, and consequently regarding cognition as out of range. 'The masculine approach to gymnastics' she claimed separates content from method. Munrow's gymnastics exercises can be directly and formally taken or informally taken. Movement gymnastics requires the intelligent co-operation of the child, rendering command-response methods obsolete . . . this represents a big break-away from the traditional approach of the 'see this' and 'do it this way' school of thought.

(Randall, 1961: 25–6)

Randall's response showed that behind the less formal methods of educational gymnastics lay an attempt to treat the pupil holistically, encouraging the simultaneous development of intellectual and creative abilities in a movement medium and relegating the physical effect of movement to a level of lesser importance.

However, the notion of body awareness, which lay at the centre of the women's scheme, suggested a theory of learning that ran directly counter to the new knowledge being produced by motor learning theorists. The educational gymnasts claimed, in much the same way as the Swedish gymnasts had before them, that the movement experience that they had to offer was a general foundation upon which more specific skills could be built. The notion of body awareness expressed this idea as generalised kinesthetic control. As early as 1949 members of the Birmingham University staff including David Munrow and Barbara Knapp questioned whether there was such a thing as generalised skill training. In her book *Skill in Sport* (Knapp, 1963), published in 1963, Barbara Knapp argued that transfer of training was most likely to occur when the tasks in question were similar, and that the best way to learn a specific action was to perform that action repeatedly over a period of time. The main point of the motor learning theorists' criticisms, which the male physical educators championed vigorously, was that skill learning is specific and that repeated practice in the same or similar conditions is the key to mastery. Taking these principles to heart, male physical educators developed an approach to teaching skills that consisted of reducing a skill to its component parts, and learning each part separately before re-assembling them gradually until the entire skill had been learned. This appeared to make nonsense of the claim amongst female physical educators that it was possible, indeed preferable, to develop a general body awareness as a foundation on which to build more specific learning.

Standards and competition in the gym

A second objection to the educational gymnasts' perspective related to the place of standards and competition in the gym. From the male point of view, it seemed unlikely that the educational gymnasts' child-centred approach could continue to stimulate pupils beyond the early stages of learning. Munrow argued that it could not challenge older boys or girls. He contended that competitive activity was essential as a stimulant or incentive for advancing learning. In *Pure and Applied Gymnastics* he complained

> Allied to a teaching philosophy which seeks actively to avoid confronting less able children with failure, is the belief that the child's own solution to the problem being always valid and right. This makes more sense with young children than with older boys and girls and with first efforts at a skill rather than with later ones . . . to leave children floundering to evolve their own technique when we could guide them is a neglect of our professional duties.
>
> (Munrow, 1955: 280–1)

In response to Munrow's view that standards were a necessary and important means of challenging pupils to strive for excellence, Randall suggested that girls, particularly in adolescence, had quite different needs to boys. She argued that the growing boy 'derives considerable prestige and social prominence through physical advantage in competitive games which his increase in height, weight and strength gives him' (Randall, 1961: 20). Girls, on the other hand, may have little to gain from competitive sport during the adolescent period.

> In the gymnastic lesson let her be free from all this competition and let her progress at her own rate and find joy and satisfaction in the slow but sure progress of controlling her body. Through her pride in the mastery of her body in the gymnasium will grow a certain independence, security and emotional stability. . . . Teaching must be geared to the individual; it must be flexible and tolerant of a wide range in aptitude . . . no longer is her worth in the gymnasium measured by whether she can get over the box in long fly or whether she can put her head on her knees keeping her legs straight; but rather can she work to surpass her own standards without being harassed or harried because she cannot conform to a common one.
>
> (Randall, 1961: 21–2)

The aims of independence, security and emotional stability contrast sharply with the desire to develop strength, endurance, flexibility and particular skills, and to use these attributes in competitive situations. The contrasts reveal starkly the contested issues that divided the male and female physical educators. It is also important to reflect upon the degree to which both sides were effectively arguing that boys and girls have different needs in relation to physical education. Notably absent in these debates is a recognition of different needs amongst either girls or boys. The image legitimated and reinforced is of two homogeneous groups aligned with stereotypical perceptions of activities and behaviours of which they are capable and in which they should be engaging.

The debate between female and male physical educators continued around these issues throughout the 1960s and into the 1970s. The development of the four-year Bachelor of Education (BEd) degree during the 1960s to replace the three-year diploma as the main qualification for teaching physical education in Britain drew heavily on exercise physiology, biomechanics and motor learning for its subject matter. This focus advantaged the men over the women whose child-centred movement focus leant itself to the Arts as a knowledge base (Fletcher, 1984). By the time the BEd was in place towards the end of the 1960s, gymnastics no longer formed the core of physical education programmes. Researcher Nick Whitehead's 1969 survey of a range of secondary schools mainly in the North of England found that the 'national sports' of soccer, rugby and cricket for boys, hockey and netball for girls, and athletics for both, now dominated school physical education (Whitehead and Hendry, 1976). Swedish gymnastics had disappeared almost completely to be replaced by Olympic gymnastics for boys which also began to compete with educational gymnastics as the main form of gymnastics for girls. So which of these gendered forms of physical education had won the day?

And the winner is . . . ?

In the mid 1970s, curriculum and assessment in Scottish secondary schools was under review. Policy-makers and curriculum writers had been influenced by the work of a number of philosophers of education (e.g. Peters, 1966; White, 1973; Hirst, 1974) who argued that some knowledge was of greater educational worth than others. These arguments led policy-makers to the view that some school subjects should be regarded as 'core' or essential and others as optional. In 1975, the Scottish Education Department (SED) and its Consultative Committee on Curriculum (CCC) set up a committee under the chairmanship of Mr James Munn to examine the curriculum of Scottish secondary schools in the years leading up to the national examinations (years 3 and 4).

The Munn Committee received submissions from interested parties during 1975 and 1976 prior to making its report the following year (SED/CCC, 1977). Given the prevailing interest in the notion of core and elective subjects based on the 'educational' criteria of the philosophers of education, members of the physical education profession were nervous about the possibility that their subject may be excluded from the core curriculum. What they chose to say 'on behalf of physical education' was clearly a matter of importance to the future of the subject.

In 1975, the Scottish Central Committee on Physical Education (SCCPE) made a submission to the Munn Committee on behalf of all of the physical education profession in Scotland (SCCPE, 1975). The SCCPE began their submission by taking issue with what they called the 'Peters/Hirst initiation model' of education arguing that this model was biased against a practical subject such as 'physical education/movement', as they called it. They proposed that the Munn committee adopt the scheme devised by another philosopher of education (Philip Phenix, 1964) whose 'realms of meaning' thesis, they claimed, offered greater scope to a movement-based subject. In laying out their view of physical education/movement, the SCCPE claimed that

> The early stages of the curriculum should attempt to help the child to become more aware of his/her own movement responses through kinesthetic feedback . . . [and should] help guide the child to an understanding of his individual movement characteristics. Cognitive understanding of underlying concepts of the activities and of individual movement responses should be established by this stage.
>
> (SCCPE, 1975: 6)

The SCCPE submission also claimed that 'the pupil should have a reasonably sophisticated body concept . . . a concept of aesthetic demands (and) a concept of the competitive nature of certain activities' (SCCPE, 1975: 7).

The emphasis that the submission placed upon understanding, cognition and conceptual development and the prominence of notions such as the aesthetic, were characteristic of the female tradition and the influence of educational gymnastics and modern dance. Significantly, the female-only Dunfermline College of Physical Education endorsed the SCCPE submission, but the male-only Scottish School of Physical Education (SSPE) did not. Indeed, the SSPE not only refused to endorse the submission, but went a step further and made a rival submission the following year. This later submission by the SSPE was altogether different to that of the SCCPE. The SSPE made no comment on the philosophy underpinning the approach likely to be taken by the Munn Committee. They made the case for physical education's inclusion in the core curriculum on the basis of its contribution to health, to the development of perceptual-motor skills through games and sports and as a preparation for life-time leisure activity. Where it was available, the men produced evidence from scientific studies to support their argument in each of these three areas.

The Munn Committee reported in 1977. Physical education was granted a place in the core curriculum of years 3 and 4 of Scottish secondary schools, though with two periods per week as compared to the five allocated to each of mathematics and English, and four to science and social studies. In Paragraph 4.17 of the Report, the Committee suggested that physical education could contribute to the development of skilful movement, to preparation for leisure, and to the health of all pupils. In justifying their decision to recommend only two periods a week for physical education, the Committee also suggested that as a 'non-cognitive activity' physical education should supplement its curriculum time through the extra-curriculum.

The similarities between the SSPE submission and the recommendations of the Munn Report were all too apparent. By the mid-1970s the male view of physical education, in Scotland in this case but arguably throughout Britain, had become the dominant perspective. The female view, it seemed, had been openly contested. The Committee countered the SCCPE's claims by bluntly stating that physical education was a 'non-cognitive activity'. The significance of this shift in the gendered definition of physical education should not be underestimated. Gender was clearly shown to be *central* to defining the subject, not merely an additional factor in this process. What the subject is today, the forms of engagement that it requires from learners and the criteria by which success should be measured, are stereotypically masculine. It follows that in order to be successful in the subject girls and women need to perform in a masculinised way, and furthermore, a particular masculinised way. This is a profound development and one that requires close and critical scrutiny since it impacts on the quality of physical education for all young people, female and male.

Conclusion

This chapter has sought to illustrate the gendered history of physical education through three episodes from the subject's recent past. I began with the notion that many adults currently accept that while there may have been gender issues in the past, physical education has now resolved these and girls are treated equally to boys. The subsequent investigation of a conference in the mid-1950s, a debate that continued in the literature into the 1960s and a crucial curriculum development process in the mid-1970s were intended to show that the optimistic view is not sustainable. On the contrary, historical investigation can lead us to no other conclusion than that physical education as it currently exists in many British schools is a masculinised form of the subject. But it is not merely masculinised. A particularly narrow vision of masculinity informs and is expressed in this masculinisation. Should this situation be a matter for concern? I believe it should. As is clearly evident in the other contributions to this book and in wider literature, this masculinised form of physical education does not meet the needs of many girls and at least some boys. A consequence is that many young people may be prevented from acquiring the knowledge, skills and motivation they need to lead active and healthy lifestyles. In schools funded by public money, such a situation is simply unacceptable.

However, we need to end with a note of caution. The male version of physical education is not a totalising discourse. This means that while it has achieved dominance, there are spaces for teachers and students to practise alternative forms of physical education that do not ascribe to the values and assumptions of stereotypically masculinised physical education. Other chapters in this book provide evidence to suggest that it is possible to expand those spaces and to provide forms of physical education that are properly educational for all young people. We must learn the lessons of history if the hopes contained in these alternative practices are to become a reality in students' later lives.

Notes

1 The partnership between the Board of Education and the Scottish Education Department was reflected in the 1903 Royal Commission on Physical Training (Scotland), a joint project and publication. This commission had an important influence on the direction of physical training throughout the UK, not only in Scotland.
2 The Scottish School of Physical Education (SSPE) was formed in 1932 to prepare male teachers of physical education, and for much of its history was part of Jordanhill College of Education, Glasgow. The SSPE was formally amalgamated with the women's college, Dunfermline College of Physical Education, in the late 1990s and survives as the Department of Physical Education, Sport and Leisure at the University of Edinburgh.

References

Board of Education (1909) *Syllabus of Physical Exercises for Schools*, London: HMSO.
Brown, H.C. (1958) The training of the man teacher of physical education, *Physical Education* 50 (91–4).
Fletcher, S. (1984) *Women First: The Female Tradition in English Physical Education, 1880–1980*, London: Athlone.
Hargreaves, J.A. (1994) *Sporting Females: Critical Issues in the History and Sociology of Women's Sport*, London: Routledge.
Hirst, P.H. (1974) *Knowledge and the Curriculum,* London: Routledge & Kegan Paul.
Kirk, D. (1992) *Defining Physical Education: The Social Construction of a School Subject in Postwar Britain*, London: Falmer.
Kirk, D. (2000) Gender associations: sport, state schools and Australian culture, *The International Journal of Sport History* 17(2/3): 49–64.
Knapp, B. (1963) *Skill in Sport*, London: Routledge & Kegan Paul.
Mangan, J.A. and Parks, R.J. (eds) (1987) *From 'Fair Sex' to Feminism: Sport and the Socialisation of Women in the Industrial and Post-Industrial Eras*, London: Frank Cass.
Ministry of Education (1952) *Moving and Growing: Physical Education in the Primary School, Part 1*, London: HMSO.
Munrow, A.D. (1955) *Pure and Applied Gymnastics*, London: Arnold.
Peters, R.S. (1966) *Ethics and Education*, London: Allen & Unwin.
Phenix, P. (1964) *Realms of Meaning*, London: McGraw-Hill.
Randall, M. (1961) *Basic Movement: A New Approach to Gymnastics*, London: Bell.
Scottish Central Committee on Physical Education (1975) Submission to the Munn Committee, unpublished paper.
Scottish Education Department/Consultative Committee on Curriculum (1977) *The Structure of the Curriculum in Years Three and Four of the Scottish Secondary School*, Edinburgh: HMSO.

Scottish School of Physical Education (1976) Submission to the Munn Committee, unpublished paper.

The Leaflet (1955) Physical Education Today and in the Future, *The Leaflet* 56(1): 6.

White, J. (1973) *Towards a Compulsory Curriculum*, London: Routledge & Kegan Paul.

Whitehead, N. and Hendry, L. (1976) *Teaching Physical Education in England: Description and Analysis*, London: Lepus.

Part II
Gender agendas

4   Difference matters: sexuality and physical education

Gill Clarke

Introduction

Earlier chapters within this collection have pointed to the specific traditions of physical education and in particular to the highly gender differentiated nature of these. These markedly conservative traditions have had a deleterious impact not only on the teaching and nature of the subject but also on conceptions of masculinity and femininity. This has contributed to a situation whereby damaging myths and stereotypes specifically about the participation of women and girls in physical education and sport have largely gone unchallenged. These prejudices centre on issues to do with the athletic body, heterosexuality and physicality. This chapter consequently seeks to raise issues around sexuality and physical education. It focuses attention on Section 28 of the Local Government Act (1988) which sought to prohibit the promotion of homosexuality within schools, and thereby illustrates attitudes towards sexuality and the impact that these have had on the educative system. Biographical research which endeavoured to make sense of the life stories of lesbian physical education teachers within the English schooling system is utilised to explore the effects of heterosexual discourses on their professional lives. Although the focus is largely on the experiences of lesbian physical education teachers it is crucial to acknowledge the impact that heterosexism and homophobia has had on boys and men and gay teachers in physical education and sport. Heterosexism

> refers to the system of beliefs, attitudes and institutional arrangements which reinforce that everyone is, or should be heterosexual; that hetero-sexuality is the only valid and worthwhile form of sexual expression; and that relationships between people of the opposite sex are vastly superior to any other lifestyle whether lesbian, gay, bisexual or single.
>
> (Labour Research Department, 1992: 4).

Homophobia is commonly defined as 'the irrational fear or intolerance of homosexuality, gay men or lesbians, and even behaviour that is perceived to be outside the boundaries of traditional gender role expectations' (Griffin and

Genasci, 1990: 211). The silences, fears and phobias that surround these issues make it difficult, if not impossible, to locate gay teachers in the macho masculine world of physical education (Clarke, 1998a). By this I mean that physical education has certain 'normalised' expectations of what it is to be male and it is these privileged ways of being that are hegemonic and often unquestioned. Those who do not explicitly portray traditional macho characteristics of toughness, aggression and physical prowess are likely to be ridiculed and their performances trivialised and marginalised by the dominant masculine group (see Parker, 1996). Thus, my attention is directed initially to specific situations within physical education that create anxiety and potential risks for lesbian teachers, in particular the supervising of changing rooms and showers. However, it is my contention that these anxieties could also be experienced by gay physical education teachers.[1] The relationships of these lesbian teachers with pupils both within the classroom and the extended curriculum, and with teaching colleagues, are examined insofar as these are locations where their heterosexual 'cover' might be blown and where specific tactics are required to protect their 'real' sexual identity. Finally, I consider how they feel the need to be seen to be 'normal' and how they deal with verbal harassment largely by pupils.

The schooling context

As the body is central to physical education, and the key vehicle for the expression of subject knowledge it is continually exposed and open to the gaze of others. Traditionally, it has been schooled along restricted and prescribed gender regimes[2] (see Scraton, 1992; Talbot, 1993). It is evident that both the content and pedagogical practices of physical education are built (and reproduced) through narrow ideologies and stereotyped visions of hetero-sexual femininity and masculinity. Accordingly, pupils and teachers learn and recognise the required 'feminine' and 'masculine' codes for acceptance within physical education and schooling more generally. These codes have to be made sense of within the confines of heterosexuality.

Lees' (1986: 145) research about sexuality and adolescent girls found that 'many girls expressed marked prejudice against them' [lesbians]. One of her subjects said 'Poofs I can tolerate but lesbians I can't. I suppose because it's my own sex' (p. 145). Lees' (1987: 177) research also revealed that 'lezzie' was the worst label that a girl could be called, far worse than a ' "slag" (a girl who sleeps around) or a "drag" (a "nice" girl who does not . . .)'. Sanders and Burke (1994: 69) also note that 'lezzie' is used as an insult and as a means to 'pressure the "other" to conform to stereotypical roles'. It is no wonder that given such pressures girls and women disengage from actively participating in physical education and sport. Boys are also pressurised into conforming. Indeed Lees (1993: 90) claims 'that it is far worse for a boy to show feminine qualities than for a girl to show masculine qualities'. Masculine identity is constructed in critical opposition to heterosexual femininity and anything deemed to be associated with femininity is subordinated and stigmatised. For a boy to be labelled a 'wimp', 'sissy', 'poofter' and or 'gay'[3] is one of the most virulent forms of insult (Askew and Ross, 1988; Duncan, 1999). As Paechter (1998: 104) points out

> the abusive form of these terms is of course derived from homophobia; the reason that it can be oppressive to be called 'gay' or 'lesbian', whether you are or not, is that lesbians and gay men are, in fact stigmatised both in and outside school.

This stigmatisation is exacerbated in England and Wales by the continued existence of Section 28 of the Local Government Act. This repressive legislation passed in 1988 by the Conservative government under the premiership of Margaret Thatcher stated that

(1) A local authority shall not:
  (a) intentionally promote homosexuality or publish material with the intention of promoting homosexuality;
  (b) promote the teaching in any maintained school of the acceptability of homosexuality as a pretended family relationship.

This legislation exemplified not only legal disapproval of lesbian and gay lifestyles but also the power of the Conservative New Right to dictate what constituted acceptable/normal sexual identity. In doing so it legitimised dominant discourses of compulsory heterosexuality. A situation which Epstein (2000: 387) notes 'both reflects and produces inequalities'.

Although Section 28 has been summarily dismissed as ambiguously worded it remains dangerously open to misinterpretation (Colvin and Hawksley, 1989). This confusion has created a situation whereby some teachers use it as an excuse for failing to act in cases of homophobic abuse (Douglas *et al.*, 1997; Epstein, 2000). Thus, whilst the provisions of Section 28 have yet to be interpreted by the courts its passing has undoubtedly had a marked effect on the teaching of lesbian and gay issues in schools.

Given this socio-political climate it is perhaps unsurprising that the largely conservative physical education profession has in the main failed to bring these issues into the public domain. Indeed, this chilly silence is also evidenced in the 'official texts' of the NCPE (2000, see chapter 7). These omissions are all the more disturbing given that earlier versions of the NCPE made specific reference to issues of 'the emergence of sexuality' (NCPE Interim Report, 1991: 17). These silences are complex and hugely powerful and signal tacit disapproval of other ways of being. Further, like Section 28 they legitimate and perpetuate hegemonic conceptions of masculinity and femininity such that it becomes difficult to challenge from either within or without. Nevertheless, the dramatic increase in homophobic bullying within schools makes it imperative that counter and more inclusive discourses are produced (Wallace,

2001). As Veri (1999: 358) points out 'counterdiscourses are needed in policies, laws, and curricula in order to strategically resist institutionalized homophobia and heterosexism.'

In order to illustrate the 'institutionalized homophobia and heterosexism' within schools I turn now to analyse the significance and impact of the context and subject matter of physical education on lesbian teachers' lives. This is identified as a major contributory factor in their feeling the need to conceal their lesbian identity from pupils, teachers, governors and parents.

Teaching physical education: a unique context

The prejudicial and discriminatory attitudes of the last Conservative Government towards lesbians and gay men has already been illustrated through reference to Section 28. This situation has left most lesbian, gay and bisexual teachers afraid to reveal their sexual identity for fear of loss of employment. In a homophobic and heterosexist world where moral traditionalist discourses about the family hold hegemonic power over other lifestyles, to be a lesbian teacher working with children is to be seen by some as 'a paedophile or pervert' (Lucy[4]). The gendered bodily culture of physical education and sport creates a unique context for denial of a homosexual identity that might not be experienced by teachers within other subject disciplines. Further, regardless of a physical education teachers' sexual identity the ways in which female physical education teachers are stereotyped as lesbian are well documented (Griffin, 1992; Squires and Sparkes, 1996). As Harris and Griffin (1997: 78) reveal this 'Labeling (or rather mis-labeling) the majority of women physical educators as lesbian is inaccurate. Such a term can be used to intimidate, discourage, devalue, and control women.'

The muscular athletic female body stands in sharp contrast to cultural conceptions of what it is to be stereotypically female, namely, passive and having a 'feminine' appearance. To transgress these bodily boundaries is to be deviant, not normal. Sport in general is associated with the defeminisation of women and the masculinisation of men, hence women and girls who participate in the male domain of physical education and sport and specifically in those activities not seen as stereotypically feminine run the risk of their sexual identity being called into question and the pejorative label lesbian applied. Many therefore seek to distance themselves from any possible suggestion of or association with lesbianism, as a result we often see evidence of what has been described as hyperfemininity (Felshin, 1974; Lenskyj, 1994). The wearing of jewellery and make-up announces a so-called 'normal' sexuality. For men and boys a 'normal' sexuality is demonstrated and proved by prowess in sport (see Connell, 1995). Failure to sustain a skilful performance and or to exhibit physical and mental toughness is to run the risk of homophobic abuse and ridicule, a situation that Parker (1996) found amongst 13–14 year old boys when their peers performed badly in competitive sport. Further, as Harris (1995, cited in Sparkes and Silvennoinen, 1999) reveals

Competitive sports can be painful for those men [and boys] who feel inferior because they cannot perform to the standards expected of them. For other men [and boys] who do not succeed, the sportsman message can cause them to doubt their worth as men [and boys].

Although prowess in competitive sport can be seen to be a marker for hegemonic heterosexual masculinity, prowess or indeed liking a physical activity that is not stereotypically masculine is a risky occurrence. Boys and men who wish to participate in dance or other related activities where they are required to display grace and exhibit emotional characteristics that are not regarded as being traditionally and stereotypically masculine also run the risk of their sexual identity being called into question and the pejorative label gay applied. Flintoff (1995: 56) has also shown how in Initial Teacher Education (ITE) male students 'do masculinity' and go

> out of their way to demonstrate their lack of commitment to 'feminine' activities like dance by fooling around, and being generally disruptive. Homophobic comments were also common, acting to reinforce the display of appropriately 'gendered' behaviour by male and female students, but also to make virtually untenable the position of any student (or lecturer) whose sexual orientation was not heterosexual.[5]

The physical nature of the subject creates particular worries for lesbian teachers since they are extremely wary as to how they may be perceived by others when they have to support and/or touch pupils. Ethel acknowledged that she felt vulnerable when she was 'Supporting female pupils in gymnastics or helping pupils hold a racket correctly (or a) piece of athletics equipment correctly . . . or generally any situation where I come into physical contact with the pupil'. Both Barbara and Caroline also confirmed that they felt anxious when they had to support pupils in gymnastics. Fay was the only teacher to indicate that she felt less wary when she had to support pupils because she believed that 'they seem to accept that you are going to have to support them anyway and so they don't seem to mind in that situation and they don't seem to feel inhibited or constricted by you touching them in those situations'.

In relation to the worries expressed by these lesbian teachers about the potential for false allegations, it is important to acknowledge that heterosexual teachers are also vulnerable to such accusations, but these lesbian women felt that it was not to the same degree. Annie believed that 'any false allegation would be less believed if the governors found they had a lovely boyfriend, but if the governors found you had a lovely girlfriend I'm sure it would open some homophobic doors'. Kay also recognised that it was a problem and she pointed out that no teacher liked to be faced with such situations. However, she was at pains to explain that it was a particularly sensitive and threatening issue for a lesbian teacher (Clarke, 1995).

Supervising changing rooms and pupil folklore

The daily routine of supervising pupils in changing rooms is another potentially threatening situation to be safely negotiated. As Caroline commented 'I don't go into the changing rooms and ever stay there, I walk in and out until they are dressed and then I speak to them.' There was also much fear over the supervision of pupils through showers, relating to concerns about being seen to be watching pupils. Consequently, all of the teachers went to great lengths to avoid being in the showering area. However, such strategies did not prevent some pupils spreading rumours about their teachers. I received a letter from Ivy (19 November 1997) in which she described a number of incidents that had occurred in the school where she teaches and which were related to her being thought of as a lesbian. One of these was associated with the issue of showering. Accordingly it seems pertinent to report it here.

> Two Year 8 girls . . . came out with the following statement to my straight colleague – who I am 'out' to. (Sorry about the pun). Basically, they said that the only reason girls don't shower was that there had been something in the paper that I had been found to be looking at girls in the showers. They had supposedly got this story from their aunty. Penny (a colleague) was terrific. They said that I must therefore be a lesbian. She replied that there had been nothing in the papers and dispelled their 'allegations'. She pointed out the supervisory nature of our role, and said because of their allegations, she would take the matter further. In consultation with me, I contacted the year Co-ordinator – who in turn told the Head – who in turn called the parents in. The parents were very apologetic, and had no knowledge of where the girls got the story from. The aunty was apparently someone whom Penny and I had both taught. The incident was handled very sensitively.

This scenario also illustrates that it is not only pupils that stereotype and label physical education teachers as lesbian. Their families may also hold such beliefs. Scraton (1992: 102) found evidence of similar parental beliefs. Her research revealed that at Townley School 'parental pressure stopped showering', as they were concerned that 'physical education staff would be able to watch their daughters in the showers'. As Scraton (1992: 102) comments, what this reaction actually implies is 'not only a concern to protect their daughter's sexuality (i.e. a protected, hidden heterosexuality), but also a homophobic assumption that female physical education teachers' heterosexuality is "questionable"'. It is also important to note that teachers may have to deal with colleagues who are not supportive.

In considering where the pupils at Ivy's school got their story from it is worth considering the place of pupils' folklore in the stories about transfer from primary to secondary school. Pugsley *et al.* (1996) found that many of these stories related to sexuality and to showers.[6] They suggest that for girls it is the most common fear about secondary school physical education. The other main 'fear' about physical education is the presence of the teacher. The following statements were written by their research subjects.

> I was told by a friend that everyone had to have a shower, watched by a teacher after sports.

> Before I went to Westhaven High school I was told by my sister that the PE teacher was gay and watched while you changed for PE and made you have a shower and watched while you had it.

> All the girls feared Miss Alexander for PE. Rumour had it she stood by the showers in the changing room, made you take your towel off and watched you showering.

It is possible that the statements made about Ivy were part of pupils' folklore, but regardless of the origin it says much about how young people view lesbians (and gay men). As Woods (1992: 91) and others have shown physical education teachers are particularly vulnerable to homophobic accusations, 'to be athletic is equated with masculinity and masculine women are labelled as lesbian. Therefore, athletic women are stereotyped as lesbian.' Hence many women in the male domain of sport and physical education learn that to be physically active, to develop muscle is to be at 'odds' with what 'real', 'normal' and 'feminine' women do. Thus, it takes 'strong' women to challenge these messages, and it could be argued that women in physical education by their very presence teaching a 'physical' subject do indeed challenge these messages (see Griffin, 1998).

Risky situations: social relations with colleagues

For the lesbian teachers in my research situations which might lead to the revealing of a lesbian identity were either avoided or closely monitored for the degree of risk. Such strategies contributed to the successful passing of the heterosexual presumption. Accordingly there was much apprehension about the kinds of questions that colleagues might ask about personal lives, most felt it safer not to say too much and to suppress their desire to talk about their home lives. Within the gendered locale of staffrooms (see Shilling, 1991) the stories that do get told are largely heterosexual ones, as Swigonski (1995: 417–18) records 'Heterocentrism structures perceptions of reality so that heterosexual ways of being define the nature of human relationships', and, I would add, the nature of many conversations. Heterosexual discourses impact on all women (and men) in teaching and on gender relations within the teaching profession (De Lyon and Widdowson Migniuolo, 1989; Siraj-Blatchford, 1993), but in this particular study it was evident how they impacted on lesbian teachers in especially damaging ways. Ivy's experiences of life in the staffroom lend support to this contention. For Ivy, who had been married for over fifteen years before 'falling in love with a woman and becoming a lesbian', the contrast was dramatic. She described how previously she was 'very free, very open', and

> had been a very chatty person about my life and saying to people 'what did you do at the weekend?' . . . I was very much a sharer in my life and other people's lives, but from that moment on I suddenly, or dramatically started to spiral inwards and closed my world entirely.

Ivy's world is no longer so closed, she has now 'come out' to a very small number of teaching colleagues and is able to talk with them about her 'private' life and her relationship with her partner. These teachers learned how to manage staffroom conversations so as to minimise the likelihood of exposure of their lesbian identity. This entailed the steering away of conversations which focused on children and partners to less threatening frames of reference. This strategy was not without its costs in terms of the nature of friendships that could be safely established within school. For Harriet this led her to 'hold back a significant part of myself all the time. I don't have any sort of intimate friendships [at work]. I suppose for fear of being exposed and for the pain that would cause'.

These narratives illustrate how the self is censored and policed and how pupils are denied the visible and positive presence of lesbian role models. The following section reveals further strategies that these lesbian teachers employ so as to appear to comply with dominant discourses of compulsory heterosexuality.

Keeping your distance: social relations with pupils and the extended curriculum

Interactions with pupils were seen as a site for the possible exposure of a lesbian identity. All the teachers commented in some detail about how they avoided getting 'too close' to pupils so as not to place themselves in risky situations. Hence, they tended to 'back off' and keep their distance in their dealings with pupils particularly in after school activities where traditionally teachers have felt able to develop less formal relationships with pupils. Several of the women did not feel quite so anxious. For instance Jay, who taught in an inner city school, which she described as having 'a lot of social problems', was rarely involved in extra curricular activities. She made the point that 'it is extremely difficult to get the girls to stay behind after school, partly because their parents are very worried about them getting home late, it's impossible to get them out on a Saturday'.

The 900 pupils in Jay's school were mainly boys of whom 70–85 per cent were Bengali, and many of the girls were Muslim. The points I am making here relate to the need to remain aware that schools are not homogeneous and hence the experiences of lesbian teachers may vary. This may be due to the location and cultural mix of the school and the attitudes of staff, parents and pupils to activities after school. Further, what is acceptable in terms of dress, physical contact/display of the body will differ amongst different cultural groups. Additionally, it should not be assumed that pupils from some ethnic minority groups are less interested than their 'white' counterparts in physical activity (Verma and Darby, 1994; see also Benn in chapter 5). As Zaman (1997: 65) states

> it is clear that a major problem surrounding participation is the ways in which sport, physical activity and physical education are organised and made available and not necessarily the activities themselves. If we genuinely want to increase the participation of Muslim young women, then Muslim values need to influence and inform the context in the way activities are structured and accessed.

It is also pertinent to this discussion to recognise that participation in the extended curriculum may be less important in some schools than others and moreover what is on offer may be at odds with the culture of young people's leisure and lifestyles (Hendry *et al.*, 1993). In the specific case of girls there is considerable evidence to support the view that the culture of physical education clashes sharply with the culture of heterosexual and emphasised femininity (Scraton, 1987; 1992).

Being seen to be 'normal'

Being seen as 'normal', that is heterosexual, meant that many of the women felt the need to introduce male figures into conversations, be they real or mythical. This adopting of dual identities, pseudo-heterosexual and lesbian, created tensions for many of the women. This identity dilemma was not experienced uniformly by all the women. Ethel who had been teaching for over twenty years felt that although she needed to be two people, as she got older it was something that was quite easy to keep going. This interface between age and sexual identity is worthy of further exploration, for it would seem to be an issue that also is not exclusively a problem for lesbian women. Indeed, single women in their 40s or 50s can experience the same pressure to engage in denial about their relationships (Clarke, 1996). Increasingly, to be deemed normal is to have a partner of the opposite sex and as such a clear heterosexual identity is evidenced. Inherent in the expectation of an established partnership are assumptions about sexual identity and what it is to be a 'real' woman. Thus, those teachers choosing to remain single may well face scrutiny.

What emerges from these stories is that the younger women generally felt that their lesbian identities were relatively safe. But being younger also meant that they were likely to be asked more personal questions by pupils. A lacuna in previous research into the lives of lesbian physical education teachers seems to be consideration of those women who are more senior members of the profession and for whom the issue of retirement becomes a key factor. This could in part be due to the 'physical' nature/culture of the subject that leads physical education teachers to think that they should be 'Growing old gracefully' (Sikes, 1988). Hence many women and men look to move away from the bodily demands of teaching physical education to other arenas within schools, such as pastoral roles and/or to teach subjects that do not require the same degree of physical competence/activity. Such moves are also likely to be related to increased promotional prospects. For Ivy it is more a matter of having fourteen years left, or as she said, 'fourteen years to survive is how I view it to be quite honest.' She wrote

> I have ten years left in teaching before I retire. I often joke that I'll be working for Stonewall, or some other L/G [lesbian/gay] organisation because I'll not be able to teach P.E. But the joke is not all light-hearted. I need the salary my job pays. At 49 there are '0' options. If I could get a job with the same salary – £24,000! I would do so at once, rather than feel under the constant pressure of losing my job, or not being able to continue in my post due to my sexuality.
>
> (Personal correspondence, 19 November 1997)

Running through most of these life stories was the feeling that within school they were living a lie, for some this had a damaging effect on their self-esteem and led to them feeling dishonest. These stories vividly illustrate the embeddedness of heterosexual discourses and the negative impact that they have on the lives of lesbian teachers.

(Hetero) sexual harassment

Many of the women had been subject to harassment because of their sexuality. Although I am unable to describe here the myriad of behaviours that constitute harassment, for the purposes of this research I utilise Halson's (1991: 99) working definition that 'Whatever its particular form, the behaviour in question is experienced as humiliating, embarrassing, threatening. . . . It offends, it objectifies, it denies autonomy, it controls.' I share Epstein's view (1996: 203) that in order to develop 'a fuller understanding of sexist harassment we need to see it within the context of . . . "compulsory hetero-sexuality"'. These points are helpful in that they draw attention to just how powerful the discourses of heterosexuality are and how institutionalised they are particularly within the educative system. Indeed, Epstein discusses how harassment can be understood 'as a kind of pedagogy of heterosexuality (ibid.: 203) . . . which schools women and men into normative heterosexuality (but not always successfully)' (ibid.: 207). In other words girls, women, boys and men are schooled into appropriate ways of behaving sexually, that is heterosexually.

The harassment the lesbian teachers had been subjected to was mainly from pupils, in school this often took the form of name calling, such as 'lezzie', 'dyke', 'homo', and/or 'queer' and in some instances graffiti also appeared around the school about a teacher's lesbianism. The women ignored the verbal comments as much as possible for fear of bringing too much attention to themselves. Ivy felt that there had been 'a shift in society', she was of the opinion that

> whereas any hint/gossip was kept amongst pupils, and whereas if you were married then there could be no question of where your sexuality was centred, now, pupils feel that it is quite acceptable to bring these issues into the public domain with little understanding of the consequences of what they are saying.
>
> (Personal correspondence, 19 November 1997)

In connection with this contention Andrews' (1990: 351) earlier research reveals how

> The more public profile of homosexuality . . . inevitably means more chat and gossip in corridors and classrooms. 'Revelations' in the popular press about a gay judge or film star, . . . reference to gay love in a GCSE text, all these may provoke hostility and controversy. If you are lesbian or gay the potential abuse is an ever present threat to your sense of safety and well-being in the world. If you decide to challenge prejudice you risk personal abuse, ridicule and adverse publicity.

Challenging prejudice for some is not worth the possible risk entailed. Further it is manifest that these physical education teachers are doubly vulnerable, as women and as lesbians.

Concluding remarks

Schools and physical education departments are powerful social and patriarchal institutions structured along heterosexual lines that operate to suppress alternative ways of being and performing. The schooling process defines and regulates what is socially acceptable through adherence to the required heterosexual gender regimes and through the activities on offer. The life stories discussed in this chapter have illustrated the oppressive power of these hegemonic heterosexual discourses to control and constrain the lives of lesbian teachers within the schooling context in general and more specifically within that of physical education. As I have demonstrated the concept of heterosexuality as compulsory is a key element in understanding and making sense of the ways in which these lesbian teachers feel the need to conceal and protect their sexual identities from exposure to the scrutiny of heterosexual 'others'. Thus, it is essential that their actions are understood both within this heterosexual matrix and the specific bodily context of physical education. Further, it is evident just how pervasive and naturalised heterosexuality is, be it in the staffroom, the changing room or in relationships between pupils and their teachers. Moreover, it is also legitimised through the discourse of Section 28. Physical education in schools and Initial Teacher Education has much to do if it is to disrupt and redress this unjust situation. A first step would be to openly acknowledge how heterosexism and homophobia act as deterrents to participation in physical education and sport. Schools in general could contribute to a more equitable and inclusive environment for both pupils and staff by subjecting the curriculum, grouping polices and teaching and learning strategies to critical scrutiny and by establishing non-discrimination and anti-harassment policies that include sexual orientation. By explicitly broadening their policies and perceptions about the multiple and contested forms of masculinity, femininity and sexual identity, physical education departments could enable all young people to begin to experience the life-long pleasures of what it is to be physically active without fear of sanction and reprisal. The recommendations that follow are intended to aid this process. They begin from the premise that homophobia is another form of discrimination that must be overcome if all pupils, student teachers, and teachers are to be provided with inclusive, effective and safe learning and working environments.

Challenging and addressing homophobia and heterosexism requires a *whole-school* commitment to:

- no form of discrimination being tolerated;
- equal opportunities policies being extended to include sexual orientation;
- non-discrimination and anti-harassment policies and practices being enacted, monitored and reviewed for their effectiveness;
- homophobic slurs/jokes/bullying/graffiti/name-calling being challenged;
- heterosexual assumptions ceasing;
- resources being available in school and the community which dispel and counter the myths and stereotypes about sexuality and physical education and sport;
- providing support for pupils, staff, coaches, governors and parents/carers;
- schools providing awareness training/education for all pupils, staff, coaches, governors, parents/carers;
- providing positive images/role models of lesbian and gay athletes/coaches/teachers;
- recognising that this is a key issue for citizenship education.

Notes

1 This difficulty led Sparkes (1997) to write an ethnographic fiction about a gay physical education teacher.

2 I use 'gender regime' in much the same way as Kessler *et al.* (1985, cited in Acker, 1994: 92) who explain it as 'the pattern of practices that constructs various kinds of masculinity and femininity among staff and students, orders them in terms of prestige and power, and constructs a sexual division of labor within the institution'.

3 Duncan (1999: 19) comments ' "Gay" seemed to have duality of meaning against boys in much the same way as "slag", "cow" or "dog" were used against girls. The word was recognised as meaning homosexual, but for most purposes it denoted a wider negative male role.'

4 The fourteen white, able bodied lesbian teachers involved in the research from 1993 to 1995 were from the outset given pseudonyms. They taught in a variety of secondary schools (i.e. mixed comprehensives, girls' schools, church and independent schools) and were aged between 23 and 47, some had just started their teaching careers, whilst others had been teaching for over 25 years. Their schools are located in inner cities, urban and or rural areas. Some of the women were single, some had been married, some were currently in long-standing relationships, and none had children. They came from a variety of working- and middle-class backgrounds. Making contact and gaining access was difficult due to the prevailing climate of fear of exposure and loss of employment that surrounds lesbian (and gay) teachers and forces many of them to remain an invisible and silent presence within our schools. Contact was therefore initially made through lesbians known to me, who contacted other lesbians, to see if they were willing to talk in confidence about their lives. This created a 'snowballing' effect where one woman put me in contact with another and so forth. Contact was also made in this manner because such are the silences and the relative secrecy that it is not always possible to identify through any other method, with any degree of certainty, those women who are lesbian.

A biographical methodology was utilised as an approach particularly well suited to gaining a closely textured account of lesbian lives within the educational system and for interpreting data generated by the life story interviews. As well as offering a detailed examination of selves in specific settings the research was additionally concerned to make visible the structural and interactional injustices confronting lesbian teachers. For more details about the research process, see Clarke, 1997; 1998b and 1998c.

5 I have written elsewhere about the experiences of lesbian physical education students and the verbal and physical abuse that they are subjected to largely by their heterosexual male peers (see Clarke, 1996; 2000).

6 Pugsley *et al.* (1996) only asked for 'scarey stories'.

References

Acker, S. (1994) *Gendered Education: Sociological Reflections on Women, Teaching and Feminism*, Buckingham: Open University Press.

Andrews, J. (1990) Don't pass us by: keeping lesbian and gay issues on the agenda, *Gender and Education* 2(3): 351–5.

Askew, S. and Ross, C. (1988) *Boys Don't Cry: Boys and Sexism in Education*, Milton Keynes: Open University Press.

Clarke, G. (1995) Outlaws in sport and education? Exploring the sporting and education experiences of lesbian physical education teachers, in L. Lawrence, E. Murdoch and S. Parker (eds) *Professional and Development Issues in Leisure, Sport and Education*, Eastbourne: Leisure Studies Association.

Clarke, G. (1996) Conforming and contesting with (a) difference: how lesbian students and teachers manage their identities, *International Studies in Sociology of Education* 6(2): 191–209.

Clarke, G. (1997) Playing a part: the lives of lesbian physical education teachers, in G. Clarke and B. Humberstone (eds) *Researching Women and Sport*, London: Macmillan.

Clarke, G. (1998a) Queering the pitch and coming out to play: lesbians in physical education and sport, *Sport, Education and Society* 3(2): 145–60.

Clarke, G. (1998b) *Voices from the Margins: Lesbian Teachers in Physical Education*, unpublished PhD thesis, Leeds Metropolitan University.

Clarke, G. (1998c) Voices from the margins: resistance and regulation in the lives of lesbian teachers, in M. Erben (ed.) *Biography and Education: An Edited Collection*, London: Falmer Press.

Clarke, G. (2000) Crossing borders: lesbian physical education students and the struggles for sexual spaces, in S. Scraton and B. Watson (eds) *Sport, Leisure and Gendered Spaces*, Eastbourne: Leisure Studies Association.

Colvin, M. with Hawksley, J. (1989) *Section 28: A Practical Guide to the Law and its Implications*, London: National Council for Civil Liberties.

Connell, R.W. (1995) *Masculinities*, Oxford: Polity Press.

De Lyon, H. and Widdowson Migniuolo, F. (eds) (1989) *Women Teachers: Issues and Experiences*, Milton Keynes: Open University Press.

Douglas, N., Warwick, I., Kemp, S. and Whitty, G. (1997) *Playing it Safe: Responses of Secondary School Teachers to Lesbian, Gay and Bisexual Pupils, Bullying, HIV and AIDS Education and Section 28*, Health and Education Research Unit, Institute of Education: University of London.

Duncan, N. (1999) *Sexual Bullying: Gender Conflict and Pupil Culture in Secondary Schools*, London: Routledge.

Epstein, D. (1996) Keeping them in their place: hetero/sexist harassment, gender and the enforcement of heterosexuality, in J. Holland and L. Adkins (eds) *Sex, Sensibility and the Gendered Body*, London: Macmillan.

Epstein, D. (2000) Sexualities and education: catch 28, *Sexualities* 3(4): 387–94.

Felshin, J. (1974) The dialectic of women and sport, in E.W. Gerber, J. Felshin, P. Berlin and W. Wyrick (eds) *The American Women in Sport*, Reading: Addison-Wesley.

Flintoff, A. (1995) Learning and teaching in PE: a lesson in gender?, in A. Tomlinson (ed.) *Gender, Sport and Leisure: Continuities and Challenges*, Eastbourne: Leisure Studies Association.

Griffin, P. (1992) Changing the game: homophobia, sexism, and lesbians in sport, *Quest* 44(2): 251–65.

Griffin, P. (1998) *Strong Women, Deep Closets: Lesbians and Homophobia in Sport*, Champaign: Human Kinetics.

Griffin, P. and Genasci, J. (1990) Addressing homophobia in physical education: responsibilities for teachers and researchers, in M.A. Messner and D.F. Sabo (eds) S*port, Men and the Gender Order*, Leeds: Human Kinetics.

Halson, J. (1991) Young women, sexual harassment and heterosexuality: violence, power relations and mixed-sex schooling, in P. Abbott and C. Wallace (eds) *Gender, Power and Sexuality*, London: Macmillan.

Harris, M.B. and Griffin, J. (1997) Stereotypes and personal beliefs about women physical education teachers' *Women in Sport and Physical Activity Journal* 6(1): 49–83.

Hendry, L.B., Shucksmith, J., Love, J.G. and Glendinning, A. (1993) *Young People's Leisure and Lifestyles*, London: Routledge.

Labour Research Department (1992) *Out at Work: Lesbian and Gay Workers' Rights*, London: LRD Publications Ltd.

Lees, S. (1986) *Losing Out: Sexuality and Adolescent Girls*, London: Hutchinson.

Lees, S. (1987) The structure of sexual relations in school, in M. Arnot and G. Weiner (eds) *Gender and the Politics of Schooling*, London: Unwin Hyman.

Lees, S. (1993) *Sexuality and Spice: Sexuality and Adolescent Girls*, London: Penguin.

Lenskyj, H. (1991) Combating homophobia in sport and physical education, *Sociology of Sport Journal* 8: 61–9.

Lenskyj, H. (1994) Sexuality and femininity in sport contexts: issues and alternatives, *Journal of Sport and Social Issues* 18(4): 356–76.

National Curriculum Physical Education Working Group (1991) *Interim Report*, London: Department of Education and Science.

Paechter, C. (1998) *Educating the Other: Gender, Power and Schooling*, London: Falmer Press.

Parker, A. (1996) The construction of masculinity within boys' physical education, *Gender and Education* 8(2): 141–57.

Pugsley, L., Coffey, A. and Delamont S. (1996) Daps, dykes and five mile hikes: physical education in pupils' folklore, *Sport, Education and Society* 1(2): 133–46.

Sanders, S.A.L. and Burke, H. (1994) 'Are you a lesbian Miss?' in D. Epstein (ed.) *Challenging Lesbian and Gay Inequalities in Education*, Buckingham: Open University Press.

Scraton, S. (1987) 'Boys muscle in where angels fear to tread' – girls' sub-cultures and physical activities, in J. Horne, D. Jary and A. Tomlinson (eds) *Sport, Leisure and Social Relations*, London: Routledge & Kegan Paul.

Scraton, S. (1992) *Shaping Up to Womanhood: Gender and Girls' Physical Education*, Buckingham: Open University Press.

Shilling, C. (1991) Social space, gender inequalities and educational differentiation, *British Journal of Sociology of Education* 12(1): 23–44.

Sikes, P.J. (1988) Growing old gracefully? Age, identity and physical education, in J. Evans (ed.) *Teachers, Teaching and Control in Physical Education*, Lewes: Falmer Press.

Siraj-Blatchford, I. (ed.) (1993) *'Race', Gender and the Education of Teachers*, Buckingham: Open University Press.

Sparkes, A. (1997) Ethnographic fiction and representing the absent other, *Sport, Education and Society* 2(1): 25–40.

Sparkes, A. and Silvennoinen, M. (eds) (1999) *Talking Bodies: Men's Narratives of the Body and Sport*, University of Jyvaskyla, Finland: SoPhi.

Squires, S.L. and Sparkes A.C. (1996) Circles of silence: sexual identity in physical education and sport, *Sport, Education and Society* 1(1): 77–101.

Swigonski, M.E. (1995) Claiming a lesbian identity as act of empowerment, *AFFILIA: Journal of Women and Social Work* 10(4): 413–25.

Talbot, M. (1993) A gendered physical education: equality and sexism, in J. Evans (ed.) *Equality, Education and Physical Education*, London: Falmer Press.

Veri, M.J. (1999) Homophobic discourse surrounding the female athlete, *Quest* 51(4): 355–68.

Verma, G.K. and Darby, D.S. (eds) (1994) *Winners and Losers: Ethnic Minorities in Sport and Recreation*, London: Falmer Press.

Wallace, W. (2001) Is this table gay? Anatomy of a classroom insult, *Times Educational Supplement*, 19 January: 9–10.

Woods, S. (1992) Describing the experiences of lesbian physical educators: a phenomenological study, in A.C. Sparkes (ed.) *Research in Physical Education and Sport: Exploring Alternative Visions*, London: Falmer Press.

Zaman, H. (1997) Islam, well-being and physical activity: perceptions of Muslim young women, in G. Clarke and B. Humberstone (eds) *Researching Women and Sport*, London: Macmillan.

5 Muslim women in teacher training: issues of gender, 'race' and religion

Tansin Benn

Introduction

The case study research that is reported in this chapter explored equity issues in relation to life-experiences, opportunities and constraints for Muslim women in teacher training, with a focus on subject experiences within physical education. The research was motivated by the fact that, despite Government efforts, ethnic minority students are still under-represented in higher education and the teaching profession (DES (1989) Circular 24/89; EOC, 1989). In England's second largest city, where part of this case study was located, it is predicted that by 2001, ethnic minorities will constitute one in three 16-year-old pupils in the schools, yet only 5 per cent of the City's teaching force. The data presented in this chapter pinpoints the complexity of overlays of disadvantage experienced by Muslim women, including inter-actions of 'race' (used, as by Siraj-Blatchford, 1993, in inverted commas to acknowledge the problematic nature of the term yet the significance of racism), ethnicity, religion, culture and gender. In the research a qualitative study with a group of Muslim women in initial teacher training, in one higher education institution (HEI) provided a 'micro' perspective of a particular group and situation. An accompanying questionnaire survey of all other higher education institutes in England and Wales offering initial teacher training with an element of physical education, was used to give a 'macro' perspective on the issues being explored. Research based in higher education is rare. Most sociological researchers pursue critical investigations of other sites in preference to their own. Siraj-Blatchford (ibid.: 35) has highlighted that 'the experiences of black students (Asian and African-Caribbean) in higher education have been largely ignored'. The data generated in this research can be seen to extend our knowledge and understanding of ways in which institutional and subject cultures, traditions, policies and practices, variously impact on particular and invariably marginalised, groups. We see the challenges that arise if teacher training is to embrace in policy and practice, conceptualisations of gender that acknowledge multiple identities and differences.

Theory and method

The research was a theoretically informed empirical study, underpinned by a process theory of identity (Elias, 1991; Mennel, 1994). This theory explores how identity is shaped and re-shaped in processes of interaction with others. As student-teachers in one HEI the Muslim women would be bound in 'figurations' or networks of mutually interested, differentially related, inter-dependent human beings. Seventeen self-declared Muslim women initially volunteered to take part in an interpretive, qualitative study. Their involve-ment in the research eventually spanned four years (from 1994 to 1998), the first two in initial teacher training the latter two in their early teaching careers. Discussion in this chapter draws upon data from the first two years of the study, gathered via interviews, participant diaries and observations. Through-out the research the focus was on the women's experiences and perceptions of the influence of others (including peers, tutors, school-experience teachers, parents, head teachers) on their professional and personal development in training. Analysis of the data highlighted the process of negotiation and change that was occurring within one HEI as a result of increasing numbers of Muslim women entering the teacher-training programme. Lecturing and management staff were making changes in the direction of providing a more compatible environment for the Muslim students, and were learning much in this process of development. Arguably, the negotiations and changes that occurred in this HEI are required in all training institutions and not only in relation to the needs of Muslim students.

The qualitative research focused on one particular group, defined by sex and religious belief. Although clearly not a homogeneous group, Muslims are united globally by the basic tenets of their faith. Whilst many are born into Islam, many others across the world choose to embrace the faith. It is not only a religion but a way of life, providing frames within which followers endeavour to live their lives as 'good Muslims', following religious guidance for men and women on diet, dress, prayer and behaviour. Respect for others, humility, and the importance of family, are key aspects of their faith. Focusing on Muslim women's experiences meant that issues of gender, 'race', ethnicity and culture, emerged alongside and inter-twined with religion. Since such terms are often confused and used loosely, later I clarify the ways in which they were approached in this study.

In order to gain a wider picture of awareness and the needs of Muslim students in higher education, lessons learned from the qualitative study were used in a subsequent questionnaire survey (conducted in the 1999/2000 academic year) of seventy higher education institutions in England and Wales offering teacher training in physical education at either primary or secondary level. The survey was directed to the relevant heads of department within these institutions and received a 50 per cent return. The heads of department were recognised as key people challenging or perpetuating institutional/ departmental ethos, policies, practices and procedures. The questionnaire focused on the extent to which, if at all, other institutions were able to meet and/or respond to the needs of Muslim student teacher-trainees. More specifically it addressed:

- awareness of numbers of Muslim students entering higher education;
- whether Muslim students had ever raised issues of religious requirements;
- to what extent the institution addressed general Islamic requirements such as single sex accommodation, dietary requirements, the honouring of Muslim Festival days or provision of a prayer room;
- whether issues of religious requirements had ever been raised in relation to participation in physical education, for example the need for single-sex groups, same-sex environments, privacy of accommodation or kit requirements;
- where colleagues had no experience to date of accommodating Muslim students' needs, hypothetical views were sought.

Although the questionnaire was designed to elicit quantitative data, questions were also incorporated that would enable colleagues to expand answers, qualitatively, where they wished. Before discussing the data generated by the research, there is a need to address my own location and identity; as a researcher, but also a lecturer in the HEI being investigated.

The researcher's position

The power differentials between researcher and researched in the qualitative dimension of this study may be seen by some as problematic. As a researcher I am positioned as a white, non-Muslim woman and head of physical education in the HEI investigated. The respondents were Muslim, predominantly of Asian heritage and students. Fellow researchers are divided over the effects of such differentials. For example, Essed (1991) suggested that black respondents would not talk freely to white researchers whilst Rhodes (1994, cited in Mirza, 1995) suggested that black respondents would be less happy talking to black researchers. Haw (1996) believes in the possibility of dialogue despite these differentials and that the future of research should be open to possibilities rather than closed by the creation of boundaries. She suggested success in cross-structural research as related to 'travelling sensitively and judiciously' (ibid.: 329).

Requirements relating to Islam would have prohibited some of the respondents from participating in one-to-one interviews with a male researcher. Ultimately, being non-Muslim appeared to be an asset since the women were not threatened by fear of any judgements on their religiosity.[1] Being non-Asian was perhaps, however, the greatest barrier in this research. There were deeply ingrained differences between myself and the participants, rooted in social habitus that limited some aspects of understanding the life-experiences of others.

The tutor/student relationship is probably best understood through the notion of relational power. As Brown and Rich (in chapter 6) also discuss, this concept is helpful in analysing power balances between groups of people, or ways in which the actions of one group enable or constrain opportunities and experiences of others. For example, gender relations denotes that changes affecting women necessarily have repercussions for men and vice versa. Process sociologists focus on shifts in balances of power within figurations, for example within gender relations, ethnic relations and other differential relations such as tutor/student. As George and Jones (1992) point out: although a tutor has more power in certain respects than students, no one is powerless. The entire qualitative research process in this study was dependent on the students, their contributions and commitment, and in that sense the students were very powerful.

Gender

Gender refers to ways in which the Muslim women's lives are affected by the socially constructed (some would argue divinely constructed) attitudes, values, beliefs, actions and behaviours expected, adopted and embodied because of their sex. For example, in the subject area of physical education, myths and assumptions exist about constraints surrounding participation, particularly of Muslim girls and women. This is partly fuelled by the fact that Muslim women do not feature prominently in major international sporting events such as the Olympic Games, and when they do they may suffer discrimination and exclusion from within their communities (Hargreaves, 1994; Scharenburg, 1999). As we see in later discussion, women's participation in sport and physical education is not anti-Islamic but is dependent on religious requirements being met in relation to issues such as modest dress, privacy for changing and single-sex environments.

Undoubtedly there is a rhetoric/reality gap between theory of Islam and lived-experiences for many Muslim women, as recognised by Sfeir (1985). Ahmed (1992) explains the difference in terms of 'ideological Islam' in which the equality of women in Islam is not disputed, and 'establishment Islam' where political/legal Islam fixes women's position as 'subordinate'. There is much that is misunderstood about the position of women in Islam, particularly when viewed from western feminist perspectives (Faruqi, 1991). This is not to deny that terrible abuses and constraints have been carried out on Muslim women in the name of Islam as described by Jawad (1998: 15):

> Women have, in many cases been deprived even of the basic human rights advocated by Islam itself. Forced marriages, arbitrary divorces, female mutilations and other abuses are sadly common in the Muslim world, as are restrictions on women's education and on their role in the labour force. In order to better their position as dignified human beings we

need to address these and other issues in the light of the contemporary position. I am not suggesting that we should abandon the tradition – only those aspects of cultural oppression that go under the name of tradition.

Jawad points to what she describes as 'authentic Islam' where, in the Qu'ran the role of women is respected and treated with justice and fairness as exemplified through the life of the Prophet, Muhammad and his family.

In England issues of racial, religious and sexist violence against Muslims and the media misrepresentation of gender and Islam are provided as evidence of prejudice and discrimination based on 'Islamophobia', that is, 'dread or hatred of Islam – and therefore . . . fear or dislike of all or most Muslims' (Runnymede Trust, 1997: 1). For women who adopt the dress code of Islam, the hijab or head-scarf and distinctive dress makes their religion visible. Evidence in the research indicated that this visibility can have positive and negative repercussions depending on context and the beliefs and values of those interacting with the Muslim women. There was no doubt that religious prejudice, related to the visibility of their Muslim dress code, created both the greatest source of tension between the respondents and their non-Muslim peers, colleagues, tutors, pupils and parents, as well as the greatest source of dignity and fellowship amongst other Muslims.

'Race', ethnicity and culture

Since the majority of British Muslims are of Asian heritage, issues of 'race' or prejudice and discrimination on the basis of skin-colour cannot be ignored (Coakley, 1994). The participants in the qualitative research were self-defined Muslims, of predominantly Asian heritage. That is, they perceived themselves as belonging to a particular group and were 'black' in the political sense used by Siraj-Blatchford (1991, 1993). We cannot and should not overlook the racialisation of religion in Britain. Acts of violence on these grounds are a reality, as evidenced in the Runnymede Trust report 1997, but not all Muslims are black. In the search for clarity of definitions, the term 'ethnic group' might be a more appropriate term indicating an element of choice in the way people define themselves (Jenkins, 1997). It is recognized that this suggestion is contentious and not yet supported in law and therefore offers no protection to Muslims as a distinct group under the Race Relations Act (as compared to, for example, that which is afforded to Jews and Sikhs).

'Culture' is used as a much broader term than 'race' or ethnicity, since it involves meanings and understandings passed on through processes of socialisation in everyday life. Culture can refer to social and institutional processes that reproduce systems of meanings, in an active way, using relational power within and between cultures to perpetuate and develop particular ways of living or cultural distinctiveness. Deciphering religious requirements from local cultural practices and influences adds to the challenge of any research in this area and has been brought about as a result of processes such as globalization and cultural assimilation. For example, the needs of all Muslims in one city would not be the same since some prefer to follow stricter traditions and practices than others. Simplistically, tradition-alists advocate strict adherence to traditional and absolute truths, modernists use modern values as a starting point for interpretation, and revivalists seek a middle way, trying to understand tradition to sift and organise meaning in relation to modern values. An important issue for British Muslims of South Asian heritage is the overlay of South Asian patriarchal cultural custom with 'a veneer of Islamic culture . . . to lend it legitimacy' (Raza cited in Lewis, 1994: 194). Whilst opportunities to study Islam enabled respondents to study for themselves and decipher 'real Islam' from cultural practice claimed to be Islamic, challenging traditions within families or communities was difficult, particularly for women.

Previous related research

Recognising the tensions and dynamic interplay between such issues as gender, ethnicity, culture and religion is important in understanding the Muslim women's perceptions of themselves and their professional and personal development in higher education. As emphasised in chapter 1, much research in education and physical education has focused on gender as an isolated factor or concept. Similar observations can be made about work that has focused upon issues of 'race' in education, sport and physical education. Here the tendency has been to focus on prejudice and discrimi-nation experienced predominantly by black youngsters of African–Caribbean heritage because of their skin-colour (Bayliss, 1989; Cashmore, 1982; Chappell 1995). Research tackling the complexity and significance of inter-action between 'race' and gender has often grown out of investigations into Asian communities. It has been very evident that religious and cultural beliefs and practices have led to differences in life-experiences for boys and girls (Brah, 1992; Brah and Minas, 1985; Carrington and Williams, 1993; Griffiths and Troyna, 1995; Jarvie, 1991). However, there have also been some tendencies to conflate 'Asian' experiences and to deny complexities within this group and important individual differences in experiences in and of physical education and sport. Some researchers (see for example MacGuire and Collins, 1998) have failed to acknowledge the very different effects that religion might have on particular groups within 'Asian communities'. Religion has sometimes emerged within studies on education, sport and physical education as an influencing factor on the lives and opportunities of young people but it has not been a main focus for studies. Growing awareness of the particular needs of specific ethnic groups, for example Muslim pupils, has stimulated some specific research focusing on religion and has given rise to acknowledgement of the need for more work in this area.

In some research, therefore, the dynamics of 'race', culture, gender and religion have been addressed (De Knop *et al.*, 1996; Haw, 1991; 1995; 1998;

Parker-Jenkins, 1995). The particular requirements of Muslim pupils in physical education have been identified (Carroll and Hollinshead, 1993; De Knop *et al.*, 1996), but the needs of those Muslim pupils who then choose to enter careers in physical education, or enter higher education more generally, have remained largely unexplored and unaddressed. Neal (1995) has suggested that the 'whiteness' of gender has contributed to rendering the position of black women in higher education 'invisible'. However, exceptions to this invisibility can be found. In 1988 Singh focused attention upon ethnic minority student-teachers, including Muslims, and revealed that they often had stressful experiences in securing and maintaining jobs. They often felt 'exploited' for their bi-lingual skills, isolated, under tight scrutiny, facing different expectations from their white colleagues and with particular difficulties surrounding prayer and dress requirements. As we will see, similar findings emerged in my research into the early teaching careers of Muslim women a decade later (Benn, 1998).

Visible yet invisible: 'Islamophobia – a challenge to us all'

The experiences, opportunities and aspirations of Muslims in the UK are relatively invisible to large sectors of society. This is due to multiple factors such as geographical location ('there are no Muslims in our area'), minority status in ethnic and religious dimensions, and superficial efforts to value and respect 'cultural diversity' in any real or meaningful way. The 1997 Runnymede Trust report 'Islamophobia – a challenge to us all' documents serious difficulties suffered by some British Muslims in terms of prejudice and discrimination, exclusion and violence. At the start of the new millennium, violence between Christians and Muslims was described as 'at its worst for generations' (Binyon, 2000: 14). With such barriers to extending knowledge and understanding it is important to use education for positive change, for example through sharing research that begins to address questions of equity, of rights and responsibilities.

Muslims and physical education

Since this research focuses on the subject of physical education and many myths still exist about Muslim participation, it is necessary to state that participation in practical sport/physical education activities is acceptable and, in fact, desirable in Islam (Niciri, 1993; Daiman, 1995; Sawar, 1994). Islam supports the maintaining of a healthy body and encourages both genders to participate in physical activity. The tensions arise at the interface of certain principles and practices within the subject, which can therefore present difficulties for some Muslims. As Carroll and Hollinshead (1993) and Benn (2000) have stressed, wider understanding may lead to a more inclusive education. For example religious requirements could be met through flexible kit that allowed coverage of arms and legs, segregating lessons for boys and girls after adolescence with a teacher of the same sex, sensitive selection of dance themes and accompaniment, options on issues such as showers, under-standing and accommodation of dietary changes during Ramadan, and flexible extra-curricular programmes.

Interestingly, the conflation of physical education and sport in current discourse (see for example, Penney and Evans, 1997) does not help children and young people in the Muslim community. The western cultural significance of sport does not have the same significance in the lives of all people and there are issues in Islam related to the display of the body and the demands of training for sporting success which can be problematic. For practising Muslims, religion is the most significant factor in their lives, and nothing can distract or come before commitment to following the path towards 'oneness with God'. But the importance of physical education in the development of all children is not disputed in Islam. Physical education in the school context is recognised as important in helping Muslim children to acquire healthy lifestyles and active participation (De Knop *et al.*, 1996). The inclusion statement in the statutory National Curriculum for Physical Education (DfEE/QCA, 1999) means that all teachers at primary level and specialists at secondary level need to respond to diverse learning needs. These include those of different cultural and ethnic groups, taking into account pupils' religious and cultural beliefs and practices, and the need to remove barriers to learning.

Addressing 'inclusion' for Muslims in higher education

The needs of Muslim students do not change as they move from secondary school to college or university. Following the path of Islam is a lifetime commitment. Are the rights of inclusion now embedded in the national curriculum present in higher education? Whilst understanding of the needs of Muslim children in schools is improving and research is contributing to knowledge about physical education and the participation of Muslim pupils, the picture nationally is not even. Despite political good-will to increase the numbers of ethnic minorities in the teaching profession, there are difficulties attracting and retaining these students in higher education. In my own institution the start of an Islamic studies variant within the religious education main subject studies of the Bachelor of Education (BEd) degree course encouraged Muslim students, predominantly women, to enter primary initial teacher training. Neither the institution nor the physical education department were ready for this. The following research charts the 'micro' learning process that ensued in terms of meeting the needs of these Muslim students. This is synthesised with survey data offering a more 'macro' picture of the position of other higher education institutions involved in initial teacher training in relation to meeting the needs of Muslim students. Specifically, the discussion and analysis that follows is structured around a number of themes that emerged through data analysis.

Emergent issues

Does higher education offer a compatible environment for Muslim students?

In my own institution the liberal thinking underpinning the launch of an Islamic studies route through the BEd degree succeeded in attracting Muslim students, predominantly of Pakistani or Bangladeshi heritage, into teacher training. The students found that the culture of the institution was not completely compatible with their religious requirements as Muslims. On reflection it is interesting that despite willingness to design courses for this specific group there was initially little 'institutional' understanding or provision for Islamic religious requirements. Staff, including the physical education department, were naïve and unprepared. What happened was a gradual process of increased awareness and an integration of changes that would enable Muslim students to feel more comfortable, and in physical education, to participate more fully, without fear or anxiety of transgressing their religious beliefs.

It is important to stress that the Muslim students were not homogeneous, with some choosing to distance themselves from those asking for change. In tracking the Muslim students' experiences it was interesting to note that the study of Islam had a positive effect on the women. They started to understand the place and opportunities for women in 'real Islam'. At the same time the religiosity of many strengthened, with some adopting hijab for the first time during their higher education period, and experiencing a growing group identity within the institution.

In terms of the basic needs of Muslim students, single-sex accommodation had to be 'reinstated'. Local houses represented one means of providing 'separate' living space for small groups. The catering department easily integrated the dietary needs of Muslim students but lack of space meant that the provision of a prayer room dedicated to Muslim students was more problematic. This issue gave rise to some resentment on the part of non-Muslim students, who viewed this as 'encroachment' in real terms on 'their space'. These early tensions have dissipated with the passage of time. Fareeda[2] recalled:

> there was uproar when we asked for a prayer room. Now this course has been going for three years and it took us two years to get a prayer room. In our eyes this is ridiculous because to us a prayer room is an essential item. We need somewhere to pray . . . obviously some students think this is preferential treatment.

Another issue that arose was that of honouring Muslim Festivals. This was raised at senior management level after difficulties during a school-experience. Muslim students had asked for permission to be able to spend Eid with their families to celebrate the end of Ramadan. Plans had been made for External Examiners to visit schools on that day and inevitable tensions arose between students, tutors and schools. Shortly after this it became policy that Muslim students would be free to celebrate this Festival as they chose.

The changes related above were notably reactive. Muslim students first raised issues, staff and managers learned and responded, seeking satisfactory solutions together. Some early tensions existed between Muslim and non-Muslim students. However, institutional intention was to enable the Muslim students to be as comfortable as possible during their time in higher education and, therefore, to meet their religious requirements wherever possible. An example of an incident that did not result in change was when requests were made by a student for long-term leave of absence to attend Hajj, one of the five pillars of faith, a duty for all Muslims. Senior managers negotiated with staff in the Islamic studies department and decided not to grant this request because the long absence would be detrimental to progress on the course. The Islamic studies staff supported the decision, suggesting that the religious requirement of Hajj needed to be undertaken only once during a lifetime and that the students would have time for this later in their lives.

During the Muslim women's time in higher education they were able to influence changes that enabled them to live their lives 'more comfortably', that is 'more Islamically', with greater consciousness in their daily lives of Islam and Islamic traditions (relating to dress and prayer practices but also underpinning thoughts, actions and interactions in everyday life). Increasing numbers of Muslim students brought opportunities to share values and beliefs. Tensions were greatest in this early period of change when decisions supporting Muslim students affected other groups. Incidents of religious prejudice did occur between some non-Muslim and Muslim students. The experiences of the Muslim women provided evidence that overt religious identity invoked more prejudice in the HEI context than racial prejudice. As Nadia explained, the vehemence of comments against those who had adopted Muslim dress, particularly the hijab, was greater than against those who were Asian but not visibly Muslim:

> other students think hijab girls are strict . . . extremists . . . they're not – they are just normal . . . I (a non hijab-wearer) am just Asian to them, not Muslim. Even though they might be a bit rude towards me they are not as rude as they are to the hijab girls, because they'd know I'd answer them back and the hijab girls would be more respectful and dignified.

By the end of their four-year initial teacher training course the women had a strong sense of belonging to the institution and a network of support within the HEI's community. They recognised the changes they had initiated and the gains they had made. Leaving this environment became a source of anxiety for some of the Muslim women as they reached the point of going into relatively 'isolating' school situations. As Rabiah explained: 'if you wanted to share something (at college/university) there was always somebody there but in schools you are alone'.

The questionnaire survey suggested that many Muslim students may be 'isolated' during training. The survey revealed that most institutions did not gather data on religious affiliation, but indicated that very few Muslim students are entering initial teacher training. Only four respondents had any direct experience of conversations with Muslim students about religious requirements and institutional practices. Awareness of Muslim students on ITT courses was therefore essentially limited to recognition by dress code or informally through informal conversations about religion. Fourteen of the thirty-five responding HEIs were aware of Muslim students who had been through their initial teacher training courses. Four were aware of men only, five of women only and five had experience of both Muslim men and women. Numbers were very small (typically one or two per year). Issues related to religious requirements had only been raised in four of these HEIs and involved dress, the provision of space for prayer and fasting.

In terms of providing environments where Muslim students were able to feel 'comfortable' (that is able to meet religious requirements on a daily basis) fourteen HEIs could offer single-sex accommodation, seventeen could meet 'dietary needs', ten honoured Muslim Festival days and ten offered a 'prayer room'. All of these requirements could be met in only six institutions. Some provision happened 'accidentally' rather than intentionally. For example single-sex accommodation was in some instances available or not on an ad hoc basis, determined by pragmatic issues rather than a concern for the needs of Muslim students. One response indicated that dietary requirements would be met but added that halal meat was not provided. This indicated that there was general accommodation of difference in dietary needs rather than provision for the specific needs of Muslim students. The extent to which provision of prayer rooms was specifically for Muslim students was not clear. Some responses indicated that a 'general prayer room' was available which would be unlikely to meet the needs of different religions.

It was therefore clear from the survey data that the majority of HEIs would not be able to accommodate the general religious requirements of Muslim students. Some could address certain needs but provision was not, as yet, happening at an intentional 'conscious' level within many institutions. This research has suggested that a lack of understanding has and does abound within traditional higher education institutes, even those espousing liberal thinking and originality in course design, including my own.

Institutional ethos and the inclusion of Muslim students

Whilst the majority of questionnaire respondents thought that there would be no resistance to changes to accommodate the needs of Muslim students, the ethos of different HEIs was raised as an issue in some. Where there was already 'a strong religious tradition' (Christian) (HEI-30) it was thought that change would be more difficult. In geographical locations with 'few Muslim people per head of population' respondents felt 'unaware of major issues' and suggested that more educational materials would be helpful (HEI-19). Other respondents suggested that 'greater communication and understanding would be beneficial' adding 'compromises have to be made by both parties' (HEI-6). Some respondents thought that staff and students would be helpful and willing to learn. One predicted 'some resistance'. Another found this question 'difficult to predict', whilst others actively sought recruitment from ethnic minorities via local schools. This picture denotes variability of experiences and expectations across institutions of higher education. There is clearly a need to pursue greater equity in relation to readiness for cultural diversity if real opportunity is to be created for more students. Due to the specific needs of this particular group a number of institutions suggested having particular HEIs specializing in provision for Muslim students. In such institutions one would imagine provision for single sex groups (for men and women) in physical education with same-sex staffing, timetabling compatible to prayer requirements, private sports spaces, changing and showering facilities. Other needs, including appropriate accommodation, honouring of Festival days, prayer rooms and provision for dietary needs, would be standard provision. Partnership schools would be fully cognisant of the needs of Muslim student-teachers in training. Such provision does not yet exist.

Muslim students 'finding a voice' in higher education

It was interesting to note that the first cohort of Muslim students at my own institution (seven), were well into the second year of their course before any mention was made of incongruity between institutional practices and their religious requirements. The second cohort (ten) were more vociferous and within months of their arrival an Islamic society was set up in the institution at their request. This became the forum through which the Muslim women were able to 'find a voice', to make their views public. If the numbers of Muslim students had not increased it is probable that the first cohort would have moved through their four-year course 'suffering in silence' rather than speaking out. In relatively isolated situations the option of 'stasis' (Menter, 1989), staying silent in preference to confrontation, was used. This coping strategy was evident in much of my research (Benn, 1998) and involved an element of retreat in terms of identity. As the Muslim women progressed in their training they became more skilful in deciding when to adopt this 'identity stasis' in the process of survival: 'You learn when to speak and when to stay silent' (Rabiah). Islamophobia and the fear that they would be labelled as 'fundamentalists' and further oppressed, underpinned and exacerbated the need for this strategy. The humility taught through Islam was recognised by one questionnaire respondent who suggested that:

There is a need to encourage more Muslims into PE in order to challenge stereotypical attitudes towards Muslims and physical ability/activity. More Muslim staff would inevitably be self-perpetuating. My experience (minimal) with Muslims in UK and abroad (in the context of PE) is of a timid approach fuelled as much by their pre-conceptions about the demands that will be made upon them by staff as by their religious teaching regarding humility and codes of dress etc.

(HEI-10)

The fact that so few higher education institutions had intentionally made changes to accommodate the needs of Muslim students reflects both institutional 'blindness' and Muslim students' own preference for 'stasis' to avoid confrontation. The women in this research felt torn between seeing higher education as a means to 'get on' in the West whilst believing that the dominant view of Islam that prevails in the West was anti-Islamic. They recognised in particular that their dress made them a potential target for prejudice and discrimination: 'people judge us as fundamentalist if we wear hijab' (Nawar).

Although this chapter is particularly concerned with Muslim women, it is necessary to recognise that Muslim men also have needs which can be invisible in higher education. When discussing the issue of the needs of Muslim students at a guest lecture in a leading higher education institution specialising in physical education teacher training, two Muslim men approached me at the end of the session. They said that they had been suffering in silence for three years because they did not feel that they had the right to ask for changes to meet their religious requirements. They had been praying daily in the gymnasium store-cupboard! Their 'stasis' had led to misunderstandings of their behaviour, misinterpretations of actions and other tensions that could have been resolved with a more open sharing of difference. Fear of negative responses and anticipation of labelling prevented the Muslim men from raising issues relating to general or subject specific ways in which their experiences in higher education could have been more compatible with their preference to be practising Muslims. Clearly, there is a need to stress that all HEIs must strive to offer environments in which students feel able to raise issues and be open about their religious identities. Particular tensions for Muslim students that are associated with the subject of physical education are the focus of the next section.

Initial teacher training, physical education and Muslim students

The Muslim women who participated in the qualitative research were in many ways the instigators of change in their HEI environment. Physical education was no exception. The women in this research entered an environment where a number of traditional practices had not been questioned. For example, mixed-sex participation in physical education including swimming was the norm, subject spaces were very public and on occasions Muslim women had been asked to remove their hijab on the grounds of safety. There is no doubt that unintentional 'institutional racism', or more accurately religious discrimination, was happening which disadvantaged this particular group and which reflected a lack of knowledge about and little sensitivity to their religious needs.

Change was not straightforward, as pragmatic organisational issues arose which affected systems, staffing and other students. Decisions for changes requested by the Muslim students were largely made within the department, but a key issue, the provision of single-sex groups for women, had wider implications. The groups for professional studies in all subjects (including physical education) were traditionally mixed. In consultation with Islamic studies colleagues and students, it was agreed that the provision of single-sex groups for some of the Muslim women would be essential to facilitating their participation. The imbalance of male/female students in primary teacher training meant the predominance of women enabled one all-female group to be established. As this decision was made mid-year it entailed some movement of women between groups and the moving of one man out of his original group. He protested that this change was unfair and 'sexist', but at the time the needs of the Muslim women were the priority. Thereafter, Muslim women were able to choose whether they wanted to be in an all-female group from the start of the course, thereby avoiding the tensions of 'changing groups'.

Other ways of accommodating the religious requirements of Muslim women were easier. The physical education 'changing rooms' have become a private meeting place for some groups of Muslim women. The issue of changing for physical education was not problematic because the layout of the changing rooms meant that privacy was possible, although showering would not have been private if any had wanted to take advantage of this facility after exercise. Kit required for primary physical education students had always been 'liberal' in that students were invited to wear whatever was comfortable. Some Muslim students wanted reassurance that loose clothing was permissible, and that the hijab could be worn, if safely secured. Clothing for swimming was more difficult. Some Muslim women wanted to wear clothing over their swimming costumes, which made the activity harder and for weaker swimmers necessitated them staying in the shallow end. These students recognised that their efforts to make their bodies less conspicuous were actually making them more conspicuous and by the end of the course most had moved to swimming in only their costumes. This became largely a confidence issue, once an all-female environment was guaranteed. For the first cohort of Muslim students who had opted to stay in mixed-sex groups (when the option was given half way through their course), participating in mixed-sex swimming was impossible. Insistence on participation could have led to an explosive situation. Course teaching methods were adapted to involve the students from the pool-side, focusing on developing their observation and teaching skills. The course emphasis was on teaching, which in swimming is normally from the pool-side, so this adaptation was considered appropriate in the circumstances by staff and students.

Due to the lack of consensus over participation in dance within Islam (see Sawar's strong 'anti' position in his guidance to British Muslims and schools, 1994: 13), some of the Muslim women faced dilemmas when undertaking the compulsory 'dance in education' training course. One reason for tensions relates to the association of dance with discos and 'dance-halls' and the visible 'use' of the body in those contexts. Dance in those contexts may be interpreted as provocative and related to promoting sexual attraction between the sexes, behaviour which would be considered anti-islamic. The dilemmas that some of the Muslim students felt before participating in the dance course, their experiences and post-course reflections were captured in diaries. Early anxieties were evident but attitudes clearly changed in a positive direction during the course as students' confidence grew and the rationale, principles and practice of dance in education became clear. The shift was such that all the students finished the course believing that there was nothing anti-islamic about 'dance in education' and that any issues raised about the appropriateness of dance in education for young children were related to misconceptions of the activity. Zauda commented that:

> it's provocative dance that is problematic. The dance we do in PE is not that sort of dance, it's movement development . . . I don't see why there should be any difficulties. . . . There will be people who object to dance, but I think when they realise it's not *that* kind of dance, they should understand about dance in education.

One of the notable characteristics of dance courses is that themes can be selected to avoid contentious issues. Experiences on this course highlighted the way in which without adequate understanding of religious and cultural traditions and practices, we will be unable to make appropriate selections of content. In one instance I made the mistake of using a story as a starting point that involved representation of gods. Although symbolic, this caused some tension for one Muslim student. I was unaware of the possible interpretation and learnt by experience.

Other issues arose in training that again necessitated reactive strategies. In one instance a male teacher accompanied a class of children with whom the all-female group would be conducting a team-taught gymnastics lesson. A small number of Muslim women were inhibited by the presence of the male teacher. They asked if it would be possible to request a class with a female teacher next time, or for them to be warned in advance so they could be better prepared, for example in terms of dress. Their concerns and request relates to a reluctance of some Muslim women to move freely in front of adult males and the importance of modest dress in such situations. Again, staff were learning from the Muslim women students in the process of the course. In-depth knowledge of Islam and religious requirements of followers would have enabled us to anticipate and therefore avoid such tensions, but at the time we were relatively uninformed and unquestioning of traditional physical education practices and their possible effects.

The survey of HEIs revealed that only two institutions could offer Muslim women the opportunity to enter single-sex groups and only one of those could guarantee to provide a female member of staff. In primary teacher training nationally, a single-sex option for Muslim women may be considered feasible but because of numbers, it would seem impossible to provide this option for Muslim men. The imbalance of men and women entering primary teacher training, in favour of women, means that pragmatic and economic constraints may prohibit single-sex groupings. One questionnaire respondent commented:

> I would foresee the principal difficulty as one of 'numbers', i.e. single-sex classes for females would not generate problems but would leave inoperable groups of males. The knock-on effect for other teaching groups might be resisted by some staff.
>
> (HEI-10)

Many questionnaire responses located constraints in 'logistics' such as demands on timetabling, 'the timetable is so tight' and pressures on staff, for example in heavy teaching loads and expectations to maintain high research profiles, increasing annually. Small departments (one physical education lecturer in some cases) meant that equitable provision for Muslim men and women in terms of single-sex groups with same-sex staff was a product of chance: 'Single-sex physical education groups would not be possible – we have so few men and I am *the* member of staff!' (female) (HEI-6).

Ideally the kit or dress code for physical education would accommodate the needs of Muslim students. For example, allowing the hijab to be worn if preferred, arms and legs to be covered in a comfortable tracksuit, allowing men to wear knee length swimming shorts and women to negotiate a way to participate in swimming, would be helpful. Twenty of the responding HEIs regarded this area as less problematic than providing single-sex groups. The majority felt that their policy was relaxed, preferring all students to be comfortable and positive about participating, with safety being their only proviso. Of the rest, nine institutions stated that they did not have provision for accommodating to the dress code requirements of Muslim students, one did not understand the question and others did not indicate a response. Qualitative comments revealed that contrasting attitudes still prevail within training institutions. For example, while one respondent commented that 'It's about time this was laid to rest for good and not just from a Muslim viewpoint! . . . students wear whatever kit they wish, as long as it is safe' (HEI-31), another individual in a leading specialist University indicated a different perspective: 'I could foresee some resistance from some staff and non-Muslim students' (HEI-33). A reflective comment from a different

University suggested: 'It would be naïve and inaccurate to suggest "there ain't no problems here." We all bring prejudices and baggage of some sort or another to any teaching/learning encounter' (HEI-30).

The culture of the subject was an issue raised by another respondent who had spent some time with Muslims. He suggested that 'the Physical Education profession needs to shake off its harsh and coarse image in order to open up the franchise to a broader community and in so doing facilitate participation amongst diverse groups' (HEI-10). This is indicative of a deeper concern about particular ways of teaching, of gendered practices, a privileged position for 'sport', dominance of competitive team games, and of subject expectations, historically endowed and still existent, particularly for men and boys. Issues of inclusion for physical education are about recognising histories, legacies, cultural practices and meanings embedded, then confronting and challenging these in terms of their appropriateness for the next millennium.

Initial teacher training, school-based experiences and Muslim students

School-based experiences for the Muslim women in the qualitative research proved difficult times for a number of reasons. The women reported feelings of isolation, meeting incidents of religious prejudice from colleagues, senior managers, pupils and parents, misunderstandings of their Muslim identity, motivations, behaviour and lifestyle and confusions about their status as 'specialists' in religious education. Partnership schools in which the Muslim students were placed for their school-based experiences, were not always appropriate. The quality of the students' experience in part depended on how welcome they felt in the school situation. This bore little relationship to the ethnic diversity within the school but was more closely related to the management style and closed or open views of Islam (Runnymede Trust, 1997) held by colleagues, pupils and parents. Students who experienced religious prejudice in staffrooms again chose identity 'stasis' as a strategy for coping. That is, they preferred not to talk about anything related to Islam or being Muslim, not to answer questions or speak their mind, in order to avoid confrontation. The preference was to 'remain silent' (Asma), 'it's not worth challenging . . . the risk is too high' (Jamilah). These were comments made about staffroom experiences by hijab-wearing Muslim teachers. Feelings of loneliness and isolation in schools were high and some of this was related to religiosity 'the more practising you become the harder it is because your purpose is different to others – to live our lives Islamically' (Rabiah).

At the other end of the spectrum, a Muslim student went into an all-white school and on the first meeting with the head teacher was offered a room adjacent to the library, as a quiet room for prayer at lunch-time if she wanted to use it. This gesture made a difference to the student's confidence in the school and led to a very successful experience. The needs of Muslim teachers are not easily addressed in schools, particularly primary schools where space is at a premium. Privacy for hygiene rituals, for changing or for prayer are difficult issues as Nawar explained:

> I'd appreciate private washing facilities. I try to keep it secret and do my ablutions in the washbasins in the staff toilet. If anyone comes in I stop and continue when they go out. Some classrooms have their own sinks but mine doesn't. I don't mind praying in the classroom but obviously I would prefer privacy.

Incidents of religious prejudice happened at every level, indicating that schools did not represent the supportive environment that we endeavoured to ensure in the training institution. There were at least four occasions when head teachers telephoned the training institution to ask if students were allowed to wear the hijab into school and to discuss possible safety implications. In an interview one head teacher suggested that this practice might encourage the Muslim girls to wear head-scarves into school, something that they were trying to ban. Class teachers spent most time with the Muslim women students and there were many conversations that involved discussing Islam. Personal and prejudiced comments were made, leaving some of the women feeling as though they were 'defending their right to be Muslim'. Comments were made about the early marriage of Muslim girls, the house seclusion of many Muslim women, issues of equality and education. Initially the Muslim women treated the opportunity for discussion positively, despite the often coloured phrasing of questions, hoping to share knowledge of 'real Islam'. However, where 'closed' views of Islam were met (Runnymede Trust, 1997) they adopted 'identity stasis' choosing not to enter dialogue about being Muslim or about Islam.

Relationships with parents were both positive and negative. Sharing language skills, religious and cultural affinity with parents in particular schools helped some of the Muslim women to feel valued. At times this was in stark contrast to experiences with colleagues and senior managers in the same school. One student, Jamilah, left a school feeling undervalued, demoralised and unfulfilled, yet accompanied by gifts and cards from pupils (in a 98 per cent Asian, Muslim school) and parents indicating their appreciation of having her at the school.

Relationships with pupils were also varied. There were common problems of acceptance in the role of 'teacher'. The over-representation of Asian women as classroom assistants meant that the Muslim women students faced many questions about their role and were asked 'when is the real teacher coming?' Interactions with Asian children were largely very positive, with some student teachers experiencing real excitement from children enjoying having a 'teacher like them', but others encountered stereotyping from the Asian children as well. For example, Zahra was asked the same three questions on all three of her school-based experiences: 'Miss, are you Pakistani?', 'Miss, are you married?', 'Miss, have you got children?'. She was from Mozambique, of African-Asian heritage, spoke Portuguese as her first language and was single with no children. She was a challenge to the pupils' perception of a 'normal Asian woman' and used this opportunity to extend their views.

Physical education school-based experiences were often better than anticipated for the Muslim women. Unfortunately, this was more often attributable to the low status of the subject in the school and the small part that it played during their school experience, than about interrogating progress of teaching this aspect of the curriculum. The Muslim women were empathetic to Muslim pupils who experienced some difficulties with mixed-sex changing. They were sometimes incensed at the rigidity they witnessed in teachers' kit expectations and strict regimes, with Muslim pupils being refused the opportunity to wear tracksuits with excuses such as 'they are dangerous because they can get caught on apparatus in gymnastics'. The women saw themselves as role models and were positive about the importance of physical education. They quickly learned that for many pupils it was their favourite subject but that for many staff it was the first subject to be dropped at the sign of a crisis elsewhere. Being a teacher of physical education in a primary school was, for the Muslim women in this research, less problematic than participating in physical education as a student-teacher in higher education. They were in a more private situation and this became even more private once qualified, when they were not observed during lessons.

As indicated above, the difficulty of the presence of adult males arose on school experience. In one instance, a Muslim women changed her dance lesson to a different time when she knew her male tutor was coming in. For some Muslim women the actual experience of having a male class teacher or tutor was regarded as 'less problematic than expected'. For others 'we would change our teaching method, we would not be able to be as practically involved with the children as we would wish to be'. The response of the institution was to offer the Muslim students a choice of a male or female tutor for school-based experiences. The concerns raised by the Muslim women have clear implications for professional development. There is a need to address, for example, the effects of the presence of male inspectors or head teachers in physical education lessons taught by Muslim women and the procedures for monitoring and advancing the professional development for Muslim women who may prefer support from female senior colleagues.

Having religious education as a main subject with a specialism in Islamic studies proved particularly difficult for the Muslim women. They met responses from teachers which intimated that being so visibly Muslim they would be incapable of being objective about delivering a multi-faith religious education. No such questions or intimations would be made of Christian teachers. This adds to the weight of insidious Islamophobia that surrounded the Muslim women in this research. Accusations of indoctrination intentions were made at any suggestion that they might contribute to religious education. Although rare, there were some experiences of positive responses to the women's Muslim identities. One moved on to become subject co-ordinator for religious education when later employed by her final school-experience school. Another respondent enjoyed a very welcoming and open attitude to her visible Muslim identity and everything that she could offer to the school, but this was not the most common experience.

Educating for equity and initial teacher training (ITT)

The fact that the Muslim women in the qualitative research experienced racial and religious prejudice from some non-Muslim student trainees during their initial teacher training is a serious issue. If attitudes are not challenged and education is not provided to increase knowledge, awareness and under-standing of equity issues in ITT then teachers' capabilities to respond to the needs of particular pupils, and colleagues, will be limited and potentially dangerous.

The questionnaire asked about ways in which issues of equity were addressed within ITT courses, with partnership schools and mentors. Twenty-five out of thirty-five HEIs addressed issues of equity within their courses. Content details were not forthcoming but some indicated times from thirty minutes to six hours being spent on issues of equity. Whether and how equity issues were addressed with partnership schools and mentors was less clear. Three HEIs stated that they adopted a 'permeation' model. One addressed this 'where there was an ethnic mix', one provided a cross-LEA 'inner City' experience, and one addressed issues 'if they were raised'. Approaches suggest reaction rather than proactivity and a likelihood of patchy awareness of equity issues amongst trainees and the future teaching profession. Many respondents identified pressures of time reductions, competing subjects and increasing centralised pressures as constraining the opportunities to address equity issues, as illustrated in the following comment: 'We would like to spend more time on such issues with trainees but there are other serious demands on our time that currently have a higher profile (e.g. PGCEs covering the fifty-four standards!)' (HEI-29).

The research has indicated that the increased responsibility of schools in the process of teacher training in England and Wales necessitates the sharing of knowledge and awareness of equity issues within and between HEIs, partnership schools, mentors and all colleagues with the power to influence the training of any teacher. Whilst the Muslim women in this study eventually felt empowered within their ITT institution they felt powerless and unable to challenge religious prejudice encountered in school-based training, indicating the need for better understanding of issues of equity amongst educators and communication between training providers. Clearly it would be helpful if schools in which Muslim student-teachers are placed are aware of their needs and of the types of experiences faced by the Muslim women in this research, so that they may be better prepared to support students in their professional training.

Conclusion

This research set out to engage with the complexity of overlapping structures of disadvantage in a particular time and place. The socio-political UK context has shaped the struggles identified as political agendas in a plural but unequal society to pursue polices of inclusion and equity. Increasing knowledge and understanding of diversity is one way to remove fear and foster positive ways forward. There are no easy answers to issues raised. Traditional practices are deeply ingrained in training institutions and therefore hard to challenge. However, change in the training context may also have the greatest long-term effects, since the training process shapes teachers and teachers shape children. My work has shown that there is a need to challenge both institutional 'blindness' and to foster more open debate with Muslim students, where previously fear and relative isolation has deterred individuals from speaking out. If we are to strive towards greater respect of cultural difference in the school curriculum (McPherson Report, 1999) it needs to start in raising consciousness and taking action to address disadvantage in the process of training the next generation of teachers.

The survey of HEIs in England and Wales indicated the current 'invisibility' of the need to address the religious requirements of Muslim students in teacher training. Government policies are driving HEIs towards ever increasing 'widening access' and policies of inclusion. But at the same time the pressures on ITT institutions for economic efficiency in provision exacerbate the pragmatic dilemmas of addressing the needs of this group, for example in the provision of separate-sex classes in a primary teacher training course. Some institutions may experience tensions in wanting to accommodate difference yet having to count the cost of provision.

The Muslim women involved in this research will be rare but vital role models for growing numbers of Muslim children in Britain. I am indebted to them and to my HEI colleagues who so willingly responded to the questionnaire. Their responses have opened the door to a broader picture and further debate.

Notes

1 Religiosity is a term used to describe a person's degree of religious conviction.
2 Pseudonyms are used for all of the students involved in the research.

References

Ahmed, L. (1992) *Women and Gender in Islam*, London: Yale University Press.
Bayliss, T. (1989) PE and racism: making changes, *Multicultural Teaching*, 7(2): 19–22.
Benn, T. (1998) Exploring experiences of a group of British Muslim women in initial teacher training and their early teaching careers, PhD thesis, Loughborough University.

Benn, T. (2000) Towards inclusion in education and physical education, in A. Williams (ed) *Primary School Physical Education*, London: Falmer Press.

Binyon, (2000) *The Times*, 4 January: 14.

Brah, A. (1992) Women of South Asian origin in Britain – issues and concerns, in P. Brahum, A. Rattonsi and R. Skillington (eds) *Racism and Anti-racism, Inequalities, Opportunities and Policies*, London: Sage.

Brah, M. and Minas, R. (1985) Structural racism or cultural differences: schooling for Asian girls, in G. Weiner (ed.) *Just a Bunch of Girls*, Milton Keynes: Open University Press.

Carrington, B. and Williams, T. (1993) Patriarchy and ethnicity: the link between school and physical education and community leisure activities, in J. Evans (ed.) *Equality, Education and Physical Education*, London: Falmer Press.

Carroll, B. and Hollinshead, G. (1993) Equal opportunities: race and gender in physical education: a case study, in J. Evans (ed.) *Equality, Education and Physical Education*, London: Falmer Press.

Cashmore, E. (1982) *Black Sportsmen*, London: Routledge & Kegan Paul.

Chappell, R. (1995) Racial stereotyping in schools, *BAALPE Bulletin* 31(4): 22–8.

Coakley, J. (1994) *Sport in Society: Issues and Controversies*, London: Mosby.

Department for Education and Science (1989) *Circular 24/89 Initial Teacher Training: Approval for Courses*, London: HMSO.

Department for Education and Employment (DfEE)/Qualifications and Curriculum Authority (QCA) (1999) *Physical Education: The National Curriculum for England*, London: QCA.

Daiman, S. (1995) Women in sport in Islam, *Journal of the International Council for Health, Physical Education, Recreation, Sport and Dance* 32(1): 18–21.

De Knop, P., Theeboom, M., Wittock, H. and De Martelaer, K. (1996) Implications of Islam on Muslim girls' sports participation in Western Europe, *Sport, Education and Society* 1(2): 147–64.

Equal Opportunities Commission (1989) *Formal Investigation Report: Initial Teacher Training in England and Wales*, London: Equal Opportunities Commission.

Elias, N. (1991) *The Society of Individuals*, Oxford: Blackwell.

Essed, P. (1991) *Understanding Everyday Racism: An Interdisciplinary Theory*, London: Sage.

Faruqi, L.A. (1991) *Women, Muslim Society and Islam*, Indianapolis: American Trust Publication.

George, R. and Jones, M. (1992) The human element in fieldwork, in A. Giddens (ed.) *Human Societies: A Reader*, Cambridge: Polity Press.

Griffiths, M. and Troyna, B. (eds) (1995) *Antiracism, Culture and Social Justice in Education*, Stoke-on-Trent: Trentham Books.

Hargreaves, J. (1994) *Sporting Females*, London, Routledge.

Haw, K.F. (1991) Interactions of gender and race: a problem for teachers? – a review of emerging literature, *Educational Research* 33(1): 12–21.

Haw, K.F. (1995) Why Muslim girls are more feminist in Muslim schools, in M. Griffiths and B. Troyna (eds) *Antiracism, Culture and Social Justice in Education*, Stoke-on-Trent: Trentham Books.

Haw, K.F. (1996) Exploring the educational experiences of Muslim girls: tales told to tourists – should the white researcher stay at home? *British Educational Research Journal* 22(3): 319–30.

Haw, K.F. (1998) *Educating Muslim Girls: Shifting Discourses*, Buckingham, Open University Press.

Jarvie, G. (ed.) (1991) *Sport, Racism and Ethnicity*, London: Falmer Press.

Jawad, H.A. (1998) *The Rights of Women in Islam: An Authentic Approach*, London: Macmillan Press.

Jenkins, R. (1997) *Rethinking Ethnicity: Arguments and Explorations*, London: Sage.

Lewis, P. (1994) *Islamic Britain*, London: I.B. Tauris.

Macguire, B. and Collins, D. (1998) Sport, ethnicity and racism: the experience of Asian heritage boys, *Sport Education and Society* 3(1): 79–88.

Macpherson, W. (1999) *The Stephen Lawrence Inquiry: Report of an inquiry by Sir William Macpherson of Cluny*, London: HMSO.

Mennel, S. (1994) The formation of we-images: a process theory, in C. Calhoun (ed.) *Social Theory and the Politics of Identity*, Oxford: Blackwell Publications.

Mirza, M. (1995) Some ethical dilemmas in fieldwork: feminist and anti-racist methodologies, in M. Griffiths and B. Troyna (eds) *Antiracism, Culture and Social Justice in Education*, Stoke-on-Trent: Trentham Books.

Neal, S. (1995) A question of silence? Antiracist discourses and initiatives in higher education: two case studies, in M. Griffiths and B. Troyna (eds) *Antiracism, Culture and Social Justice in Education*, Stoke-on-Trent: Trentham Books.

Niciri, M. (1993) The Islamic position in sport, in *Sport in the Modern World – Chances and Problems*, Scientific Congress, Munich Olympics, Berlin, Springer Verlag.

Parker-Jenkins, M. (1995) *Children of Islam*, Stoke-on-Trent: Trentham Books.

Penney, D. and Evans, J. (1997) Naming the game: discourse and domination in physical education and sport in England and Wales, *European Physical Education Review* 3(1): 21–32.

Runnymede Trust (1997) *Islamophobia – a Challenge for All of Us*, London: Runnymede Trust.

Sawar, G. (1994) *British Muslims and Schools*, London: Muslim Education Trust.

Scharenburg, S. (1999) Religion and sport, in J. Riordan and A. Kruger (eds) *The International Politics of Sport in the Twentieth Century*, London: E & FN Spon.

Sfeir, L. (1985) The status of Muslim women in sport: conflict between cultural traditions and modernisation, *International Review for Sociology of Sport* 20(4): 283–304.

Singh, R. (1988) *Asian and White Perceptions of the Teaching Profession*, West Yorkshire: Bradley and Ilkley Community College, UK.

Siraj-Blatchford, I. (1991) A study of black students' perceptions of racism in initial teacher education, *British Educational Research Journal* 17(1): 35–50.

Siraj-Blatchford, I. (1993) *Race, Gender and the Education of Teachers*, Buckinghamshire: Oxford University Press.

6 Gender positioning as pedagogical practice in teaching physical education

David Brown and Emma Rich

Introduction

In recent years a growing body of empirical work has helped develop our understandings of masculinities and femininities in education, physical education and school sports contexts (see for example, De Knop *et al.*, 1996; Tsolidis, 1996; Salisbury and Jackson, 1998; Wright, 1997; Hickey *et al.*, 1998; Ennis, 1999; Hargreaves, 2000). However, to date, rather less of this empirical work has considered the nature of gendered positions of Physical Education teachers themselves (see Evans *et al.*, 1996; Brown, 1999). In this chapter we consider some of the insights that are emerging from two studies that focus on the social significance of gendered physical education teacher identity. We present a view of teachers that acknowledges them not merely as the products of a brief period of initial teacher education, but as knowing subjects with lives and identities already strongly shaped by the time they enter the profession (Tabachnick *et al.*, 1984; Templin and Schempp, 1989; Grenfell and James, 1998). Our perspective also positions physical education teachers as key intermediaries in the social construction and transmission of what counts as 'gender legitimate' knowledge dispositions and practices. As such they can be considered as 'living links' (Brown, 1999) between generations of encultured gendered practice in the profession. We contend that a better understanding of this process of enculturation is crucial if we are to move towards more gender inclusive futures in physical education.

Our main concern in this chapter is to show the ways in which gendered student teacher identities, masculine and feminine, are 'positioned' and deployed as pedagogy, in response to the socio-cultural forces brought to bear on them during their period of Initial Teacher Education (ITT) and beyond. However, a point to note about our analysis is our concern to move from a critique that is essentially passive in its outlook, to one that engages with the possibilities for future practices that arise from our enhanced understandings. We therefore make the case that gender needs to be viewed as an integral part of the teacher's pedagogical repertoire (Gore, 1990; Luke and Gore, 1992) and that the positioned, gendered, self identity becomes a significant pedagogical resource. We are therefore viewing difference as a resource (see Evans, 1993) to be utilised in the further development of pedagogy in physical education.

A relational perspective of gender in physical education

Earlier chapters pay testimony to both the historical but also contemporary prevalence of gender inequities and exclusion within the fields of physical education and school sport (see also Kirk, 1992; Evans, 1993; Talbot, 1993). Following Messner and Sabo (1990) we contend that viewing this situation in terms of a relational 'Gender Order' provides a useful basis from which to gain insights into the issues of inclusion, exclusion, reproduction and change. They comment:

> A relational conception of gender necessarily includes a critical examin-ation of both femininity and masculinity as they develop in relation to each other within a system of structured social inequality.
>
> (Messner and Sabo, 1990: 13)

Humberstone (1990: 202) has highlighted that 'the complex web of inter-connections between cultural values, gender identity development and gender stereotypes surrounding sport are mediated through the PE curriculum'. Relational approaches attempt to gain insights into these interconnections and their implications for social reproduction and change. As Edley and Wetherell (1995) point out the relational nature of men and women (and similarly, other social categories) implies that changes to the position of one group will cause ripples, effecting the lives and positions of the others. These 'ripples' provide a key relational focus, as they are points of interconnections between masculinities and femininities. From a relational perspective, gender power relations operate in similar ways to Gramsci's (1971) observations on class hegemony, in that they are never total or absolute, but contested in social arenas such as schools and physical education classes. While we have to acknowledge that hegemonic forms of masculinity remain the dynamic ideological form around which western patriarchal relations are constructed, legitimised and defended (see for example, Brittan, 1989; Brod and Kaufman, 1994; Siedler, 1997; Pease, 2000; Whannel, 2000), we can also recognise multiple constructions of masculinities and femininities as men and women implicitly and explicitly are positioned and position themselves in relation to dominant ideological forms of hegemonic masculinity (Connell, 1995). Although it is necessary to clarify that women are *most* disadvantaged by a Gender Order dominated by hegemonic masculine ideology, it is equally vital to acknowledge that many men and boys are also marginalised and subordinated in and by this order. This prompts the deconstruction of over-simplified 'binary' male/ female gender boundaries from which categories of 'other' are constructed (Young, 1990). As Connell (1987) points out:

'Hegemonic masculinity' is always constructed in relation to various subordinated masculinities as well as in relation to women. The interplay between different forms of masculinity is an important part of how a patriarchal social order works.

(1987: 183)

In the analysis that follows we draw specifically on Connell's (1995) relational work on masculinities. Connell's work provides a useful heuristic that explores the dynamics of a patriarchy constructed around hegemonic masculine power and the ways in which individuals are positioned relative to it. We see hegemony, domination/subordination and complicity on the one hand and marginalisation/authorisation on the other (1995: 81). The former relations define the internal Gender Order with women, homosexual men and effeminacy being actively subordinated. A further position, complicity, refers to those who might not actively promote hegemonic masculinity but whose lives and dispositions benefit from the advantage men in general gain from the subordination of women (and of 'other' men). The second set of relations, marginalisation/ authorisation is caused by the, 'interplay of gender with other structures such as class and race' (ibid.: 80). These positions might be tentatively represented by the model below.

The ascendancy and 'logic' of this Gender Order also connects gender with sexuality through symbolic association. For example in physical education, where links between female/feminine and male/masculine are disrupted, sexuality is called into question. Men who do not demonstrate competitive, aggressive and dominant aspects of 'hegemonic' masculinity in contexts such as teaching physical education risk being positioned as 'effeminate' or 'gay'. Alternatively, women who do not act in 'appropriate feminine' ways might similarly be positioned outside the heterosexual other, which in physical education has historically meant 'lesbian', a powerful label and pejorative discourse that affects and limits all women, in terms of their gendered, sexual and professional identities (Griffin, 1992; see also Clarke in chapter 4). Neither this chapter, nor the studies that informed it, focus directly on issues of sexuality in teaching physical education. However, we acknowledge that the gender positioning that we identify in practice has implications for sexualities and their concomitant positions in a Gender Order based on heteronormativity. In short, the Gender Order constructs 'the other' through a series of oppositions that render dominant heterosexual forms of masculinity central but invisible and silent (Rutherford, 1988).

Notwithstanding the criticisms of Connell's model (see Peterson, 1997) for the way in which it might be interpreted as essentializing and reductionist in its categorization of masculinities and femininities, we sense nonetheless that, when viewed as a dynamic heuristic (i.e. context dependent, fluid and individualised rather than fixed and generalised), the framework offers a useful starting point in positioning the relative forms of gender that are in evidence in teaching physical education and sport. Moreover, it offers the

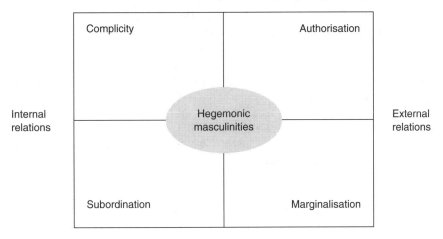

Figure 6.1 The Gender Order: internal and external relations

opportunity to expose the previously 'invisible centre' of the Gender Order that works relationally to legitimise certain gendered pedagogies, and render marginal or subordinated, the many possible alternatives.

Viewed through these relational lenses the domination of the contemporary social landscape of physical education and school sport in England and Wales by a particular European, elite middle class, heterosexual masculine ideology becomes more clearly visible. We begin to see an ideological ideal producing a series of discourses and practices which have long served as a benchmark for the legitimate uses of the body, standards of performance, modes of physical and emotional expression, patterns of interaction, curriculum organisation and so on (see for example Mangan, 1981; Hargreaves, 1986; Fletcher, 1987; Mangan and Walvin, 1987). Acknowledging such processes Connell (1995) stresses that:

> Any curriculum must address the diversity of masculinities, and the intersections of gender with race, class, and nationality, if it is not to fall into a sterile choice between celebration and negation of masculinity in general. The importance of education for masculinity politics follows from the onto-formativity of gender practices, the fact that our enactments of masculinity and femininity bring a social reality into being.
>
> (Connell, 1995: 239).

Locating the studies and the participants

The empirical data for this work have been drawn from two parallel studies that focus respectively on male and female student teachers as they progress towards becoming and being teachers of physical education on a

Postgraduate Certificate in Education (PGCE) course in an English university. The two studies have some important (and shared) methodological characteristics. Primarily the studies have utilised life history analysis of biographical data gathered from intensive semi-structured interviews conducted at intervals during and after their training. The constructions of gendered self-identity have been analysed from the positioned gendered stories that the participants reconstruct about themselves as a result of their previous, current, and future-anticipated life experiences. Here we cannot represent all of these stories. Instead we focus upon key moments and positions from the stories of four participants that are indicative of the dilemmas faced by all the participants.

In mapping masculinity and femininity onto identity we remain anxious to avoid falling into the essentialist trap mentioned above, by suggesting 'fixed' identities or types of men and women, however consistent they may appear. Femininities/masculinities can no longer be made sense of as unitary, static 'wholes'. Gendered multiplicity is a phenomenon observable across societies, cultures and history and it is also in evidence at the individual level. Finally, our use of the term 'positioning' as an active as well as passive verb is intentional. Analysis of the participants' life stories consistently indicates that positioning genders in teaching contexts has an active as well as passive dimension; it does involve agency. The student teachers are thus shown to draw on their own identities and experiences to make sense of gendered encounters and merge them with their developing pedagogies to *take, assign and receive* gendered positions.

Our participants here are two men and two women, whom we refer to by pseudonyms; Derek, Trevor, Christie, and Robin. While these participants talked explicitly about the 'positioning of their gender' within their teacher education, narratives of sexuality and sexual identity were either absent or silent. Participants made connections between gender-appropriate behaviour and sexual identities of others, acknowledging for example the myth of 'PE teacher as lesbian' (Griffin, 1992; Squires and Sparkes, 1996; Sparkes, 1997). The silences that we observed were largely indicative of culturally predominant discourses of heteronormativity, where perspectives of hetero-sexuality are considered implicit and taken for granted.

All of these individuals either were, or still are, active elite performers, involved respectively in athletics, semi-professional rugby union; county level badminton and netball, and elite level university football. In spite of these elite experiences, at the outset of their teaching careers all of these participants expressed a concern to be teachers who could provide equal opportunities for all pupils to access positive experiences of physical education and school sport. The following comments capture their beliefs:

> I'm going to be a teacher you know, who teaches PE, so I want to go into a school and be someone that kids can talk to, someone that they can

learn from, someone that they want to listen to, or maybe they can learn a few things about PE, about growing up, about handling themselves about respecting themselves, about doing what they want to do and about meeting challenges, which is, I mean, that's what it's all about. . . . So I want, I feel quite strongly that I could be a good teacher and then . . . because I love sport.

(Trevor)

I think what it needs to be is to be able to work with children. I always get a great buzz working with passing on all the knowledge and experiences I have had in PE . . . and you know, think about the sport for all especially . . . and I want everyone to have positive experiences in my classes.

(Derek)

PE is actually trying to show people the benefits of what they can get from it, whether it be physically, socially, success in something. It's something that can be available to anyone and there's so many different types of sports or activities. I am a games player and that is what I love, but there are so many types of being physically active that are beneficial and that is what PE should be about.

(Christie)

Robin made an explicit reference to masculinity and femininity, saying:

I think they are really important [the meanings of femininity/masculinity] because I am teaching PE, it's important to not have a stereotypical view of the body; so I am trying to get to grips with perhaps the correct terms to use. I haven't finalised anything definite. . . . I want to give other people the chance to realise their potential and to realise that they are individuals that can achieve things. . . . Enjoyment for everyone to feel safe, secure and happy.

(Robin)

All of these comments arguably reflect 'intellectual' and 'liberal' stances in relation to equal opportunities in physical education. The central perception of their role is to facilitate access and opportunity as key objectives, rather than to critically address the nature of the opportunities[1] themselves. As a cognitive, intellectual position a belief in gender equality and inclusion represents a very positive personal stance. However, as we shall see, the stance is not always retained when teaching. We see that how the student teachers position themselves, others, and how others position them, has implications for the reproduction of the Gender Order and reveals limitations in their shared liberal notions of equal opportunities.

The double bind of practice: gender positioning as pedagogy

Being positioned

The life histories indicate that 'gender positioning' is being practised and consolidated in these students' teaching placements and in subsequent teaching jobs. This pedagogical practice forms a part of what Templin and Schempp (1989) and others have referred to as 'professional socialisation' where the bringing together of personal and professional identities is a strongly gendered process. All of the participants reported *being in, taking and assigning* gendered positions according to the context in which they found themselves and fusing these positions with and within their teaching pedagogies. In spite of their intellectual intentions for equality, the participants experience forms of double bind or entrapment that forces them into positions complicit with dominant masculine norms. Derek experienced this early in his first teaching placement when he asked his head of department 'how much dance do you want me to do?' and received the answer, 'Oh none, I don't believe boys should do that.' Derek is implicated in this positioning and specifically, denied the experience and pedagogical practice of teaching dance. This is in spite of his own increasingly positive views about the value of dance in the physical education programme and its applicability to all pupils. Moreover, he was denied the opportunity to show and develop other dimensions to his own teaching identity and to forge alternative ways of fusing it with his practical pedagogies.

Trevor had similar experiences of being positioned at the outset of his teaching career. He explained the context that he encountered, saying:

> I mean the PE department that I was in was almost like the cadets you know, it was very structured, very rigid and very like, testosterone like, you know. You couldn't . . . it was charged, it was a charged atmosphere more than the second school . . . the first mentor at [school name], he was excellent, he was quite hard taskmaster, he was like old authoritarian schools, he was quite old fashioned . . . and he was good. . . . He always like said, oh you're too nice, you got to be this that and the other, do know what I mean? And I think part of that was it was just my first experience of teaching.
>
> (Trevor)

In this context Trevor's relaxed and friendly approach was immediately called into question, with the implication that being 'nice' was a sign of weakness and not the way that male physical education teachers should act. Trevor had to re-position his approach to teaching boys physical education towards something 'harder' and more authoritarian, and in line with the institutional culture. Consequently, Trevor's formative experiences of teaching boys physical education were based around dominant, authoritarian displays and pedagogies. He has 'learned' how to teach in these ways and they are the pedagogies that he continues to deploy, and that he is now comfortable with. Furthermore, as his judgement of 'excellent' above indicates, he has also come to value their 'effectiveness'.

In a similar but perhaps more oppressive way, Christie's and Robin's stories also feature the experiences of being positioned by other members of staff and pupils in their practice institutions:

> There was one bloke there [male physical education teacher] and he was very funny, and he was a good laugh but some of the comments that he made to the kids were very derogatory, you know one of the lads had a buckle on his shoe and he was calling him a, I can't remember what he called him now . . . a dancer. He was saying, oh you look like a . . . I don't know if he actually called him a poof, but it was some term along that line. And I'd think, I don't really think you should have quite put it like that, and they make some comments to me about, you know, football, of what do you know about football. And just I'd give as good as I got for a bit, and then I'd just be like, oh carry on.
>
> (Christie)

The comments made by Christie's male mentor are a good illustration of how the Gender Order operates to position everyone relationally in terms of an implicit dominant masculine norm, with femininity and homosexuality actively subordinated here. Furthermore, when the gendered positioning is direct and personal as in Christie's case, her response again demonstrates the double bind or entrapment experienced by those who would seek to challenge the Gender Order and work towards more inclusive perspectives and practices in education and physical education. If she challenges the Gender Order operating in this situation, Christie risks being stigmatized and actively subordinated as a non-complicit female and student teacher. But by not offering a challenge to the order, she accepts a complicit role and implicitly reinforces the established order. The following extract further illustrates her dilemma:

> To be honest I've been amazed by some of the stuff that I've heard at the school. I mean the other day, there is this one teacher, a male, and he is supposed to be one of the best teachers in the school. Anyway, we were all in the staff room and they've got exams on at the moment and this guy was talking about the fact that when the kids sat at their desks, during exams, the girls skirts like come up and he was going on about the fact that he could see the girls' knickers. They even call them slappers and things like that, and you know, it's just not appropriate, but everyone laughs, everyone joins in and that's it. How are you supposed to fight that? I really want to just walk out of the room, but then it would just be the

case that the tables would have been turned around onto me, and I would be the one to look bad, you know?

(Christie)

We can wonder how many other teachers in these staff rooms felt the same way as Christie, but also chose silence? What does it cost these young women to speak their minds, to challenge the status quo? The discourses within physical education and sport attempt to normalize heterosexuality for girls and women in ways which assert a heterosexuality that bonds sex and gender together (Sykes, 1998). Acting in 'female appropriate' ways therefore tacitly implicates 'sexuality'. Where female and feminine are not clearly linked, questions of sexuality are raised. Speaking up in these contexts means challenging the status quo, and those who disrupt gender binary logics run the risk of being positioned outside the heterosexual self as 'other'. Historically, this 'other' in physical education has meant 'lesbian'. These complex dilemmas of 'speaking up' and the dynamics of interaction illustrate the difficult if near impossible situation of exerting particular expressions of agency, in the face of potential stigma. Attempts to dispel the 'masculine' (read lesbian), stereotype which have haunted the profession not only compromises female teachers' actual identities but also dis-empowers them in terms of the Gender Order. Acting in ways that are gender appropriate, and that appear as safely heterosexual, positions them in the gender order as subordinate 'sexualised' females in these contexts. These dynamics further mediate the pedagogical advice offered by many teachers, wherein gender positioning features heavily. Robin recalls the following strong advice from her mentors about the way to behave and how to position herself when teaching physical education:

You've got to treat them like dogs. I talk to them like I do my own dog and that's the way that it has got to be because you've got to get them in a position whereby you've disciplined them, you've got control and they're ready to get on and learn. That's what they are there for. You have to remind them of the fact that we've all got to do things that we don't want to do but that's the way it is sometimes. You need to go right. You over there bang (points). You need to take a teacher-centred approach.

(Female teacher from Robin's teaching practice)

Here Robin is being prompted to develop a masculinized teaching identity, that in symbolic and practical terms draws on confrontational, authoritarian and didactic pedagogical approaches associated with dominant masculinities. Like her fellow student teachers, Robin is being denied the opportunities to adopt alternative gender positions and pedagogies. Moreover, these women are aware that to engage in particular pedagogical practices is to risk their personal identities, making the projection of a professional a process fraught with complexity and difficulty:

The lady that was there before [physical education teacher in school], I can't say she was stereotypical because she was married not single, and she wasn't particularly butch. She was hard and aggressive and a lot of the girls I remember used to call her a bitch and they thought she was very hard and aggressive, she wasn't butch looking but she was quite . . . well, you know.

(Christie)

Taking and assigning gender positions

As well as being positioned, participants in the study all had to engage in the practical *taking and assigning* of gendered positions themselves. Again, it is important to reiterate that these student teachers, like their more experienced mentors, are behaving reflexively in context, endeavouring to balance many priorities of their duties, such as trying to include, motivate, keep control, structure and deliver content knowledge in their classes. Such experiences, it would seem, again present a series of practical double bind situations, through which the gendered status quo remains unchallenged. Consider Derek's experiences of teaching girls:

It was different . . . I don't know, they tended not to go off tasks so easily, as much as mess around . . . and to motivate them, but yes, you had to deal with them a bit more sensitively I think – do it a bit quieter during your teaching . . . when you are talking to them, and plenty of praise for the ones that weren't so motivated, and teach in a slightly lower tone perhaps, I don't know. . . . I saw that with my mentor especially, the more caring side, with the girls you would tend to have to be a bit more, um, not so macho perhaps. . . . Especially in the mixed PE situation, they [the girls] challenge the boys and they adopt some of the characteristics that perhaps they [the boys] have got.

(Derek)

In this situation Derek positions both himself and his pupils in notably gendered ways and again inherent dilemmas are apparent. The basis for his differentiation is a gendered assumption, reinforced by his mentors, that the girls need a different approach to boys to make them participate and learn. However, in stating 'not so macho' Derek is also reflexively positioning himself, in order to offset the dominant masculine position which he accepts is also available to him and sometimes expected of him. His actions are likely to reconstruct the Gender Order. Derek also demonstrates how masculine discourses occupy an invisible centre through the use of this pedagogy; the girls will acquire some of the boys dispositions thereby showing how the boys' characteristics are implicitly being used as the benchmark against which others are judged.

Trevor's experiences are similar, as is the reflexive way in which he engages in positioning and specifically, the management of his own gendered teaching identity:

> Sometimes, I mean to be honest, in school it is quite handy as well because the kids [boys] that are a lot of trouble in a lot of other classes aren't trouble in PE because they look to do PE, and then if you have got them in other classes or other areas of the school you can take that with you, because you have got more control over them where they are prepared to at least listen to what you say, where they wouldn't listen to what the maths teacher or English teacher because they hate maths and English, so in a way that is useful.
>
> (Trevor)

Here we see Trevor actively gravitating towards a dominant position in response to his perception of the needs of the situation based around mentor and pupil expectations. Like Derek, Trevor is also caught in a double bind; while the need to keep control is not an exclusively masculine threat, it nevertheless represents a particularly acute threat to stereotypically dominant masculine assumptions of how 'strong men' and 'real male physical education teachers' should act in the face of challenges to their authority. This next extract seems indicative of a masculinity under threat, with Trevor drawing on dominant aspects of his own identity ('if you've got the tools') to position himself as a dominantly masculine teacher, in spite of his intentions to explore alternative pedagogies which reflect his preferred 'more laid back' masculine identity:

> Yes I think so, I think it does make it easier to teach and I think especially in a classroom if you've got those lads then you've got the class. You know what I mean, if you've got the tools, if you keep them quiet then everyone else is going to be quiet. . . . Well, I mean, a lot of young lads obviously, you know, that's what they look up to and that's what they lock onto.
>
> (Trevor)

Connell (1995) refers to such action as the 'patriarchal dividend'; the implicit strategy of many men to benefit from the Gender Order that they don't necessarily subscribe to in order to offset any chance of being marginalised or subordinated, that they would risk, should they engage in less obviously dominant displays of masculinity. The important lessons that these men are embedding through practice is that a fusion of their dominant masculine selves and their teaching pedagogy is not only a legitimate, but a necessary identity resource, as Trevor points out in the following comment:

> Everybody teaches differently, I think but it's like a continuum, I think, . . . and obviously you've got 'masculine of masculine' which would be

male, obviously wouldn't be a female, but there would be some women that maybe teach in a more masculine way than some men; you know there's a whole range. You know I put myself towards that end of it but not at that extreme.

(Trevor)

Explicit here is the firmly gendered view and apparent status and identity of particular pedagogies.

A similar series of positioning practices and gender relational binds is also in evidence in the experiences of the female student teachers represented here. The ways in which Christie and Robin take and assign positions are particularly significant since, of all the female student teachers studied, their educational philosophies were perhaps most strongly allied to a critical child-centred feminist approach. Their biographical narratives suggest that these women see themselves as having a particular form of agency for changing gendered practices, which they believed would form the basis of their pedagogical creativity. Despite this, they go on to describe situations during their teacher training in which they have failed to exercise any such agency. As a football player Christie found herself particularly caught up in relational dynamics of gender positioning by pupils when she taught boys football. Pedagogical positioning was made more problematic by the gendered institutional, structural features of Christie's teaching environment. Her positioning was clearly compromised by the need to gain credibility in male dominated arenas of physical activity:

This was core PE that was mixed, and this was just they had no experience of having been taught by women since Year 7 until they got to Year 10 and suddenly they had a female there and they had no respect for, I don't know whether they had no respect for women or whether it was women sports people, whether it was because I was female teacher or whether it was because I was a sporting female, but they had very little respect for me even though I probably could sort of, you know, in terms of skill-wise been a lot better than any of them.

(Christie)

Christie's natural reaction, to demonstrate herself as a competent performer, has consequences for the relational dynamics of this educational situation, and is typical of both the active positioning and the double bind that is central to this discussion. As a competent performer Christie implicitly challenges the masculine stereotypical orthodoxy of males play football better than females, if she does not – she reinforces it. But in challenging the orthodoxy in this way Christie has to demonstrate the very same set of values and practices that would qualify as a 'good' male performance, and thereby aligns herself with the dominant gender position and its associated values and practices that she wishes to play a part in changing:

I took an all-boys football group, and it was quite interesting the way that they [the boys] reacted. One of the balls rolled over to me, and naturally I did take a flick and then a few keepie-ups and, you know, that was it, you know all the lads were like, 'Miss do you play football?' And I had my women's football top on, and then the lads started taking the mick out of one of the other boys in the group saying, 'Miss is better than you'.

(Christie)

Here we see that Christie's feminine physicality is defined in *relation* to and *comparison* with male standards, while the boys compare themselves with a 'women' rather than 'a competent performer'. A similar situation arose in basketball:

Yeah, the height thing can be a bit of a problem, like in basketball I had to do a couple of lay ups and a couple of three-pointers before I could even get them to listen and it was like, yeah, she can play basketball.

The demonstration of physical ability in these particular sports and contexts is in sharp contrast to the cultural conception of what it means to be stereotypically female. The disruption to the heterosexual logic of female/feminine brings sexual identity into question. Christie's competence as a woman is therefore positioned by the male pupils (and perhaps others) as an anomaly, as deviant, and she risks being defined as 'masculine' (read, lesbian). Consequently, Christie and doubtless other female teachers have the option of either taking a subordinated feminine position or a complicit position in a Gender Order, both of which ultimately suppress the alternative gendered identities that could be brought to teaching and learning physical education. In summary, while these women can position themselves in ways which allow them to access the masculine cultural project, significantly they have limited means to challenge its secular legitimacy, and in so doing embrace new ways of 'doing male things'. For the men, the fusion of their dominant masculine selves and their teaching pedagogy is a legitimate, expected and even demanded identity resource. For the women the expectation is that they become instrumental, dominant, authoritarian as teachers, whilst remaining stereotypically feminine women. In order to gain the available status and credibility, they have to fully embrace the symbolic gender dualisms, working towards a position of instrumental control, identifiable with a masculine tradition which has a disdain for that coded as feminine. Thus despite being female and challenging particular male orthodoxies, they also maintain the Gender Order through their paradoxical derogatory depictions of 'softer' forms of femininity. What we see in the next extract is the way in which Christie draws upon a segregation not only between the sexes but within, demonstrating a disdain for traditional subordinated forms of femininity. She comments that:

It's difficult to play games when there are only two out of a class of twenty-four, and ten are not doing it because they don't want to break their nails.

In addition, she makes sense of her own participation in sport through aligning herself more to masculinity than femininity:

We [her and her sister] are very different . . . can I say she is a typical girlie-girl? She is very, sort of, feminine with the short skirts and doing the hair. . . . The fact that I had a male friend growing up, I suppose I was a complete tomboy.

(Christie)

While Christie has taken important steps in gaining access to male orthodoxies, her use of oppositional gendered criteria to position herself and pupils only serves to reproduce the polarised stereotypes currently predominant and that underpin the continued marginalisation of pupils that she and her fellow student teachers are so clearly committed to attempt to include and motivate.

Challenging the gender order: connecting the self, pedagogy and the politics of change

When considered as a heuristic device, the notion of gender positioning that emerges from this empirical work is useful for revealing the linkages between individuals and the gendered social worlds that they inhabit and consciously or subconsciously contribute to reconstructing. Particularly with the women here, it would be easy to regard these people, and many others like them, as merely victims of forms of oppression by what Brod and Kaufman (1994) refer to as the central invisible discourses of dominant masculine ideology in the field of education, physical education and sport. We would not entirely refute this interpretation. In many ways they all are victims. However, we would also suggest that the gendered positions taken might be viewed as the *unintentional consequences* of human agency (Giddens, 1984, 1990) as carried out by 'knowledgeable actors' behaving reflexively in the contexts of their lives. This latter view gives cause for some optimism about the potential for reconstructing alternative expressions of gender identity in teaching physical education that might facilitate a more gender inclusive future for the subject. Specifically, we argue that there a series of connections that need to be made between the gendered self, pedagogy and the politics of change in gender relations. We sense that these connections would offer these teachers a broader range of 'identity resources' that would help them become more 'active agents' in confronting the dilemmas of gender positioning in teaching physical education. These would seem to include:

1   An awareness of a socially constructed Gender Order in society, sport and physical education and its implications for positioning individuals within that order.
2   An awareness that challenging the Gender Order through teaching physical education involves taking a micro-political stance and developing carefully considered courses of action.
3   A broader range of personal practical and experiential identity 'resources' that can support intellectual commitments to develop alternative ways of teaching physical education.

An acknowledgement of the Gender Order in our society and its relational implications for everyone is crucial if change is to be initiated and sustained from the level of the individual teacher, cascading upwards and rippling outwards, through pupils, other teachers, future student teachers and so on.

The work of Sparkes (1991) on the subjective dimensions of educational change provides further qualitative insights into these connections and the means of exploring them. These participants and, we suspect, other similarly committed physical education teachers need assistance if they are to be aware of the micro-political nature of challenging the Gender Order in their teaching and its implications for their own self-identities. It is important to move beyond classic 'liberal' (equality of access) notions of political agency that is in evidence in Christie's aspirations to 'control' football in the school she teaches in:

> This other school, I would have been in charge of all the football, like boys and girls, all years and that would have been fantastic to have got that position as a female. To go in and just do that job. I mean it would be brilliant to go out onto the pitch, like at a league match, or something and you could just predict what would happen. I mean the other male teacher would come in with his lads and look at me and then look around and probably say to me 'Where is he then?' [referring to a male PE teacher]. And I'm just the sort of person to love that, to be able to go in and challenge that.
>
> (Christie)

While the success in gaining access to this arena would promote visibility and provide opportunity for change, ironically it will do little to challenge the Gender Order if Christie's own discourses and practices merely mimic dominant masculine pedagogies in evidence earlier. The opportunity here is for Christie to strategically challenge the status quo from within, by innovating with techniques and practices that challenge conventional dominant masculine positions and practices in this and other activity areas. Such action is far from easy and furthermore, requires considerable support and professional preparation.

Our third focus in pursuing notions of challenge relates to the nature of gender itself. Trevor's comments below show that 'lived' understandings of gender are necessary if articulate micro-political strategies are to be developed:

> It's quite . . . I think . . . I don't know, I try not to think of teaching girls and boys because I haven't got younger sisters or anything, also I haven't got any children, so, it's a bit difficult, sort of, this is how I teach girls as opposed to boys – I just try and teach them.
>
> (Trevor)

Trevor's position here as elsewhere in his biography is entirely laudable, but it is unlikely to sufficiently empower him to develop inclusive pedagogies without succumbing to positions complicit to hegemonic masculinity. A key resource here is reflection on one's own possible identities. These reflections can be used to inform the development of alternative pedagogies, but in order to do so they must extend beyond binary visions. This shift in thinking is crucial if we are to move towards the development of differentiation pedagogies and positions not based on assumptions of gender but on judgements of individual need. 'Difference' therefore, becomes a more situated, lived understanding of gender and physical education, in which Davies (1989) suggests:

> A first step is the conceptual separation of lived masculinities from the idea, and the idealisation of that idea, of hegemonic masculinity. A second is the realisation that males and females can equally take up what have been defined as masculine and feminine positioning without that being a moral blot on their character. A third and vital step is the recognition of multiple masculinities and femininities, most of which bear little or no relation to the genitals of the person taking them up.
>
> (Davies, 1989: 111)

Connecting the self, pedagogy and the Gender Order involves drawing on lived experience as a gender identity resource. The evidence emerging from these student teachers is that they do not always possess sufficient alternative gender identity resources, in the form of 'other' gendered experiences (including, internalised subject knowledge, communication skills and alternative narratives of the self, see Sparkes, 1999), to facilitate the transference of the inclusive cognitive beliefs into practical pedagogies. By way of example, Derek's comments pay testimony to the need for further 'lived' identity resources:

> No, my background was totally single sex, at the start it was slightly alien to me, but I totally came round to it, maybe gymnastics and dance

especially, if I was teaching in an all-boys group for both of those I just wouldn't have got the quality.

(Derek)

By 'quality' Derek was referring to the embodied physical expression of himself as a dance teacher, the movements, language and dispositions and ideas which come with involvement and experience. We agree with Kenway (1998) and Vertinsky (1992) who contend we should be encouraging a wide variety of ways of being female and develop and promote alternative and non-violent (or dominant) ways of being male, and we should expect students (and teachers) to take *risks* with their own gender identities. Relations of power operate in multiple directions, and through experimenting with gender identities we might begin to move outside, across and inside the gender divide. Given that dominant discourses within physical education assert a heterosexuality which bonds sex and gender together (Sykes, 1998), these qualifications might have implications for issues of sexuality in physical education. Specifically these practices may assist in challenging the silencing which has been central to the experiences of lesbian and gay physical education teachers (Khayatt, 1992; 1994; Sparkes, 1994a; 1994b; Squires and Sparkes, 1996; Clarke, 1998; Sykes, 1998).

Further, as Wright (1997) suggests, we should be concerned with finding ways of empowering women and girls, and men and boys, so that they feel confident and skilled in using their bodies in all aspects of life, rather than being restricted by narrow gendered forms of embodiment and practices. These are all embodied and experiential resources which lay much broader cross-gender foundations for what individuals feel comfortable doing and saying, and they facilitate the reconstruction of embodied agency (Shilling, 1999).[2] This also draws attention to the need for physical education (in schools' curriculum and in initial teacher training) to draw from a wider spectrum of activities and physical culture that is already represented in society (Kirk, 1999). As Penney and Chandler (2000) note, it also calls into question the current activity-based framework which dominates curriculum organisation and the subject matter of teaching and learning in physical education[3] in the United Kingdom.

In conclusion, our empirical work suggests that a vision for gender inclusive futures in physical education strongly implicates physical education teachers' gendered identities. While the quality and commitment of our participants' approach to their profession is not in doubt, the dimensions of their gendered identities which they drew upon during the difficult circumstances of teaching are implicitly strategic enactments that tend to fit into, rather than challenge the Gender Order in society, sport and physical education. In response, and in contribution to an inclusive agenda for change, we consider as imperatives, that the above connections between the Gender Order, the self, pedagogy and the politics of change should more explicitly underpin Initial and In-service teacher training. In addition, if the aggregate experiences of these teachers' biographies is indicative of wider patterns, subsequent generations of students, teachers and mentors will need to be encouraged to develop and internalize a greater range of practical, embodied and experiential gendered identity resources, including, alternative gendered modes of communication, movement skills, subject knowledge and narratives of the self. With these in place these teachers would be in a stronger and more flexible position to embrace their own and facilitate the development of their pupils' multiple masculine and feminine identities and in so doing take action to challenge the Gender Order.

Acknowledgement

We would like to thank the participants in this study, whose co-operation made this work possible. We would also like to thank Dr. Dawn Penney and Professor John Evans for their constructive comments on earlier drafts of this chapter.

Notes

1 The primary concern of liberal approaches to equal opportunities is with equality of access to valued social and cultural goods/opportunities – such approaches stop short of providing a critique of elements such as patriarchy, oppression or domination through which those goods are given value in the first place. By contrast critical approaches to equal opportunities retain the belief in equal access but question the nature of the opportunities we have access to.
2 Shilling argues that our understanding of an individual's ability to act in society has been based on cognitive-only models of 'rational' actors. But that the agency provided by the body is a crucial missing link – between agency and structure debates, and can help alter the way we think about human agency and its potential.
3 The specific reference here is to the NCPE in England and Wales but the activity-based model is also in evidence in many other physical education curricula around the world.

References

Brod, H. and Kaufman, M. (eds) (1994) *Theorizing Masculinities: Volume 5*, Thousand Oaks: Sage.
Brown, D. (1999) Complicity and reproduction in teaching physical education, *Sport, Education & Society* 4(2): 143–60.
Brittan, A. (1989) *Masculinity and Power*, Oxford: Basil Blackwell.
Clarke, G. (1998) Queering the pitch and coming out to play: lesbians in physical education and sport, *Sport, Education and Society* 3(2): 145–60.
Connell, R.W. (1987) *Gender and Power: Society, the Person and Sexual Politics*, Sydney: Allen & Unwin Pty Ltd.
Connell, R.W. (1995) *Masculinities*, London: Polity Press.
Davies, B. (1989) *Frogs and Snails and Feminist Tails: Preschool and Gender*, Sydney: Allen & Unwin Pty Ltd.

De Knop, P., Theeboom, M., Wittock, H. and De Martelaer, K. (1996) Implications of Islam on Muslim girls' sports participation in Western Europe, *Sport, Education and Society* 1(2): 147–64.

Dillabough, J.-A. (1999) Gender politics and conceptions of the modern teacher: women, identity and professionalism, *British Journal of Sociology of Education* 20(3): 373–94.

Ennis, C. (1999) Creating a culturally relevant curriculum for disengaged girls, *Sport, Education and Society* 4(1): 31–49.

Edley, N. and Wetherell, M. (1995) *Men in Perspective: Practice, Power and Identity*, London: Prentice Hall.

Evans, J. (ed.) (1993) *Equality, Education and Physical Education*, London: Falmer Press.

Evans, J., Davies, B. and Penney, D. (1996) Teachers, teaching and the social construction of gender relations, *Sport, Education and Society* 1(1): 165–84.

Fletcher, S. (1987) The making and breaking of a female tradition: women's physical education in England, 1880–(1980), in J. Mangan and R. Park (eds) *From the Fair Sex to Feminism*, London: Frank Cass.

Giddens, A. (1984) *The Constitution of Society: Outline of the Theory of Structuration*, Cambridge: Polity Press.

Giddens, A. (1990) *The Consequences of Modernity*, Cambridge: Polity Press.

Gramsci, A. (1971) *Selections from the Prison Notebooks*, London: Lawrence & Wishart.

Griffin, P. (1992) Lesbian and gay educators: opening the classroom closet, *Empathy* 3: 25–8.

Gore, J. (1990) *The Struggle for Pedagogies: Critical and Feminist Pedagogies as Regimes of Truth*, University of Wisconsin-Madison.

Grenfell, M. and James, D. (1998) *Bourdieu and Education: Acts of Practical Theory*, London: Falmer Press

Hargreaves, J. (1986) *Sport, Power and Culture: A Social and Historical Analysis of Popular Sports in Britain*, Cambridge: Polity Press.

Hargreaves, J. (2000) Gender, morality, and the National Physical Education Curriculum, in J. Nansen and N. Neilsen (eds) *Sports, Body and Health*, Odense University Press.

Hickey, C., Fitzclarence, L. and Mathews R. (eds) (1998) *Where the Boys Are: Masculinity, Sport and Education*, Geelong, Victoria: Deakin Centre for Education and Change, Deakin University.

Humberstone, B. (1990) Warriors or wimps? Creating alternative forms of physical education, in M. A. Messner and D. F. Sabo (eds) *Sport, Men and the Gender Order: Critical Feminist Perspectives*, Champaign, IL: Human Kinetics.

Kenway, J. (1998) Masculinity studies, sports and femininism: fair play or foul?, in C. Hickey, L. Fitzclarence and R. Mathews (eds) *Where the Boys Are: Masculinity, Sport and Education*, Geelong, Victoria: Deakin Centre for Education and Change, Deakin University.

Khayatt, D. (1992) *Lesbian Teachers: An Invisible Presence*, Albany, NY: State University Press of New York.

Kirk, D. (1992) *Defining Physical Education: The Social Construction of a School Subject in Postwar Britain*, London: Falmer Press.

Kirk, D. (1999) Physical culture, physical education and relational analysis, *Sport, Education and Society* 4(1): 63–73.

Luke, C. and Gore, J. (eds) (1992) *Feminisms and Critical Pedagogy*, London: Routledge.

Mangan, J.A. (1981) *Athleticism in the Victorian and Edwardian Public School: The Emergence and Consolidation of an Educational Ideology*, Cambridge: Cambridge University Press.

Mangan, J.A. and Walvin, J. (eds) (1987) *Manliness and Morality: Middle-class Masculinity in Britain and America, 1800–1940*, Manchester: Manchester University Press.

Messner, M. and Sabo, D. (eds) (1990) *Sport, Men and the Gender Order*, Champaign, IL: Human Kinetics Press.

Pease, B. (2000) *Recreating Men: Postmodern Masculinity Politics*, London: Sage.

Penney, D. and Chandler, T. (2000) Physical education: What future(s)?, *Sport, Education & Society* 5(1): 71–88.

Peterson, A. (1997) *Unmasking the Masculine: Men and Identity in a Sceptical Age*, London: Sage.

Rutherford, J. (1988) Who's that man?, in R. Chapman and J. Rutherford (eds) *Male Order: Unwrapping Masculinity*, London: Lawrence & Wishart, pp. 21–67.

Salisbury, J. and Jackson, D. (1998) *Challenging Macho Values: Practical Ways of Working with Adolescent Boys*, London: Falmer Press.

Shilling, C. (1999) Towards an embodied understanding of the structure/agency relationship, *British Journal of Sociology* 50(4): 543–62.

Sparkes, A. (1991) Exploring the subjective dimension of change, in Armstrong and A. Sparkes, (eds) *Issues in Physical Education*, London: Cassell Education.

Sparkes, A. (1994a) Life histories and the issue of voice: reflections on an emerging relationship, *International Journal of Qualitative Studies in Education* 7: 165–83.

Sparkes, A. (1994b) Self, silence and invisibility as a beginning teacher: a life history of lesbian experience, *British Journal of Sociology of Education* 15(1): 93–118.

Sparkes, A. (1997) Ethnographic fiction and representing the absent other, *Sport, Education and Society* 2(1): 25–40.

Sparkes, A.C. (1999) Exploring body narratives, *Sport, Education and Society* 4(1): 17–30.

Squires, S. and Sparkes, A. (1996) Circles of silence: sexual identity in physical education and sport, *Sport, Education and Society* 1(1): 77–102.

Sykes, H. (1998) *Teaching Bodies, Learning Desires: Feminist Post-structural Life Histories of Heterosexual and Lesbian Physical Education Teachers in Western Canada*, unpublished Doctoral thesis, Vancouver, BC: University of British Columbia.

Talbot, M. (1993) Gender and physical education, in J. Evans (ed.) *Equality, Education and Physical Education*, London: Falmer Press.

Tabachnick, B., Zeichner, R. and Kenneth, M. (1984) The impact of the student teaching experience on the development of teacher perspectives, *Journal of Teacher Education* 35(6): 28–36.

Templin, T. and Schempp, P. (eds) (1989) *Socialization into Physical Education: Learning to Teach*, Indianapolis: Benchmark Press.

Tsolidis, G. (1996) Feminist theorisations of identity and difference: a case study related to gender education policy, *British Journal of Sociology of Education* 17(3): 267–77.

Vertinsky, P.A. (1992) Reclaiming space, revisioning the body: the quest for a gender-sensitive physical education, *Quest* 44(3): 373–97.

Wright, J. (1988) Reconstructing gender in sport and physical education, in C. Hickey, L. Fitzclarence and R. Mathews (eds) *Where the Boys Are: Masculinity, Sport and Education*, Geelong, Victoria: Deakin Centre for Education and Change, Deakin University.

Whannel, G. (2000) Sport stars, narrativization and masculinities, *Leisure Studies* 18: 249–65.

Wright, J. (1997) The construction of gendered contexts in single sex and co-educational physical education lessons, *Sport, Education and Society* 2(1): 55–72.

Young, I.M. (1990) *Justice and the Politics of Difference*, Princeton, New Jersey: Princeton University Press.

Part III

Gender and physical education: policies and practice

7   Gendered policies

Dawn Penney

Introduction

This chapter focuses on what we conventionally regard as 'policy' in physical education; 'official texts' produced by governments or curriculum agencies that provide the reference point for the development of physical education in schools. However, it locates these texts as part of the complex process of policy development that we described in chapter 2. The discussion therefore highlights a number of important points in relation to investigations of the ways in which gender issues are represented in policies for physical education. In particular I stress that we need to look at physical education policy developments in the context of political influences and agendas, and in the light of pragmatic concerns relating to education and to physical education. Not for the first time we see that policy making always involves compromises and that these reflect the positions that particular people and particular interests either have or are denied in the policy process. In pursuing the representation of gender issues in physical education policies I also direct attention to what can *not* be said in policy debates and what is excluded from policy texts relating to physical education. I argue that silences can certainly speak louder than words and that neither silence, nor the use of 'neutral' language, is in any way neutral. In policy developments in education decisions to retain silences or to use particular language are conscious and political decisions that have important implications for future practice. These characteristics will influence the degree to which policies serve to demand or encourage that established and inequitable practices and beliefs are rendered a thing of the past, and new practices developed that signal a conscious commitment to better representation of individuals who are currently marginalised in and by physical education.

My discussion focuses upon texts associated with the development of the National Curriculum for Physical Education (NCPE) in England. However, the issues raised are ones that can be pursued in the investigation of other policies, at other times or in other places. The potential value of adopting a comparative perspective in policy studies is worthy of note. Often it takes a comparative perspective to reveal what could be different, or what is missing from the policies that we are most familiar with and may well have come to view unproblematically. In several respects an investigation of the progressive development of the NCPE in England through the 1990s illustrates the value of a comparative perspective. I deliberately focus attention upon an official text that has long since disappeared from view: the Interim Report produced by the original NCPE working group in 1991. It is a text that highlights what has not been said in relation to gender and equity in subsequent NCPE texts, but that also itself featured silences that it is important to pursue. I encourage readers to consider whether in implementation there is the scope for teachers and teacher educators to 'fill silences' that remain a feature of the official National Curriculum texts and to thereby extend the gender agendas inherent in physical education curricula and teaching. In 1993 Graham and Tytler expressed the view that 'The National Curriculum is a potent tool for change and for bringing about equality of opportunity. Its potential is largely unrealised as yet' (p. 132). This chapter provides some insights into that potential in the context of physical education. It also provides an important backdrop to the chapters that follow in this section. Harris and Penney (in chapter 8) and Williams and Bedward (in chapter 9) present data that illustrate the ways in which silences inherent in the official texts of the NCPE have been variously 'filled' and also overlooked by teachers. Both chapters show that policy texts issued by governments are far from finished and that they can and will be read and responded to in various ways, for better or worse in relation to gender equity.

My initial discussion comes in two parts. First I consider those instances in which equal opportunities, equity and/or specifically, gender equity, has been addressed explicitly within NCPE texts issued by the central government and/or curriculum agencies in England. In the second part of the chapter I turn to the ways in which other features of these texts have had important implicit messages in relation to gender issues in physical education. As many of the explicit references to equal opportunities, equity and gender have been removed as the development of the NCPE has progressed, this exploration of 'hidden messages' is particularly important. Recognising the ways in which particular requirements and particular language serve to legitimate inequities in gender relations in contexts of physical education and sport is crucial if we are to design policies that give different messages and/or encourage 'alternative readings' of notably conservative official texts.

A National Curriculum for Physical Education: the promise of progress

The development of a National Curriculum for all children in all state schools in England and Wales was heralded as securing 'an entitlement for all' (DES, 1989). It was a development that appeared to promise much in relation to equal opportunities in education. But since the launch of the National Curriculum several things have become clear about the 'entitlement' that was secured by the Education Reform Act of 1988. The relative absence of debates about the nature of the educational entitlement outlined in the National Curriculum, about whose and what interests the new statutory requirements were directed towards and set to provide for, or whose educational needs and interests may be being overlooked by the requirements, is not insignificant. In the rush of development and revision of the National Curriculum attention has invariably been fixed upon the practicalities of implementation rather than any need to pose critical questions of principles underlying requirements. Has it been a policy that has embraced the varied needs and interests of girls and boys, coming from different class, cultural and religious backgrounds, with different sexualities? Has it positioned those differences as a resource or a problem for the teachers charged with providing all children with their statutory entitlement? Have the official texts outlined an entitlement in physical education that would challenge long-established sex-differentiated patterns of curriculum provision and staffing in physical education and provide children with a physical education capable of reducing the dominance of gender stereotyped attitudes, beliefs and patterns of participation in physical activity and sport? It is these questions that underpin my exploration of various versions of the NCPE that have emerged throughout the 1990s in England. The discussion seeks to pursue the direction and/or encouragement that official texts (including non-statutory guidance materials issued by government agencies) have given teachers to engage with gender issues in contexts of physical education.

The Interim Report 1991: putting gender on the agenda

As others have noted, the Interim Report from the NCPE working group provided what has to now be seen as extensive commentary on 'equal opportunities in physical education' (Hargreaves, 1994; 2000; Talbot, 1993). Subsequent texts featured a dramatic loss of depth in discussion and a reduction in the strength of the messages being sent out to teachers about what action is expected of them in relation to equal opportunities in physical education. The Interim Report stood out for not only identifying equal opportunity as 'a leading and guiding principle for physical education' (DES/WO, 1991a: 16) but also clearly embracing a commitment to equity within this principle. The group specifically drew attention to the need for teachers to focus upon the individuality of pupils and furthermore, to view this positively. They explained that:

> All children will have their own individual gifts to contribute, some of which may be derived from or expressive of their backgrounds. These can be used to their own advantage and to enrich the experience of the group, but should never be used as a basis for restricting access to, or opportunity for, any learning experience in physical education.
>
> (ibid.: 16)

In addition, the group highlighted some of the complexities of gender and of pedagogical relations in physical education, and the challenges that engaging with these posed for schools and teachers within them. They stressed that:

> mere *access* cannot be equated with real *opportunity*. The distinction between access and opportunity is crucial. In some schools, girls and boys, able-bodied and disabled, from a range of cultures and ethnic background may be said to have the same *access* to the physical education curriculum: no children are prevented by virtue of their sex, religion, ability or race from taking part. But even when this desirable state of affairs exists, do children also have equal *opportunities* to learn and express themselves through and in physical education? The effects of attitudes and expectations of teachers, the preconditions of access, the interactions within mixed-sex, mixed-ability and multi-cultural groups, and the previous experiences and relative ranges and levels of the skills, knowledge and understanding of the children must also be considered.
>
> (ibid.: 17, original emphasis)

In a further move that openly questioned the legitimacy of common practices and perceptions in physical education, the group identified a number of issues that in their view, demanded 'particular thought and consideration' and upon which they would expand in their final report. These were:

(a) the public nature of success and failure in physical education;
(b) the competitive nature of many physical education activities;
(c) the legacy of single-sex teaching and teacher education in physical education;
(d) moves towards mixed-sex grouping, sometimes without an educational rationale, and without consideration of the conditions under which mixed-sex teaching and single-sex teaching might be more successful or appropriate;
(e) the biological and cultural effects of being female or male on the behaviour considered appropriate for girls and boys of different cultures;
(f) the physical nature of physical education, and the emergence of sexuality during key stages 2, 3, and 4, providing both problems and opportunities for physical education in challenging body images, sex stereotypes and other limited perspectives which constrain the choices and achievements of disabled children, and of both girls and boys;
(g) the effects of some culturally restricted interpretations of masculinity on the place and value of dance in the school curriculum, and on boys' opportunities for dance experience and education;
(h) the barriers to young people's involvement caused by the restrictive ways some sports and forms of dance are portrayed and practised;

(i)   the rich potential for physical education to transcend categories of race, sex and learning need, through nurturing the value of individual contributions in group situations, and through presenting a wide range of cultural forms and experiences which reflect our multi-cultural society; and

(j)   the treatment of physical education in sex discrimination legislation and the varied levels of understanding of its effects on curriculum physical education, extra-curricula activities and school sport.

(ibid.: 17)

The group acknowledged the complexity of these issues, but also stressed the need for teachers and teacher educators to engage with the complexity. They reiterated that 'mixed *grouping* (ability, sex, cultures) is not the same as mixed ability, multi-cultural or co-educational *teaching*' (ibid.: 18, original emphasis) and stated that:

Working towards equality of opportunity in physical education involves not only widening and ensuring access. It involves the understanding and appreciation of the range of pupils' responses to femininity, masculinity and sexuality, to the whole range of ability and disability, to ethnic and cultural diversity, and the ways these relate for children to physical education.

(ibid.: 18)

The limits of the existing understanding of these issues amongst both teachers and teacher educators was implicit in their comment that 'This will entail, both in initial and in-service training of teachers, the critical review of prevailing practice, rigorous and continuous appraisal and often the willingness to face up to long held beliefs and prejudices' (ibid.: 18).

True to their word, the working group further highlighted the importance and scope of equal opportunities in physical education in their final report (DES/WO, 1991b). They dedicated a chapter of the report to what they maintained was a 'guiding and leading principle' for the subject. They identified that the role of teachers should be 'to foster respect for fellow human beings; to question the stereotypes which limit children's behaviour and achievements; and to challenge, whenever necessary, instances of sexism and racism' (ibid.: 15). Once again they stressed the distinction between access and opportunity and the potential for enrichment by virtue of individuality, whilst also acknowledging the challenge that responding to these issues represented for the profession. They stated in no uncertain terms that legacies from the past continued to constitute a significant barrier to progress towards gender equity in physical education, saying that:

the different ideologies and content of programmes of the former single sex institutions, and commonly for men and women in mixed courses, continue to affect not only teachers' attitudes, but also the ability of both men and women teachers to teach across a balanced programme of physical activities. In-service training will need to address this issue to avoid future undesirable sex stereotyping of activities (for example, with women teaching all dance and men teaching all contact sports).

(ibid.: 57)

Returning to the matter of grouping, they explained that 'Choices of mixed- or single-sex groupings in physical education should be made for educational reasons, and after considering the conditions under which they might be most successful and appropriate' (ibid.: 57). Notably, they pointed to the need for moves to address gender in schools to also engage with experiences (and inequities) beyond them, with 'recognition of the different opportunities which are available for girls and boys to acquire particular sets of skills outside of the school curriculum' (ibid.: 57). The report thus made it clear that different grouping would be appropriate in different contexts and that a move away from sex-differentiated curricula should not be interpreted as demanding wholesale adoption of mixed-sex grouping. However, they also warned of the tensions that may arise between policies adopted within schools and those beyond them, specifically in relation to 'the exclusionary practices and rules of some sports governing bodies on competitive school sport' (ibid.: 58). If not part of the education service, competitive sport may be exempted from the Sex Discrimination Act of 1974, with provision outside of the curriculum thereby potentially giving rise to contradictory messages for pupils. As O'Sullivan and colleagues note in chapter 10 of this text, competitive sport in the USA has, in contrast, been legally required to engage with sex discrimination issues.

On the matter of 'kit' for physical education, the report prompted further challenges to stereotypical conventions. The group stated that 'Considerations of safety, comfort and freedom of movement should override conventions associated with being male or female' (ibid.: 58). In later discussion of 'cultural diversity' the report also identified the need for negotiation to facilitate participation and enjoyment within particular religious conventions and drew attention to the need for teachers to be sensitive to the costs of clothing and equipment for physical education. Here the text thus acknowledged the importance of the constant interplay of issues of gender, ethnicity and class in relation to equal opportunities in physical education.

In a further effort to extend understandings of gender issues and counter stereotypical images and understandings, the group linked the breadth of experiences incorporated in the curriculum with the potential for the subject to extend current (and limited) perceptions of masculinity and femininity in relation to physical activity and sport. They stressed the need for schools to 'include equal opportunities considerations among the criteria by which they select the content of the physical education programmes, so that all children have the opportunity to experience a range of physical activities within both

National Curriculum physical education and extra-curricula school sport' (ibid.: 58) and stated that 'In particular, a broad and balanced programme of physical education, sensitively delivered, can help to extend boys' restricted perceptions of masculinity and masculine behaviour' (ibid.: 58). While not denying this potential, there is a need to recognise that it is not only boys who may have notably narrow perceptions about these issues. We need to engage both girls and boys in efforts to extend understandings of both masculinities and femininities.

Obscuring the agenda?

As indicated, we need to value the extent of the group's commentary on equal opportunities and see its inclusion in an 'official text' issued by the government as a significant achievement on the part of the group. However, in celebrating the commentary we are in danger of overlooking some characteristics of the final report that are important in relation to the degree to which it would succeed in securing equal opportunities as a 'guiding and leading principle' in the implementation of the NCPE. Would the progressive intentions of writers be reflected in practice? In this respect several points are worthy of note, not least of which is the physical position of much of the above commentary within the final report. The status and potential impact of many of the points made by the group in relation to equal opportunity in physical education seemed compromised by what can only be seen as 'relegation' to an appendix of the report. This location appeared contradictory to the claimed lead status of the principle. Furthermore it was a position that undoubtedly placed in jeopardy the expression of equal opportunities in practice. The appendices of any text do not carry comparable weight to the main text and points raised in the group's discussion of, for example, 'sex and gender' and 'cultural diversity' may have simply never been read by many teachers. Understandably, attention would be upon the specifics of statutory requirements rather than accompanying commentary.

Separate or focused discussion on 'equal opportunities' has 'pros and cons' wherever positioned in the text. The separation can be seen as reflecting the importance of equal opportunities as an issue for the subject and the profession. However, it is also a position that may lead to the issue being totally overlooked or given limited attention amidst a focus upon what were perceived as more immediate concerns, such as the general requirements established for the subject,[1] the programmes of study[2] outlined for each of the identified areas of activity within the curriculum, or the assessment framework provided for the NCPE. It is when we explore these other sections of the NCPE that we can begin to appreciate the extent to which policy texts always feature compromises between different interests, not all of which have equal status in policy developments (Ball, 1990; Bowe *et al.*, 1992; Penney and Evans, 1999). In addition, we see the significance of omissions and the way in which they may give rise to contradictions or inconsistencies in the messages being given out to readers. If we are concerned to promote equal opportunities within physical education, consistency and reinforcement of messages seem crucial.

Before expanding upon some of these issues in relation to the NCPE texts, I should acknowledge another important characteristic of the development of the NCPE. The working group's final report was not a text that the group had autonomy over, in relation to either form or content. Like similar documents produced for other subjects and subsequent national curriculum texts produced by other government agencies, it was instead a text that openly reflected the politics of policy development in education and a process that was far from neutral (Evans and Penney, 1995; Penney and Evans, 1999). The demands for writers to produce documents that would be acceptable to civil servants and ministers have been vividly described by the Chairman and Chief Executive of the National Curriculum Council,[3] Duncan Graham. Graham's commentary on the development of the National Curriculum makes it very clear that government officials required a particular content in a particular form from the groups that had been appointed to advise them on the National Curriculum (Graham with Tytler, 1993). The compromises and contradictions that we see in texts such as the NCPE final report therefore need to be acknowledged as not entirely of the group's own making, but as nevertheless, significant characteristics of the text. The following discussion of such characteristics is illustrative rather than exhaustive. Furthermore, it is a critique applicable to other policy texts relating to physical education. Many of the omissions and contradictions noted are ones that have been replicated in more recent official publications. Certainly, there is a continued need to explore silences, compromises and contradictions in physical education policies. As Noble (1999) has explained, readers interpret silences as well as words. They can have powerful meanings and important implications for future practice.

Limiting and excluding agendas

Above, I identified sections of the NCPE official texts that for many teachers would be their priority and hold their attention. One such section was the 'recommended programmes of study' for physical education. This section of the working group's final report addressed the breadth and balance of the curriculum. However, here the text failed to reinforce the commentary incorporated within the sections specifically dedicated to 'equal opportunities in physical education'. In outlining their recommendations regarding the areas of activity to be incorporated within the various key stages of the curriculum, the group made no reference to the need to consider issues of gender or cultural diversity. Instead their attention focused on the practicality of their recommendations and the flexibility that they accorded to schools, 'as requested by the Secretaries of State' (DES/WO, 1991b: 26). The impression was that pragmatic rather than educational or specifically, equal opportunities issues, would be the first and legitimate point of reference in curriculum design.

The section of the text that addressed the programmes of study associated with each specific area of activity could similarly be viewed as 'full of omissions'. For example, given the emphasis above that dance could 'help to extend boys' restricted perceptions of masculinity and masculine behaviour' (DES/WO, 1991b: 58) we could expect the programme of study for dance to feature explicit prompts to teachers to explore this potential. The absence of reference to gender and sexuality in recommendations such as those below has to be seen as not only an omission, but also a loss – in the status accorded to equal opportunities and of an opportunity to prompt its expression in practice. For key stage 3 dance (for pupils aged 11–14), it was recommended that pupils should:

- be taught to perform set dances showing an understanding of style;
- develop and use appropriate techniques and styles to communicate meanings and ideas;
- be guided to create and perform short dances showing sensitivity to the style of accompaniment;
- be taught to describe, analyse and interpret dances recognising stylistic differences, aspects of production and cultural/historical contexts; and
- be taught to support their own dance compositions with independently researched material, and, where appropriate, record dance in words and symbols.

(DES/WO, 1991b: 33)

The text relating to identified 'general requirements' that were applicable to all of the key stages and relevant to all of the areas of activity, was a further section devoid of mention of equal opportunities. The need for pupils to be physically active, to understand safety issues, to 'be taught to cope with both success and failure', to 'observe the conventions of fair play', engage in problem solving, 'be given the opportunity to consolidate their skills through repetition' and 'be made aware of the importance of good posture' were all matters that, unlike equal opportunities, gender or sexuality, were identified as 'general requirements' to be addressed in implementation of the programmes of study (DES/WO, 1991b: 28).

Requirements and guidance relating to assessment is another area in which there is both the opportunity and arguably a critical need for issues of equal opportunity to be addressed. Once again, there was a silence in the NCPE working group's text. The final report identified a number of 'issues in assessment'. Several of these could be seen as demanding that attention be directed to equal opportunities considerations. However, equal opportunities and/or gender issues did not feature in the discussion of criteria for assessment, or in the group's emphasis that the context of assessment needed to have meaning for pupils (DES/WO, 1991b: 42–3). Both the criteria for assessment and the context of assessment are important considerations if we wish to promote greater gender equity in physical education. The tendency may well be for a 'gender blind' or 'same for all' approach to be viewed as the desirable or defensible approach. However, it is an approach that ignores important differences between pupils that we should be actively responding to in teaching and assessment if we are to maximise opportunities for all pupils to progress and enjoy success in the subject.

Further absences in the text could be identified in the discussion of 'partnerships in provision'. Despite the group's stated belief that 'partnerships have a major role to play in furthering the aims of physical education' (DES/WO, 1991b: 49), the critical need for collective and co-ordinated action to challenge inequities in provision seemed underplayed (see also Macdonald, chapter 12 in this text). There was important recognition that ability can restrict pupils' access to extra-curricular physical education and sport and the need to use the extra-curricular arena to extend the breadth of pupils' experiences. But there was no prompt for teachers to move from the commonplace practice of male staff taking responsibility for organising extra-curricula activities for boys and female staff doing likewise for girls, with the result that extra-curricula programmes invariably promote stereo-typical images of masculinity and femininity and narrow perceptions of the range of physical activities that men and women can participate in (see Penney and Harris, 1997; Bass and Cale, 1999).

Sustained silence: the statutory orders for the NCPE

Absences such as those identified above have featured in texts that have superseded the NCPE working group's final report. The silences became progressively more obvious and more significant as cuts were made to the length of policy documents and the scope of discussion inherent in them. As the development of the NCPE progressed much of the commentary specifically directed to equal opportunities issues disappeared altogether, or was relegated to accompanying and notably *non*-statutory guidance texts. Far from being portrayed as a leading principal, equal opportunities and more specifically gender issues were hard to find in the consultation report issued in 1991 (NCC, 1991), the statutory order published in 1992 (DES/WO, 1992) and the revised order issued in 1995 (DfE/WO 1995). The bland impression was that equal opportunities and gender issues were simply not worthy of sustained commentary in the NCPE. Figueroa (1993: 100) reflected that 'The closest the National Curriculum Council Consultation Report – on which the statutory order, that is, the legal requirement, is based – gets to issues of multi-cultural and antiracist education is in mentioning, sparingly and in the broadest terms, such concepts as "fair play" and "cultural issues".' Meanwhile Evans and Davies (1993: 19) observed that 'there is little in the recommendations of the NC for PE to ensure that the practice of differentiating the curriculum for boys and girls will not continue' and Barton (1993) pointed to the relative lack of sophistication in the conceptualisation of 'disability' (and therefore, of equal opportunity) being presented by the text. Barton stressed the need for clearer engagement with the complex interaction of equal opportunities 'issues', explaining that 'the difficulties of and responses to being disabled are influenced by class, race, gender and age factors. These can cushion or compound the experience of discrimination and oppression' (p. 45). He was thus pointing to the clear failure of policy to promote sophisticated understandings of equal opportunities and equity. Such understandings are a crucial pre-requisite to the development of practices that respond to the individual needs of pupils. Later in the chapter I consider whether the latest version of the NCPE can be regarded as an advancement in relation to these concerns. First, however, I explore some of the less explicit gendered characteristics of the NCPE established as the entitlement for all children in state schools in England and Wales.

Gender off the agenda?

In the context of consistent gaps and omissions in the commentary on equal opportunities, equity and gender in the various versions of the NCPE, the implicit messages inherent in and portrayed by the official texts take on an enhanced significance. Following others (Hargreaves, 1994, 2000) I suggest that in its form and content the NCPE has been openly gendered and has repeatedly failed to prompt an extension of notably limited understandings of gender in physical education. The discussion below pursues some key characteristics of the NCPE in relation to these claims. The aim is to illustrate that even if apparently excluded from the texts, gender issues were very much embedded in them, and set to arise from them.

One of the issues that has consistently featured prominently in debates about the NCPE has been the breadth and balance of the curriculum outlined as a statutory entitlement. Previous commentaries have pointed to the progressively privileged position that was accorded to games following the government's response to the working group's Interim Report (see Evans and Penney, 1995; Penney and Evans, 1999) and the parallel reduction in requirements for other areas of activity to feature in the entitlement curriculum. The privileging of games is significant in relation to our interest in gender on at least two counts; curriculum content and organisation. Invariably the two issues are inextricably linked. Games remains an area of physical education frequently associated with sex-differentiated patterns of provision, with sports stereotypically regarded as exclusively 'men's' or 'women's' being provided for boys and girls respectively, and typically also staffed by male and female teachers respectively. The 'flexibility' of the NCPE requirements has enabled this practice to continue.

Many factors may contribute to the continuation of stereotypically gendered provision. Pragmatic issues of timetabling groups and staff (with differing expertise) may mean that patterns of provision that break with tradition are not regarded as a realistic possibility. Parent and pupil expectations may also be seen as a barrier to provision that deviates from stereotypical norms. The fundamental link between curriculum content and the established pattern of extra-curricula provision focusing upon the performances of school teams in stereotypically gendered sports (see Penney and Harris, 1997) may also be a driving force in curriculum design. However, there are opportunities to challenge these patterns of provision and the inequities inherent in them. Williams and Bedward (in chapter 9) illustrate that silences in the NCPE need to be seen as presenting important opportunities for change, not only barriers to progress. Silences may mean that texts fail to require or offer encouragement for progressive developments, but they certainly do not prevent such developments. The requirement for all children to experience invasion, striking/fielding and net/wall games can be fulfilled in ways that openly reproduce and legitimate stereotypically gendered patterns of provision and participation, or in ways that actively seek to challenge such practices and the perceptions about participation in particular activities and about masculinity and femininity that they generate amongst both girls and boys. Thus while Hargreaves (2000: 140) has stressed that:

> the 'hidden curriculum' of competitive team games, more than any other aspect of the physical education curriculum, replicates conventional notions of gender differences. Male bonding is encouraged, aggression and sexism are endemic, and boys quickly learn that the sporting man is a symbol of masculine character; those who are poor sportsmen are despised and ridiculed as 'less than male'

we need to balance this with recognition that games can be a context in which very different attitudes and behaviours are celebrated and encouraged. Not for the first time, the crucial role that initial teacher training has to play in the translation of policy 'into practice' is apparent. Initial teacher training remains the key forum in which 'alternative' readings of and responses to conservative policies can be encouraged and nurtured. However, as Flintoff (1993) has previously stressed and Rich and Brown reinforce in chapter 6, we cannot assume that there will be interest in or support for such action in initial teacher training. Notably, recent government policies relating to initial teacher training have served to openly dissuade deviations from conservative readings of the National Curriculum.

In addressing the breadth and balance of the curriculum, the privileging of games is only one dimension of debates. The marginalisation of other areas of activity, that in some instances are no longer a compulsory part of the entitlement curriculum, is equally important in relation to gender issues. Once again, we need to acknowledge that the absence of a requirement for coverage does not preclude schools extending provision in ways that will openly engage with gender equity concerns. The statutory order for the NCPE presented schools and teachers within them with some key choices in relation to these concerns. For many teachers, one of the most welcome features of the order issued in 1992 was the choice to include or alternatively omit dance from the curriculum at key stage 3, for girls, boys or both girls and boys. In Hargreaves' (1994, 2000) view the government's rejection of the NCPE working group's recommendation that dance should be a *compulsory* activity within the curriculum for all pupils signalled the loss of an opportunity to radically reshape many physical education curricula and specifically, to challenge the gender stereotyping inherent in them. Some teachers in some schools are challenging boys' and girls' perceptions about dance, about who can and should participate in what forms of dance. But in others, the picture of provision, the opportunities arising, and the attitudes promoted are very different and far less progressive. There is every potential for boys to be 'systematically shut off from an expressive movement experience and are schooled into physical robustness and aggressive competition, whilst girls are schooled into creativity and co-operation' (Hargreaves, 1994: 153).

Outdoor and adventurous activities is another area of activity worthy of note in relation to the flexibility of the NCPE requirements. There is the scope to include outdoor and adventurous activities within the NCPE, but not a requirement to do so. From a gender equity perspective the flexibility can be seen as a further loss of an opportunity to ensure experience of activities that may offer particular potential to extend understandings of and attitudes towards gender in physical education (Humberstone, 1993). However, in the case of both outdoor and adventurous activities and dance, we should avoid the temptation to assume that a different activity in and of itself, will signal greater gender equity in physical education. McFee and Smith (1997: 70) make the point that ' if we seek to make dance more accessible to males by ensuring ". . . masculinity through athletics in dance" (Hanna, 1988: p. 217) we are in danger of simply reinforcing traditional images of masculinity: thereby bringing about no more than the situated rebirth of ideology'.

One of the other characteristics of the NCPE that previous policy analyses have drawn attention to is the privileging of discourses of sport over discourses of health (Penney and Evans, 1997; 1999). With interests in gender equity in mind we need to critically reflect upon how sport is being defined and portrayed in the NCPE. The tendency for policies to feature a narrow conceptualisation of sport that openly celebrates stereotypically masculine values and behaviours is significant. However, as Harris and Penney illustrate in chapter 8, we cannot assume that discourses of health are any more equitable or progressive than those of sport.

The new NCPE: new principles; new prospects?

The year 1999 witnessed yet another revision to the NCPE, this time under a Labour rather than a Conservative government. The revision came at a time when it was widely acknowledged that teachers wanted stability in national requirements rather than further upheaval (QCA, 1998, 1999a). Thus, much that was familiar and established remained intact in the 'new' National Curriculum, and NCPE specifically. From a gender equity perspective the mix of 'old' and 'new' discourses inherent in the revised NCPE can certainly be seen as having 'pros and cons'. The new requirement for pupils at key stage 4 to follow programmes of study in at least two different areas of activity (as compared to two activities that could both be from the same area) may be celebrated as a direct challenge to the dominance of games in many curricula. However, as was emphasised early in the development of the NCPE, it is naïve to assume that extending the range of activities required will guarantee more equitable provision and experiences. Other areas of activity can reinforce narrow perceptions of masculinity and femininity in relation to physical activity and sport as much as games.

We also have to consider the dominant messages relating to gender issues that arise from the overlying frame of the NCPE. The retention of the six established areas of activity and the continued privileging of games through-out key stages 1–3, arguably reflect and portray a narrow (and culturally specific) conceptualisation of sport and physical activity. The framework does not embrace, for example, martial arts and nor does it provide a clear location for various activities (such as weight training, aerobics classes, recreational cycling) frequently associated with participation in physical activity primarily for health and/or social reasons. Exclusions such as these have important implications for the degree to which the NCPE can be seen as providing for the needs and interests of all girls and boys and it is notable that the new NCPE in Wales has recategorised activities at key stage 4 to embrace 'exercise activities' (National Assembly for Wales/Awdurdod Cymwysterau Cwricwlym Ac Asesu Cymru, 2000).

The programmes of study within the new NCPE in England, together with the accompanying non-statutory 'schemes of work' issued by the QCA (2000) have raised the profile of participation in 'other roles' in sporting contexts, such as the role of official or coach. The development of skills, knowledge and understanding in relation to these roles has thereby been formally established as 'legitimate knowledge' within the new NCPE. Diversifying teaching and learning to promote experience of 'other roles' may help to make physical education a subject that more girls and more boys may enjoy and experience success in. However, if those children (girls and boys) who have traditionally felt marginalised by the dominance of performance discourses are to now feel that they and their particular skills and interests are valued, there is a need to challenge the portrayal of the 'other roles' as the (inferior) 'other' to performance. Furthermore, we need to be aware that gender stereotyped images and understandings can be promoted amidst a focus on leadership or officiating as much as performance. How will boys react to a girl taking on a coaching role for their warm-up or skill-practice? Will girls feel that they can legitimately coach boys? Will boys be willing to undertake choreography for a dance performance and would girls accept a boy in this role? Questions such as these demonstrate the scope for the curricula developed from the new NCPE to either reinforce or alternatively, actively challenge and extend pupils' perceptions about who can legitimately 'do what' in physical education and sport.

In other respects discourses of elite performance have been privileged in new requirements, at times quite openly and on other occasions more subtly via 'hidden silences' in the text. For example, at a first glance the direct linkage between knowledge, skills and understanding relating to 'evaluation' and 'improving performance' that was written into the requirements may not seem problematic. That is, until we recognise the scope for notions of evaluation to be directed towards the social dynamics and relationships within learning contexts, and the gender inequities inherent in those dynamics and relationships. Thus, the particular definition of 'evaluation' presented in and promoted by the text of the NCPE and accompanying guidance material (QCA, 1999b) is important. The exclusion of 'other discourses', particularly of social justice, from notions of 'evaluation' is a far from neutral act. Physical education syllabus texts developed elsewhere and particularly in Australia and New Zealand (see Wright, chapter 11 in this text; Kirk *et al.*, 1998) demonstrate that in different political contexts, these 'other' discourses can come to the fore in the subject.

In some respects the influence of a change in government and new political agendas was very obvious in the new National Curriculum in England. The government made much of the fact that the new National Curriculum formally set in place an agenda for 'inclusion'. Specifically, it established that in all subject areas teachers must pay 'due regard' to the following three principles for inclusion:

- Setting suitable learning challenges
- Responding to pupils' diverse learning needs
- Overcoming barriers to learning and assessment for individuals and groups of pupils.

(DfEE/QCA, 1999: 28)

Each of these principles can be used as a focus for addressing gender equity issues in physical education, but currently there is little guarantee of such a response. Once again it is notable that the commentary on inclusion came after the detail of the programmes of study within the NCPE text and may be in danger of being overlooked. Silences on gender equity issues in other sections of the text seem to be echoed in early implementation. The principles of inclusion have been notably absent from discussions relating to the implementation of the NCPE order. The initial impression is that teachers have not regarded the principles as a priority in implementation (Penney, 2001). Professional development work seems essential if the opportunities inherent in the revised NCPE to promote greater understanding of the complexities of gender equity in physical education and to facilitate advancement of practice that embraces these complexities, are to be explored. Currently, the commentary on gender equity within the text is marginally positioned and provides very few insights into how teachers can respond to the complexities of gender in their teaching. It is explained that teachers should respond to pupils' diverse needs by creating effective learning environments in which:

- the contribution of all pupils is valued
- all pupils can feel secure and are able to contribute appropriately
- stereotypical views are challenged and pupils learn to appreciate and view positively differences in others, whether arising from race, gender, ability or disability.

(ibid.: 29)

As O'Sullivan and colleagues observe in chapter 10, such commentary leaves it to teachers and teacher educators to pursue the matters of how, when and where this can be achieved. Furthermore, we see a failure to embrace sexuality in the above guidance. In England education has mirrored the 'sports establishment' in failing to

> create a discourse to explain and deal with discrimination against homosexuals and, more specifically, against lesbians in sports. Silence implicitly condones taken-for-granted ways of thinking and behaving, which occur subtly and during informal activities, and which are hurtful and harmful to non-heterosexuals.
>
> (Hargreaves, 1994: 260; see also Clarke, chapter 4 in this book)

Conclusion: gendered policies; what prospects in practice?

The bottom line in the implementation of the National Curriculum for Physical Education and one that overseas observers may particularly view as contradictory, is that the statutory entitlement is different in different schools and may well be different for different pupils within the same school. The flexibility in the statutory requirements for the NCPE may be argued as essential given the very different school contexts in which implementation has to occur. Undoubtedly, if we are looking for openings for progressive practice that will further gender equity in physical education, it is an invaluable characteristic of the NCPE. However, as I have emphasised, it can also be seen as a further inherent weakness of the official texts, since by its very nature the flexibility does not ensure that all teachers or all teacher educators will engage with gender issues. There is extensive scope for 'slippage' (Bowe *et al.*, 1992) in the interpretation and implementation of the NCPE. It is a policy that was designed and destined to be interpreted differently in different schools, by different teachers, with varying resources and personal expertise to draw upon. The 1990s have clearly demonstrated that this has presented the potential for both conservativism and creativity in practice and this remains the case in the context of teacher's implementation of the 'new' NCPE. So what are the future prospects for gender equity in the context of the NCPE?

As Penney and Evans (1999) have emphasised, responses to policies need to be understood in relation to the political, economic and institutional contexts in which they occur. In important respects, contemporary contexts can be seen to offer limited support for creativity in implementation, and presenting instead considerable pressures for teachers to reinforce the dominance of established (and gendered) discourses, that promote and celebrate elite performance in a narrow range of games. In England, changes to the funding and structure of Local Education Authorities have considerably reduced the support available for teachers interested in innovation, while arrangements for inspection of schools discourage experimentalism. The direction of developments is towards teachers adopting a technicist approach within safe and clearly legitimate frames of reference. There seems little encouragement or support for risk-taking or deviations from texts that inspectors will recognise, or texts that parents (whose custom is to be attracted and nurtured in the education market, see Bowe *et al.*, 1992; Penney and Evans, 1999) will also recognise and value. In these circumstances the claimed 'spaces for action', freedom and flexibility in implementation may effectively be closed down. Space for action that will signal resistance to stereotypical patterns of provision, images and attitudes, that will enable masculinit*ies* and femininit*ies* to be expressed in and promoted via physical education and sport, and that will prompt various social, cultural and religious values to be embraced and celebrated, may regrettably be not merely unexplored, but unexplorable amidst other expectations and priorities. Mahony's (2000) observation of the absence of discourses of gender equity amidst discourses of effectiveness is important. The two need not be mutually exclusive, but regrettably:

> Conceptions of the 'effective teacher' and headteacher are being redefined in ways which render invisible the role of schools in contributing to the construction and maintenance of gender inequalities. Teachers' responsibilities to challenge these and other inequalities are being removed as the purposes of schooling are articulated around a narrow form of economic instrumentalism.
>
> (ibid.: 239)

Undoubtedly, there are pockets of progressive practice. But that is a far cry from what seemed promised with the introduction of 'entitlement for all'. As indicated above, initial teacher training remains the key arena in which readings of official texts are shaped and in which future teachers will develop opinions about the readings that are both possible and legitimate. It is a forum in which student teachers can be encouraged to actively explore the 'scope for slippage' and 'fill the silences' inherent in official texts in ways that serve to challenge the dominance of established gendered discourses and introduce and/or and raise the profile of alternative discourses. It is where boundaries to thinking and actions should be openly debated, challenged and extended if we are to succeed in establishing 'new gender agendas' in physical education in the years ahead – within and despite the constraints posed by a still largely conservative official National Curriculum text. Thus we can lament, but must also continue to actively oppose the degree to which requirements for initial teacher training in England serve to erode opportunities for creativity in the interpretation and implementation of the NCPE (Evans *et al.*, 1996).

Notes

1 General requirements applied to all key stages and were to be taught through all areas of activity. These requirements supplemented the general and activity specific programmes of study (DES/WO, 1992).
2 Programmes of study were designed to set out 'the matters, skills and processes which are required to be taught to pupils of different abilities and maturities during each key stage' (DES/WO, 1992: 4).
3 The National Curriculum Council was the agency established to advise the government on the original content of the National Curriculum in England and Wales.

References

Ball, S.J. (1990) *Politics and Policy Making in Education: Explorations in Policy Sociology*, London: Routledge.

Barton, L. (1993) Disability, empowerment and physical education, in J. Evans (ed.) *Equality, Education and Physical Education*, London: Falmer Press, pp. 43–54.

Bass, D. and Cale, L. (1999) Promoting physical activity through the extra-curricular programme, *European Journal of Physical Education* 4: 45–64.

Bowe, R. and Ball, S.J. with Gold, A. (1992) *Reforming Education and Changing Schools: Case Studies in Policy Sociology*, London: Routledge

Department for Education/Welsh Office (DfE/WO) (1995) *Physical Education in the National Curriculum*, London: HMSO.

Department for Education and Employment (DfEE)/Qualifications and Curriculum Authority (QCA) (1999) *Physical Education: The National Curriculum for England*, London: HMSO.

Department of Education and Science (DES) (1989) *National Curriculum: From Policy to Practice*, London: HMSO.

Department of Education and Science (DES)/Welsh Office (WO) (1991a) *National Curriculum Physical Education Working Group Interim Report*, London: DES.

Department of Education and Science (DES)/Welsh Office (WO) (1991b) *Physical Education for Ages 5–16: Proposals of the Secretary of State for Education and the Secretary of State for Wales*, London: DES.

Department of Education and Science (DES)/Welsh Office (WO) (1992) *Physical Education in the National Curriculum*, London: HMSO.

Evans, J. and Davies, B. (1993) Equality, equity and physical education, in J. Evans (ed.) *Equality, Education and Physical Education*, London: Falmer Press, pp. 11–27.

Evans, J. and Penney, D. (1995) The politics of pedagogy: making a National Curriculum physical education, *Journal of Education Policy* 10(1): 27–44.

Evans, J., Penney, D. and Davies, B. (1996) Back to the future? Education policy and physical education, in N. Armstrong (ed.) *New Directions in Physical Education. Change and Innovation*, London: Cassell Education, pp. 1–18.

Figueroa, P. (1993) Equality, multiculturalism, anti-racism and physical education in the National Curriculum, in J. Evans (ed.) *Equality, Education and Physical Education*, London: Falmer Press, pp. 90–104.

Flintoff, A. (1993) Gender, physical education and initial teacher education, in J. Evans (ed.) *Equality, Education and Physical Education*, London: Falmer Press, pp. 184–204.

Graham, D. with Tytler, D. (1993) *A Lesson for Us All: The Making of the National Curriculum*, London: Routledge.

Hargreaves, J. (1994) *Sporting Females*, London: Routledge.

Hargreaves, J. (2000) Gender, morality and the national physical education curriculum, in J. Hansen and N.K. Nielsen (eds) *Sports, Body and Health*, Odense, Denmark: Odense University Press, pp. 133–48.

Humberstone, B. (1993) Equality, physical education and outdoor education – ideological struggles and transformative structures?, in J. Evans (ed.) *Equality, Education and Physical Education*, London: Falmer Press, pp. 74–89.

Kirk, D., Burgess-Limerick, R., Kiss, M., Lahey, J. and Penney, D. (1998) *Senior Physical Education: An Integrated Approach*, Champaign, IL: Human Kinetics.

Mahony, P. (2000) Teacher education policy and gender, in J. Salisbury and S. Riddell (eds) *Gender, Policy and Educational Change: Shifting Agendas in the UK and Europe*, London: Routledge, pp. 229–42.

McFee, G. and Smith, F. (1997) Let's hear it for the boys: dance, gender and education, in A. Tomlinson (ed.) *Gender, Sport and Leisure: Continuities and Challenges*, Aachen: Meyer & Meyer, pp. 63–80.

National Assembly for Wales/Awdurdod Cymwysterau Cwricwlym Ac Asesu Cymru (ACCAC) (2000) *Physical Education in the National Curriculum in Wales*, Cardiff: ACCAC.

National Curriculum Council (NCC) (1991) *Physical Education in the National Curriculum. A Report to the Secretary of State for Education and Science on the Statutory Consultation for the Attainment Target and Programmes of Study in Physical Education*, York: NCC.

Noble, C. (1999) Silence: absence and context, in I. Parker and the Bolton Discourse Network, *Critical Textwork. An Introduction to Varieties of Discourse and Analysis*, Buckingham: Open University Press, pp. 191–200.

Penney, D. (2001) The revision and initial implementation of the National Curriculum for Physical Education in England, *The Bulletin of Physical Education* (in press).

Penney, D. and Evans, J. (1997) Naming the game: discourse and domination in physical education and sport in England and Wales, *European Physical Education Review* 3(1): 21–32.

Penney, D. and Evans, J. (1999) *Politics, Policy and Practice in Physical Education*, London: Routledge.

Penney, D. and Harris, J. (1997) Extra-curricular physical education: more of the same for the more able ? *Sport, Education and Society* 2(1): 41–54.

Qualifications and Curriculum Authority (1998) *Developing the School Curriculum. Advice of the Secretary of State and his Response on the Broad Nature and Scope of the Review of the National Curriculum*, London: QCA.

Qualifications and Curriculum Authority (1999a) *The Review of the National Curriculum in England. The Secretary of State's Proposals*, London: QCA.

Qualifications and Curriculum Authority (1999b) *Terminology in Physical Education*, London, QCA.

Qualifications and Curriculum Authority (2000) *Physical Education: A Scheme of Work for Key Stages 3 and 4*, London: QCA.

Talbot, M. (1993) A gendered physical education: equality and sexism, in J. Evans (ed.) *Equality, Education and Physical Education*, London: Falmer Press, pp. 74–89.

8 Gender, health and physical education

Jo Harris and Dawn Penney

Introduction

This chapter explores the expression of gender in the context of policies and practices in physical education specifically directed towards health. Perhaps to the surprise of some readers we show that work within physical education curricula that is associated with health (and are therefore typically termed health-related exercise (HRE) or health-related fitness (HRF)) may be as likely to express and promote stereotypically gendered attitudes and images as sex differentiated games settings. Thus, while we are anxious to point to the potential for health-related work in physical education to extend pupils' understandings of gender issues, we stress that it cannot be assumed that either policies or practice will promote these progressive ideals. Research reported here has revealed the way in which teachers and the school and curriculum structures that they are working within, may act to reproduce and legitimate narrow and openly gender stereotyped understandings of health issues in contexts of physical education and physical activity. We therefore identify teacher training and continuing professional development as having a key role to play if health-related work is to contribute to the development of more equitable educational practices and learning environments in physical education.

Our analysis focuses on the National Curriculum for Physical Education in England.[1] As Penney (in chapter 7), we draw attention to a number of omissions in these texts. The significance of the omissions becomes vividly apparent in our accompanying presentation of data from research that has explored teachers' development of health-related work in the context of their implementation of the NCPE. The data demonstrates that in some instances this work openly legitimates and reinforces very narrow understandings of gender in relation to participation in physical activity and sport. We illustrate distinct differences in the respective approaches of male and female heads of physical education departments towards the development of health-related exercise in physical education, and in the curricula provided for girls as compared to boys. We see very clearly the centrality of teachers in policy and curriculum development and the ways in which their understandings and values will have a key role to play in determining the extent to which curricula advance gender equity in physical education. It is notable that the practices reported here occurred in the context of implementation of the National Curriculum for Physical Education in England: the provision of the 'entitlement curriculum' for *all* pupils in state schools. The entitlement is shown to be very different for different children, with gender issues playing a part in shaping those differences. The data thus reveals the way in which the gaps and flexibility that Penney (in chapter 7) identified as a key characteristic of the NCPE, may provide opportunities for creativity in curriculum design and teaching, but can equally present opportunities for the retention of openly inequitable practices. The notion of 'slippage' in the implementation of policy (Bowe *et al.*, 1992; Penney and Evans, 1999; chapter 2 in this text) is thus central to our analysis.

The concept of discourse (see chapter 2 in this text) also underpins our critical examination of the interests and values that are promoted or in contrast, marginalised or excluded in the policies and practices that we explore. We show that there are *many* discourses of health in physical education and that there are direct linkages between these and stereotypically gendered discourses of the body, of health and of physical activity 'for' men and women. Furthermore, there are clear associations between particular contemporary discourses of health in physical education and the gendered history of the profession and the subject (see Kirk, 1992; chapter 3 in this text). We therefore reaffirm the role that history has played in shaping both the policies and practices of the NCPE. The historical exploration of the gendered dimensions of health in the context of physical education in the United Kingdom serves to reveal the different discourses 'of health' that are variously expressed in physical education, the association of particular discourses with either 'men's' or 'women's' training, and with physical education for either boys or girls. Locating health amidst this historically gendered development of the subject is vital to understanding the contemporary policy developments and responses to them that we describe later in the chapter.

Health and physical education: historically gendered

An examination of the historical association of health and physical education reveals that it is an inherently gendered one. The post-war period witnessed the emergence of health education as a school subject in its own right and the development of two contrasting approaches to health within physical education; one developed by female physical education teachers for girls and the other by male physical education teachers for boys. The former version was developed within some private girls' schools and was expressed through a form of Swedish gymnastics which was strongly associated with the 'harmonious development of the whole body' (McIntosh, 1968: 120). The 'whole body' in question was a particular body, with the association between physical education and health clearly framed in terms of traditional images of femininity. The focus of the activities provided for girls was their capacity to develop elegance, poise and posture, and to provide physical preparation for child-bearing. In sharp contrast to this focus and these activities for girls, the approach developed by men centred on the role of exercise in developing strength and endurance as a basis for 'fitness'. Fitness in this instance, was fitness for engagement in activities that would demand muscular strength and endurance. This particular view of the exercise–health relationship was thus embedded in, and an expression of the 'new' scientific functionalist approach to physical education (see Kirk, 1992 and chapter 2 in this text). Within this approach, 'physical fitness' was linked to a mechanistic view of the body and development of its efficiency via circuit training and later weight training. Male physical education teachers were the pioneers of physical education with this orientation, while the sex-differentiated pattern of schooling meant that the practices that they developed only featured in physical education curricula for boys.

McNair (1985) has provided further insights into the very different orientation towards the body, health and fitness that was expressed in and pursued during the 1940s and 1950s by male and female teacher training colleges respectively. The protagonists of Ling's Swedish system of gymnastics, middle-class formally-trained young ladies, were looking to develop harmonious movement to enhance poise, posture and elegance. Male training colleges were in pursuit of very different notions of a physically fit body, and of fitness for very different purposes and aligned themselves with different practices. Tough experienced retired army officers from working-class backgrounds supported the more vigorous McLaren-based system of physical training. The Ling or Swedish system of gymnastics was invented by Per Henrick Ling in the early nineteenth century and consolidated into a system of physical training which involved mostly free-standing exercises that sought to systematically exercise each part of the body through intricate flexions and extensions (Kirk, 1992). The McLaren system of physical education was introduced by Archibald McLaren in the mid-1800s and comprised precise physical exercises that worked through the entire range of possible movements of the joints and actions of the muscles in a systematic way (Kirk, 1992).

Traditional stereotypical images of masculinity and femininity were thus both embedded in and openly promoted by the respective practices; the 'different knowledge' being defined as physical education 'for boys' as compared to that 'for girls', and the different knowledge respectively gained by future male and female teachers. Men and women positioned themselves and in turn, positioned boys and girls, as having distinct and furthermore, essentially homogeneous, educational needs. There was little acknowledge-ment of either the respective value of the practices developed by the two groups, or the need for either boys or girls to have access to 'the other' body of knowledge. As McNair (1985) recognised, the controversy between the two groups had the unfortunate effect of inhibiting 'the appreciation that each group had something to contribute to fitness and health' (p. 114).

The more recent history of health in physical education: health-related fitness and health-related exercise

As many readers will be aware, the 1980s saw a new wave of interest in health amongst physical educationalists in the United Kingdom. 'Health-related fitness' or HRF as it was commonly termed, became a new element of work in many physical education curricula. The terminology that was typically used in the early developments was significant in relation to our concern with gender issues. It is always vital to acknowledge that health-related work was developed in different ways in different schools. However, the critical commentary that followed much of the early development work clearly points to the tendency for HRF to be directed towards arguably narrow notions of 'fitness' that had many similarities to the notions inherent in the scientific functionalist approach previously pursued in the male training colleges. The focus of attention was invariably measurement of strength, speed and endurance, with improvement of these aspects of fitness portrayed as an individual responsibility to be instilled in children (Biddle, 1987).

It is only if we compare this focus with subsequent developments in the UK, and with developments overseas (see Wright, chapter 11 in this text), that some of the issues and interests effectively marginalised in early HRF become apparent. Circuit training, fitness testing and/or weight training were new activities introduced in many curricula, alongside activity-based units of work. The activities were directly linked to concerns for physical education to be promoting improvements in physical fitness, but we need to recognise these as particular aspects of fitness. They were aspects that clearly related to concerns to extend understanding of the importance of physical dimensions of fitness in relation to participation and performance in sport but that often had less obvious connections with interests in long-term health.

The association of particular activities with particular outcomes becomes clearer when we consider subsequent development of health-related work in physical education in the UK through the 1980s and into the 1990s. The adoption of a different terminology of health-related exercise (HRE) was symbolic of a different orientation in health-related work, with attention shifting towards the role that physical education may play in promoting regular participation in physical activity with interests in lifelong health uppermost in mind. Those advocating the development of HRE recognised the linkages between fitness and performance in sport, but sought to extend visions to make clear connections between aspects of fitness, involvement in physical activity and long-term health. With our interests in gender in mind, probably the most significant characteristic of the moves to develop HRE as compared to HRF, was the extended range of activities that HRE became associated with. Aerobics was by no means a feature of all HRE programmes developed in schools. Nevertheless, it became firmly linked with the growth in HRE in physical education. Several points need to be noted in relation to this association. First, it meant that HRE was associated with an activity that was widely regarded as primarily if not exclusively for girls and women, rather than boys and men. Aerobics was specifically seen as having important potential to regenerate interest in physical education and physical activity amongst teenage girls. Its popularity as a leisure time activity amongst young women was a key factor in relation to the perceived appeal to girls, providing important credibility for the activity. Second, we need to recognise that the different discourses (of fitness and health) that were being expressed and promoted via the introduction of aerobics were thus destined to themselves become viewed as inherently gendered. The version of health and fitness being promoted would be seen as primarily if not exclusively, one 'for women'. Finally, we have to acknowledge the criticisms that in some instances have been directed at the introduction of aerobics into curricula. Some lessons and by association, aerobics as an activity and in turn, HRE, have been deemed recreational and not educational, and described as a 'modern form of drill' involving repetitious, mindless, 'follow my leader' exercises' (Clay, cited in SCAA, 1997: 36). Practices and discourses that were particularly associated with the interests of girls, but that were also seen as contrasting to, rather than compatible with, a focus on performance in sport, were under fire here.

Several commentators have previously drawn attention to a mix of practices that were variously established in curricula under the banners of HRF and/or HRE during the 1980s (Biddle, 1987; Harris, 1997a). However, the stereotypically gendered dimension of the emerging practices and furthermore, the different discourses of fitness and health that were variously privileged, appears largely unexplored. The research that we report below leads us to the view that the gendered history of the subject of physical education and the profession has had a very significant influence on the emerging relationship between physical education and health in the context of contemporary policy and curriculum developments. Our data has prompted us to acknowledge the way in which HRF and HRE, together with their respective sets of interests and different foci, could quite neatly be accommodated within the sex-differentiated pattern of provision of physical education in many schools. Following Penney and Evans (1999) we therefore point to strong elements of accommodation of new policy requirements within largely unchanged practices in physical education. We suggest that in relation to the development of health-related work in physical education, this accommodation may have particular significance for gender equity.

HRE in the NCPE: policies and prospects

In now turning attention to policies and practices associated with the National Curriculum for Physical Education, we should first note a further important historical feature of developments within the subject relating to health. During the 1940s and 1950s the focus upon physical fitness that was dominant within the male training colleges became clearly linked with sports performance. Health, associated with the notion of 'fitness for sport', was tied with concerns over the national standing in international sport, focusing primarily on males (Kirk, 1992). In the development of a National Curriculum for Physical Education in England and Wales at the end of the 1980s, sport was the reference point for the structure and focus of curriculum requirements (Penney and Evans, 1999). As we explain below, from the outset 'health' was positioned in relation to the central focus on sport. Discourses of sport, not health, provided the foundation for the NCPE. Any analysis of the position and nature of health in the context of the NCPE needs to acknowledge this characteristic. The dominance of discourses of sport can be seen as not only setting a frame for the development of health in the NCPE, but as setting an openly gendered frame for development, that would have implications for the particular discourses of health that would be deemed (by policy-makers and by teachers) to have a legitimate place in the policies and practices of the NCPE.

In a similar way to which equal opportunities was identified as of central importance in the development of the NCPE and yet at the same time seemingly marginalised in the texts issued (see Penney, chapter 7 in this text), health-related exercise can be seen to have suffered a similar fate. The NCPE working group identified 'an urgent need for a coherent programme of education about exercise in order to establish its relevance and stimulate increased activity patterns' (DES/WO, 1991: 62). Yet, neither the working group's final report nor the statutory order that followed in 1992 provided an outline of such a programme. The commentary addressing implementation of requirements relating to health-related exercise remained at the level of broad guidance and pointers for prospective development. There was acknowledgement that there were many instances and different contexts in which health-related exercise could be incorporated in implementation of the NCPE. The need for 'reinforcement' of health-related concepts in the various areas of activity was also stressed, but as we explain below, the extent to which this need was pursued in the programmes of study for the respective areas of activity was limited. Health-related exercise was not *an* area of activity within the NCPE, but rather, was a matter that the working group acknowledged could and should be addressed in the context of requirements relating to the specified areas. We suggest that both this relational position and the lack of specificity about when, where and how teachers should develop health-related exercise work in the context of physical education, were key characteristics of the NCPE in relation to our interest in gender equity. In particular, we see these as characteristics that have meant that important potential for health-related work to extend the gender discourses expressed in physical education has not always been realised in practice. Furthermore, they have meant that health-related exercise could be developed in ways that reinforced stereotypical images and understandings relating to men's and women's participation in physical activity.

The working group noted that work focusing on health-related exercise shared with all other work in physical education the requirement for the experiences provided to 'respect pupils as individuals with different experiences, capabilities and preferences' and added that 'there is an important message that everyone can succeed in exercise' (DES/WO, 1991: 62). In the light of the data below, the absence of a comment to the effect that planning and teaching of health-related exercise work should also seek to challenge stereotypical attitudes and beliefs that may constitute a barrier to engagement in particular forms of exercise, was a notable omission.

Recalling our discussion of historical developments, the use of the term health-related *exercise* in the NCPE working group's final report was not insignificant. It signalled a privileging of particular discourses in preference to others. It appeared to legitimate and promote a focus upon holistic orientations towards health, acknowledging physical, affective and cognitive dimensions, and recognising the social and cultural construction of health (Stacey, 1988) in contexts of physical education. We contrast this orientation with the comparatively narrow orientation embraced in developments previously associated with health-related fitness (HRF). The focus on HRE can also be seen to reflect concerns about levels of physical activity in young people's lives and desires for education to be directed towards encouraging participation in regular exercise of moderate intensity (Blair and Connelly, 1994) as a feature of lifestyle (Armstrong and Welsman, 1997; Sports Council and Health Education Authority (HEA), 1992). The government's strategy for the health of the population of England (Department of Health, 1992) that was issued at the time of the introduction of the NCPE identified schools as key settings for health promotion and highlighted the role that physical education had to play in teaching the skills and understanding associated with adopting active lifestyles. Again, we can note the contrast with previous developments and specifically, tendencies for HRF to be associated with effective performance in high intensity activity in contexts of competitive sport. However, as we will see, the absence of detailed development of HRE requirements in the NCPE meant that there was no guarantee that the broader conceptualisation would be developed in practice. The flexibility inherent in the NCPE requirements relating to the development of health-related exercise (that can also be read as a lack of clarity) meant that there was the scope for discourses more aligned with HRF than HRE to come to the fore in implementation, and furthermore, be positioned alongside and in contrast to discourses of HRE in an openly gendered way.

As explained above, HRE was not identified as an area of activity in the NCPE. Instead, it was addressed in the context of general programmes of study outlined for each of the four key stages of teaching and learning[2] and also, within the statements developed to describe 'the knowledge, skills and understanding which pupils of different abilities and maturities can be expected to achieve at the end of the key stage in question' (DES/WO, 1992: 5). Programmes of study were designed to set out 'the matters, skills and processes which are required to be taught to pupils of different abilities and maturities during each key stage' (ibid.: 4). In physical education these comprised 'general' programmes of study for each key stage and activity-specific programmes of study for each key stage that related to the six areas of activity established within the NCPE (of athletic activities; dance; games; gymnastic activities; outdoor and adventurous activities; and swimming). The following requirements relating to key stage 3 illustrate the way in which HRE was positioned and articulated within the NCPE. Among the end of key stage statements for this key stage was the statement that pupils should be able to 'understand the short- and long-term effects of exercise on the body systems and decide where to focus their involvement in physical activity for a healthy and enjoyable lifestyle' (ibid.: 8). The following points were then incorporated in the general programme of study for this key stage; that pupils should:

- be given the opportunity to plan and undertake simple and safe health-related exercise in the context of different areas of activity, understanding the principles involved;
- be taught to understand the short- and long-term effects of exercise on the body systems;
- be made aware of the increasing need for personal hygiene in relation to vigorous activity;
- be taught how to prepare for and recover from specific activity.

(ibid.: 8)

When and where these points would be addressed in implementation of the NCPE, and specifically, fulfilment of the activity specific programmes of study, was a matter for teachers to decide upon. The activity specific programmes of study did not expand upon or make any clear linkages to the above points relating to HRE. Instead they focused upon the development of movement skills specific to the area of activity and understanding relating to particular aspects of performance in that area of activity (such as sequencing of movements in gymnastics, or tactical aspects of game play).

The data that we discuss below needs to be viewed in the context of this 'flexibility' (and arguably, lack of clear direction) relating to the implementation of HRE in the NCPE. Notably, the research that we draw upon did not set out to investigate gender issues in that implementation. Rather, it produced data that revealed them as 'an issue' in the implementation of HRE in the NCPE. After providing some key insights into the gendered patterns of development of HRE in contexts of implementation of the NCPE we return to our investigation of policy texts to examine the degree to which more recent NCPE texts have provided prompts to challenge the stereotypical practices that we describe.

Gendered PE: gendered HRE

Between 1993 and 1995 Harris undertook multi-method research addressing the implementation of HRE in the NCPE. This comprised a questionnaire survey of heads of physical education departments in 1000 secondary schools in England, and interviews, participant observation and documentary research in three selected case study schools. The survey aimed to provide data that would describe the provision of HRE in schools and explore factors potentially influencing this provision. Utilising focused interviews with physical education staff and documentary research, the case study investigations sought to provide further insights into teachers' views, approaches and practices relating to HRE in physical education. Three mixed-sex state secondary schools (11–16 age range) randomly selected in each of the South, Midlands and North of England were used for this phase of the research. Further details of the research methods are reported in Harris (1995, 1997a) and findings have been the subject of several previous publications (see for example Harris, 1995, 1997a, 1997b, 1998; Harris and Penney, 2000; Penney and Harris, 1997, 1998).

Scraton (1987) has described school physical education as overtly reinforcing gender differences in terms of the activities offered, and covertly through the attitudes of policy-makers and practitioners. Although it was not specifically directed towards the exploration of equity issues, Harris' research revealed the way in which implementation of the NCPE was occurring within clearly gendered patterns of curriculum organisation and gendered frames of reference. Overall, data supported Scraton's (1986) notion that separate and different physical education programmes remain a central and institutionalised feature of education in England, reflecting stereotypical assumptions about the respective educational needs, interests and abilities of girls and boys. Harris identified distinct differences in the curriculum provided for boys as compared to girls and found evidence to suggest that the NCPE was being developed differently by male and female staff respectively. The context of implementation of HRE within the NCPE was one in which sex-differentiated patterns of provision and staffing remained intact in physical education and in many instances, seemed destined to reinforce stereotypical images of masculinity and femininity and of the physical activities that men and women can participate in. For example, Harris' data revealed that boys had access to a broader and different range of games than girls, that girls and boys were introduced to different styles of gymnastics and that dance, if offered at all, was provided only, or predominantly for, girls and was usually delivered by female staff (see Harris, 1997a). Below we explore the ways in which sex-differentiated provision was evidenced in HRE specifically.

The first point to stress is the complex dynamic between staffing arrangements, grouping strategies and curriculum provision in physical education. The practicalities of timetabling (of staff, pupils and facilities) have very clear influences upon the provision that is deemed possible. However, when we address staffing arrangements in physical education and decisions relating to the activities that children will experience and the grouping strategies that will be employed in provision, we invariably encounter gender issues. Gender issues underpin and/or are inextricably bound up with decisions that are often described in relation to pragmatics of provision. For example, a teacher at one of Harris' case study schools explained that:

> The last couple of years there has been a problem – it's tended to be one man and two women. . . . Next year, we're going to have to go to mainly mixed groups . . . you can't have one member of staff being left with forty-odd. We'd quite like to keep it single sex – I think it suited both pairs of staff. We got on with what we had to do and they got on with what they had to do. We've got no real preference apart from, say, major games where we want single sex because you don't really want the girls around when you're doing rugby or football.
>
> (Male Head of Physical Education,
> State Comprehensive School, 1995)

The reference to games and the specific desire for this to be an area in which sex differentiated provision is retained, is important. In some schools, this desire may determine (and constrain) the grouping arrangements adopted for other aspects of the physical education curriculum. One head of department illustrated the way in which logistical issues associated with the privileging of games have these wider-reaching effects on the physical education curriculum:

> You can do them (health-related blocks) mixed and we'd be happy to do that but because of the structure of the timetable it would mean that we can't, we don't have the resources for everybody to do the health unit at the same time. So, that means that two groups can be doing the health module using the space that is required and two groups would be doing a games module. What that means, then, is the games module has to be a single sex module, then the health module has to be a single sex group. Once you've got a single sex module working with one group you can't mix it with the other group, you're tied in, as much as you might want to do it . . . I think I would prefer to have mixed lessons on that (health module), but . . . there are the practical problems.
>
> (Male Head of Physical Education,
> State Comprehensive School, 1995)

In the majority of mixed-sex schools, HRE was delivered in mixed-sex discrete units for the younger years and that over half of schools had mixed-sex units for the older years. Interestingly, Harris' research showed that more male than female heads of physical education organised HRE in mixed-sex groups for most year groups. This latter finding was consistent with that of Caldecott (1992) who reported that male teachers were in favour of mixing

Table 8.1 HRE theoretical content within the PE curriculum in secondary schools in England

HRE theoretical content	%
Stamina/Cardiovascular health	92.0
Suppleness/Flexibility/Stretching	87.4
Muscular strength and endurance	84.2
Fitness testing	61.0
Designing exercise programmes	46.6
Weight management	29.0
Relaxation/Stress management	21.4
Other	4.7

Percentage figures represent the proportion of the sample of secondary schools (N = 728) involved in the various activities. The sample comprised 41 per cent (299 out of 728) female and 59 per cent (429 out of 728) male responses.

boys with girls for health-related lessons whereas female teachers were of a more divided opinion. Harris' research suggests that there is also a link between teachers' grouping preferences and the age of pupils, with developmental issues being the key concern here. One teacher explained the thinking and subsequent grouping arrangements, saying that:

> I think keeping them (Year 9s) separate was a better idea with the fitness . . . with the (Year) 9s I think, because, obviously, going through puberty and so on, I think that would work better single sex.
>
> (Female teacher responsible for Girls' Physical Education,
> State Comprehensive School, 1995)

Other data from Harris' work leads us to call for further investigation of the implications of sex differentiated staffing and/or grouping arrangements for HRE. Data relating to the theoretical aspects of HRE respectively developed by male and female teachers and the practical activity contexts that they respectively utilised in their teaching of HRE, indicates that if single sex grouping is adopted in the older years and if this is accompanied by sex differentiated staffing arrangements, girls and boys may receive very different versions of 'HRE'. More specifically, they may receive versions of HRE that openly legitimate and reinforce stereotypically gendered discourses of 'fitness', 'health' and 'exercise' in physical education.

With respect to the *theoretical content*[3] associated with HRE, table 8.1 illustrates the range of content variously featuring in the HRE developments within the schools in Harris' research.

The survey revealed statistically significant gender differences[4] in the theoretical content respectively addressed by female and male heads of physical education departments. More female heads of department included relaxation and stress management in HRE, while more male heads of department included strength work and fitness testing. Female teachers in two case study schools acknowledged that they were paying minimal attention to strength work within their HRE units and expressed the concern that 'formal' testing may adversely affect pupils' attitudes towards physical education. Questionnaire data showed that male heads of department included more fitness testing in curricula than their female counterparts, and revealed differences in the emphasis placed upon specific components of fitness by male and female teachers respectively. More female teachers incorporated flexibility tests and more males included upper body strength tests. Further, more males than females utilised measurement instruments such as flexibility testers, weighing scales, 'sit and reach' boxes, heart rate monitors, skinfold calipers and dynamometers.

Alongside these observed differences it is important to also register the overall privileging of particular content and the apparent marginalisation of other knowledge and understanding relating to HRE. The relatively few instances of teachers incorporating weight and stress management into HRE seem worthy of note. If physical education is concerned with lifelong issues, there are clearly arguments for raising the profile of both issues and further-more, to do so in the curricula provided for both girls and boys. In the case of weight management particularly, there are dangers that this may be regarded as something that is only relevant to girls and that therefore should only feature in the HRE provided for girls. While weight management may be a matter which has particular resonance with many girls, which features heavily in many women's involvement in physical activity, and which will demand particular sensitivity in the design of learning experiences, it is clearly an issue of relevance to all young people. If physical education (and HRE specifically) is to contribute towards the reduction of social pressures upon young people (both boys and girls) to be a particular shape, to challenge the tendencies that pupils themselves may have to accord very different social status to different bodies, and to extend understanding of the complex relationships between physical activity, fitness, health, weight and body shape, we need curricula for both girls and boys that actively engage them with these issues. We therefore see the predominance of content that appears to link with discourses of scientific functionalism as a concern for the education and lives of many girls, but also, many boys.

As indicated, statistically significant gender differences were also noted in the *practical activity focus* of HRE. The range of activities featuring in HRE within the schools in Harris' research are detailed in table 8.2.

In the compulsory physical education curriculum, more male than female heads of department included cross-country running, circuit-training, weight-training (both fixed and free weights) and keep fit in the compulsory physical education curriculum. More female heads of department included skipping in the curriculum. With respect to optional activities within curricula, more females offered aerobics and skipping, and more males offered cross-country running. Case study findings revealed similar differences in the

Table 8.2 HRE practical activities in the PE curriculum (compulsory and optional) and extra-curricular programme in secondary schools in England

HRE practical activity	Compulsory %	Optional %	Extra-curricular %
Cross country running	61.5	21.4	40.0
Circuit training	56.2	25.8	19.1
Aerobics	40.5	49.5	34.1
Skipping	29.1	10.2	5.6
Jogging	25.3	15.4	17.0
Weight training (fixed weights)	21.2	36.8	26.5
Keep fit	13.0	13.2	8.9
Weight training (free weights)	12.4	21.8	17.2
Step aerobics	6.2	17.4	12.1
Water exercise	6.2	7.4	4.3
Other	1.8	0.4	1.1

Percentage figures represent the proportion of the sample of secondary schools (N = 728) involved in the various activities. The sample comprised 41 per cent (299 out of 728) female and 59 per cent (429 out of 728) male responses.

activities respectively provided for girls and boys, pointing to the significance of underpinning sex differentiated patterns of staffing, whereby female staff take responsibility for developing a curriculum for girls, while men do likewise for boys. For example, in one school, at key stage four, the girls' HRF[5] course covered a range of aerobic-type activities while the boys' course focused on 'sporting activities'.[6]

Similar differences were observed in the content of extra-curricular programmes. The survey revealed that more female heads of department offered aerobics and step aerobics, while in contrast, more male heads of department included weight training (see Harris, 1997a for further detail of the data). Furthermore, in each case study school, aerobics and step aerobics were selected primarily if not exclusively by girls. The absence of boys participating in these activities can obviously be associated with the fact that the activities were only introduced in the curriculum for girls and were delivered only by female teachers.

Throughout Harris' data we see a tendency for girls and boys to be viewed as having quite distinct needs and interests, which, particularly as they get older, are deemed such that separate provision and/or different curricula are seen as appropriate. Further research is needed to pursue the degree to which single-sex grouping is accompanied by sex-differentiated staffing and/or curriculum provision. This needs to incorporate critical reflection upon the degree to which such provision may be limiting the educational experiences, knowledge and understanding, but also, future life chances, of some girls and some boys. There are certainly strong arguments for developments that raise the profile of activities that have particular appeal as leisure activities for women and that will appeal to many girls (see Flintoff and Scraton, 2001;

Markula, 1995; McDermott, 1996; Obel, 1996; Talbot, 1993; Whitson, 1994). However, issues of appeal and relevance in pupils' eyes need to considered within the context of concerns to introduce both girls and boys to a broad range of activities and in so doing, to be challenging narrow stereotypical preconceptions about who may legitimately participate in particular activities. In Wortley's (1994) view the elimination of gender bias in provision and developing a wide variety of activities for all pupils is a prerequisite to the successful development of healthy active lifestyles. In Harris' research girls and boys were talked about as homogenous groups and simplistic generalisations about, for example, the health-related activities that 'suit' girls or boys respectively, appeared to be informing planning. Thus, while HRE was an arena that at times clearly directed attention towards the individual (for example, with pupils developing personalised training programmes) it seemed to be largely failing to acknowledge some key individual differences. The data has prompted us to question whether teachers and pupils are engaging with the complexities of gender and with multiple femininities and masculinities within and via HRE, and how issues of ethnicity, sexuality and class are being addressed in HRE provided for either girls or boys. In the next section we explore whether revisions to the NCPE have provided any prompts for these issues to be addressed in the development of HRE. We explain how HRE has been repositioned in the context of two revisions of the NCPE and describe specific changes made to the requirements relating to HRE. Once again we pursue from a gender equity perspective, the particular discourses of health and fitness being privileged, or alternatively, subordinated, in the official texts.

HRE in the NCPE: repositioned; redefined?

The first revision of the NCPE (DfE/WO, 1995) saw few changes to the specific content of HRE. Instead, the changes were largely structural, with references to health-related work being repositioned as part of new 'introductory statements' for each key stage and within the 'End of Key Stage Descriptions' which summarised what pupils should know, understand and be able to do by the end of each key stage. The extract below, which again relates to requirements for key stage 3, shows that this change in position was not accompanied by notable changes in terminology or focus. Furthermore, the continued absence of comprehensive guidance relating to how teachers should develop HRE within their implementation of the NCPE meant that the re-positioning was likely to have very little effect upon established patterns of provision and approaches to teaching HRE.

The revised requirements for key stage 3 featured an introductory statement to the programmes of study that stated:

> Throughout the key stage, pupils should be given opportunities to engage in health-promoting physical activity, where possible within the local community. They should be taught: how to prepare for particular

activities and to recover afterwards; the short-term and long-term effects of exercise on the various body systems; the role of exercise in establishing and maintaining health.

(DfE/WO, 1995: 6)

The End of Key Stage Description identified that by the end of the key stage:

Pupils devise strategies and tactics for appropriate activities, and plan or compose more complex sequences of movements. They adapt and refine existing skills and apply these to new situations. Pupils show that they can use skills with precision, and perform sequences with greater clarity and fluency. Pupils recognise the importance of rules and apply them. They appreciate strengths and limitations in performance and use this information in co-operative team work as well as to outwit the opposition in competition. *They understand the short-term and long-term effects of exercise on the body systems, and demonstrate how to prepare for particular activities and how to recover after vigorous physical activity.*

(DfE/WO), 1995: 11, our emphasis)

Again, discourses that can be related back to the gendered history of the subject, that celebrate certain values, and certain bodies, were foregrounded in contemporary policy. Discourses relating to health-related exercise were also clearly positioned in a supporting relationship to discourses of performance in sport.

The more recent revision of the NCPE in 2000 (Department for Education and Employment (DfEE)/Qualifications and Curriculum Authority (QCA), 1999) has arguably further reinforced these characteristics. 'Knowledge and understanding of fitness and health' was one of four aspects of skills, knowledge and understanding that were established as a focus for the development of programmes of study relating to each of the key stages and to the various areas of activity. The other aspects identified were:

- acquiring and developing skills;
- selecting and applying skills, tactics and compositional ideas; and
- evaluating and improving performance.

(DfEE/QCA, 1999: 6)

In this revision of the NCPE, eight level descriptions replaced the previous end of key stage descriptions. By the end of key stage 3 the majority of pupils are expected to have reached or exceeded level 5, which was described in the following terms:

Pupils select and combine their skills, techniques and ideas and apply them accurately and appropriately, consistently showing precision, control and fluency. When performing, they draw on what they know about strategy, tactics and composition. They analyse and comment on skills and techniques and how these are applied in their own and others' work. They modify and redefine skills and techniques to improve their performance. *They explain how the body reacts during different types of exercise, and warm up and cool down in ways that suit the activity. They explain why regular, safe exercise is good for fitness and health.*

(DfEE/QCA, 1999: 42, our emphasis)

The changes in terminology here are important when we recall (from Harris' data) the language typically being used by male and female teachers respectively when talking about their health-related work within the NCPE. The predominantly male focus on physical fitness for performance in sport has been legitimated while other interests, expressed more often by female teachers, are absent. An accompanying text issued by the QCA, entitled 'Terminology in physical education' reinforces the specific focus being promoted in and via the NCPE. The QCA defined fitness as 'sufficient bodily function to carry out [a] specific task safely', and described 'fitness for purpose' via the following examples:

• Sufficient bodily capacity and function to carry out a task efficiently without strain;
• Strong enough to prop up a scrum;
• Strong enough to control or 'spot' a landing when jumping off apparatus;
• Enough stamina to maintain rapid pace for more than 30 seconds.

(QCA, 1999: 7)

Our interest here is in how these particular discourses of 'fitness and health' relate to established and stereotypical discourses of the body, of health, and of physical activity 'for' men and women – or HRE/F 'for' girls and boys. We question the degree to which the official texts can be regarded as promoting the development of practices in physical education (and health-related work specifically) that will be inclusive of all children's needs and interests, and specifically, their lifelong health interests. Recent research by Cale and colleagues[7] has reaffirmed that sex differentiation remains a characteristic of the NCPE in some schools and more specifically, that the new requirements relating to 'knowledge and understanding of fitness and health' are, in some instances, being expressed in ways that openly reinforce gender stereotyping. For example, a male head of physical education explained that:

We deliver a slightly different programme in KS3. Boys do not do dance. Boys do no gym in Year 9. KS4 choices operate, mainly restricted to football, basketball, cricket, athletics for boys; netball, aerobics, badminton, tennis, rounders, athletics for girls.

(Male Head of Department, State Comprehensive School, 2000)

In relation to health-related work specifically, teachers variously explained that

> the use of the multigym has a different emphasis for boys and girls generally – i.e. strength development *v.* toning and muscular endurance. In cardiovascular type work, the emphasis tends to be on running activities for the boys and aerobics type work for the girls.
> (Male Head of Department, State Comprehensive School, 2000)

> Girls – aerobics and step aerobics. Boys – more work in multi-gym on strength and power.
> (Female Head of Department, State Comprehensive School, 2000)

> Boys and girls taught separately but content is the same at KS3. At KS4 girls more towards aerobic type exercise than boys.
> (Male Head of Department, State Comprehensive School, 2000)

These quotations illustrate the way in which the flexibility inherent in the NCPE requirements can result in continued gender inequity within and beyond physical education. In this context, guidance and training clearly has a key role to play in extending awareness and understandings in ways that will prompt the development of practices that challenge narrow and gender stereotyped images and understandings relating to men's and women's participation in physical activity and sport, what constitutes a healthy body, and what it is to 'be fit'. In the final section of our discussion we therefore turn our attention to guidance material that has been specifically developed to support teachers' development of health-related exercise in the context of their implementation of the revised NCPE.

Guidance and gaps: resistance and reproduction

The guidance material, authored by Harris (2000), was the product of a working group that included primary and secondary school teachers, lecturers, advisers/inspectors, consultants and representatives of national organisations relating to health, sport, exercise and the curriculum. Given the shift in terminology in the NCPE, the retention of a focus on health-related *exercise* is in itself notable. Definitions of terms further reinforce the way in which the guidance material has been designed to 'go beyond' the 'official discourses' of fitness and health. In contrast to the QCA's definition, Harris (2000) describes fitness as 'a capacity or a set of attributes that individuals have or achieve that enable them to participate in and benefit from physical activity' (p. 1) and adds that 'Fitness has physical and mental dimensions' (ibid.: 1). Harris also makes explicit that fitness can be associated with various interests, referring to 'fitness for life' and 'fitness for health' as well as 'fitness for performance' and 'skill-related fitness' (ibid.: 1). The concern to broaden thinking and to encourage the development of health-related work that extends beyond an exclusive focus upon a supporting function for perform- ance in sport is evident throughout the materials. Encouraging and enabling all young people to participate in physical activity within and beyond schools, and ensuring that they enjoy doing so in the context of physical education, are principles underpinning the guidance offered to teachers about their approach to the development of HRE in the NCPE, their teaching approaches and assessment. Harris specifically addresses the need for teachers to consider notions of 'developmentally appropriate' and suitably differentiated physical activity. The guidance goes on to explicitly consider the ways in which health- related activities within physical education can be 'inclusive'. Harris (2000) states that:

> To promote current and future involvement in physical activity effectively, exercise experiences should be offered that meet individual needs and preferences. In practising and promoting the principle of equity, it is necessary to integrate all pupils including the least active, least competent and those with learning, physical or sensory impairments or specific health conditions.
>
> (p. 20)

Although Harris stresses that 'Often, the main barrier to participation in physical activity is not a specific medical condition or impairment but the attitudinal, economic and environmental barriers that society places in the way' (p. 21), the absence of any commentary on the way in which gender issues may be at the heart of much practice and many barriers seems a missed opportunity to raise awareness and prompt changes in practice. The silence on the issues that have emerged and continue to emerge from research, may be in danger of leaving a door open for stereotypical practices to continue in contexts of HRE within the NCPE.

Conclusion

Previously it has been proposed that a health-related approach to the develop- ment of physical education in schools is more likely to provide an equitable environment for pupils (Carrington and Leaman, 1986; McKenzie *et al.*, 1996; Williams, 1989) and that a health-based physical education programme can allow girls and less skilful students to feel more centrally involved in lessons (Velert and Devis, 1995). The findings from our research clearly call into question any assumed links between a focus on HRE and more equitable educational experiences. We stress that the practices that we have described should not be regarded as a feature of provision of HRE in *all* schools in England. Nevertheless, we regard it as noteworthy that our investigations have pointed to the existence of distinct 'female' and 'male' versions of HRE, considered appropriate 'for girls' and 'for boys' respectively. At least in some schools it seems that girls and boys are being given opportunities to develop quite *different* knowledge, understanding and skills in relation to health, fitness and physical activity. In these respects, the impression arising from the research is that the introduction of and subsequent revisions to the NCPE has had very little impact upon long-established beliefs and practices. The strength of the gendered divisions within health-related work in physical education and, more importantly, the absence of any prospect of change to this situation were highlighted by the following teacher who commented that:

> with regard to some areas such as HRF, we have different approaches to some of our work. This may not be politically correct but it has been discussed at length, without agreement, and the situation remains.
>
> (Male head of physical education,
> State Comprehensive School, 1993)

The extent and impact of the differences that we have identified in the respective approaches of male and female teachers and in the skills, knowledge and understanding that is being pursued by them in their development of HRE, are well worthy of further exploration. There is also a need to develop better understandings of what underpins the differences that we have observed. Clearly, the very conservative discursive frame (Penney and Evans, 1999) for curriculum development that has been set by the NCPE does not encourage the development of 'alternative' discourses of health, fitness and physical activity. Initial teacher training is an arena in which important foundations can be laid to enable and encourage teachers to explore the flexibility inherent in the NCPE (and specifically in its requirements relating to 'fitness and health') in ways that actively promote gender equity. However, the discursive frames shaping practices in initial teacher training in England are also extremely conservative (Evans *et al.*, 1996). HRE invariably remains marginalised in initial teacher training, subsumed within and subordinate to an overriding focus upon the development of skills, knowledge and understanding relating to particular areas of activity. The discourses of HRE that emerge from such contexts are likely to be ones that are compatible with and that serve to legitimate and reinforce the dominant discourses of elite sport performance.

Continuing professional development thus seems the key forum in which to promote alternative readings of policies and the development of practices that privilege discourses that are currently subordinated. If we are serious about gender equity, we cannot be content with the uncritical acceptance of the dominance of established discourses of fitness and health within the ongoing implementation of the NCPE. In failing to respond to the dominance, physical education teachers and teacher educators will be failing to respond to sustained inequities in schooling and in society and, furthermore, will be playing a part in the reproduction of those inequities. As others, we do not pretend that challenging and/or changing the dominance of particular discourses within and beyond the profession is easy. There are clearly many ideological, political and organisational barriers to overcome (Goodson, 1993, 1995; Penney and Evans, 1997). However, we also see a need to acknowledge that silence on these issues is by no means a neutral stance. We remain committed to a view that teaching and learning in HRE *can* be an arena in which we may actively challenge, deconstruct and reconstruct in new ways, views and images of the physical activities that girls and boys can legitimately pursue. Flintoff and Scraton (2001) have stressed the need for physical education to offer opportunities for young women to develop physical identities that are 'other than the antithesis of men – less able, less strong and less competitive' (p. 8). However, enabling and encouraging the development of a broader range of physical identities is important for the inclusion of many boys as well as many girls. It is a critical issue to address if physical education is to succeed in providing learning environments 'in which young people (girls and boys) acquire respect for themselves and each other' (Humberstone, 1993: 218) and in which we promote 'reciprocal under-standing and valuing between girls and boys' (ibid.: 218). We are very aware that training and ongoing support for teachers will be essential to such progress in physical education, and in HRE specifically. The relationship between difference in provision and equity in provision is far from straight-forward. The issues are complex and as we have seen, there appears at times 'remarkable resilience to change' (Williams and Bedward, 1999: 31) within physical education. But as Macdonald discusses in this text, the action required extends beyond physical education and beyond schools. We need change not only 'in the form and content of PE in schools but also a change in the deep structures of communication throughout education and society' (Humberstone, 1993: 219).

Acknowledgement

This paper draws on the following research project which is funded by the Nuffield Foundation: Cale, L. and Harris, J. (2001) *The Impact of Health-related Exercise Guidance Material on Secondary School Physical Education Teachers in England and Wales*. The support of the Nuffield Foundation is greatly appreciated.

Notes

1 The specific reference to England acknowledges that although early National Curriculum texts were developed for all state schools in England and Wales, subsequent separate documentation and requirements has been specific to each country.
2 The NC proposed a new nomenclature for the years of schooling comprising four key stages (KS): KS 1 (reception, Years 1 and 2, age 5–7 years); KS 2 (Years 3–6, age 7–11 years); KS 3 (Years 7–9, age 11–14 years; KS 4 (Years 10–11, age 14–16 years) (DES, 1989).

3 This term reflects an ongoing tendency within physical education in England and Wales, to disassociate disciplinary knowledge from practical activity, and thus to refer to 'theory' and 'practice' as distinct elements of curricula.

4 In this paper, only statistically significant differences (at the conventional 0.05 level) are reported from the research. See Harris (1997a) for more detailed information on the data.

5 It is notable that the term HRF was retained here, in preference to HRE.

6 Interview data did not indicate the specific activities referred to here.

7 Research by Cale, Harris and Leggett during 2000 examined the impact of the HRE guidance material on provision of HRE within secondary schools in England and Wales. A questionnaire was administered to a stratified sample of heads of PE departments in 500 state secondary schools in England and Wales. The questionnaire data were analysed using SPSS (Norusis/SPSS Inc., 1990; Cale and Harris, 2001).

References

Armstrong, N. and Welsman, J. (1997) *Young People and Physical Activity*, Oxford: Oxford University Press.

Biddle, S. (ed.) (1987) *Foundations of Health-Related Fitness in Physical Education*, London: Ling Publishing Company.

Bowe, R. and Ball, S.J. with Gold, A. (1992) *Reforming Education and Changing Schools: Case Studies in Policy Sociology*, London: Routledge.

Caldecott, S.W. (1992) A study of teachers' practices, perceptions and further intentions regarding health-related fitness, *Bulletin of Physical Education* 28(1): 33–9.

Cale, L. and Harris, J. (2001) *The Impact of Health-Related Exercise Guidance Material on Secondary School Physical Education Teachers in England and Wales*, Nuffield Foundation Research Project Report, Loughborough University.

Carrington, B. and Leaman, O. (1986) Equal opportunities and physical education, in J. Evans (ed.) *Physical Education, Sport and Schooling: Studies in the Sociology of Physical Education*, London: Falmer Press, pp. 215–26.

Department for Education/Welsh Office (DfE/WO) (1995) *Physical Education in the National Curriculum*, London: HMSO.

Department for Education and Employment (DfEE)/Qualifications and Curriculum Authority (QCA) (1999) *Physical Education: The National Curriculum for England*, London: HMSO.

Department of Education and Science (DES) (1989) *National Curriculum: From Policy to Practice*, London: HMSO.

Department of Education and Science (DES)/Welsh Office (WO) (1991) *Physical Education for Ages 5–16: Proposals of the Secretary of State for Education and the Secretary of State for Wales*, London: DES.

Department of Education and Science (DES)/Welsh Office (WO) (1992) *Physical Education in the National Curriculum*, London: HMSO.

Department of Health (1992) *The Health of the Nation: A Strategy for Health in England*, London: HMSO.

Flintoff, A. and Scraton, S. (2001) Stepping into active leisure? Young women's perceptions of active lifestyles and their experiences of school physical education, *Sport, Education and Society* 6(1): 5–21.

Goodson, I. (1993) *School Subjects and Curriculum Change. Studies in Curriculum History* (3rd edition), London: Falmer Press.

Goodson, I.F. (1995), *The Making of Curriculum: Collected Essays* (2nd edition), London: Falmer Press.

Harris, J. (1995) Physical education: a picture of health?, *British Journal of Physical Education* 26(4): 25–32.

Harris, J. (1997a) *Physical Education: A Picture of Health? The Implementation of Health-Related Exercise in the National Curriculum in Secondary Schools in England*, unpublished doctoral thesis, Loughborough University.

Harris, J. (1997b) Good practice guidelines for HRE, *British Journal of Physical Education* 28(4): 9–11.

Harris, J. (1998) Health-related exercise: rationale and recommendations', *British Journal of Physical Education* 29(3): 11–12.

Harris, J. (2000) *Health-Related Exercise in the National Curriculum: Key Stages 1 to 4.* Champaign, IL: Human Kinetics.

Harris, J. and Penney, D. (2000) Gender issues in health-related exercise, *European Physical Education Review* 6(3): 249–73.

Humberstone, B. (1993) Equality, physical education and outdoor education: ideological struggles and transformative structures?, in J. Evans (ed.) *Equality, Education and Physical Education*, London: Falmer Press, pp. 74–89.

Kirk, D. (1992) *Defining Physical Education: The Social Construction of a School Subject in Postwar Britain,* London: Falmer Press.

Markula, P. (1995) Firm but shapely, fit but sexy, strong but thin: the postmodern aerobicizing female bodies, *Sociology of Sport Journal* 12: 424–53.

McDermott, L. (1996) Towards a feminist understanding of physicality within the context of women's physically active and sporting lives, *Sociology of Sport Journal* 13: 12–30.

McIntosh, P. (1968) *Physical Education in England since 1800*, London: Bell & Sons.

McKenzie, T.L., Nader, P.R., Strikmiller, P.K., Yang, M., Stone, E. and Perry, C.L. (1996) School physical education: effect of the child and adolescent trial for cardiovascular health, *Preventive Medicine* 25: 423–31.

McNair, D. (1985) The historical concept of health and fitness: a review, in *British Universities Physical Education Association Conference Proceedings*, Belfast: Queens University, pp. 99–119.

Norusis, M. J./SPSS Inc. (1990) *SPSS Base System User's Guide: SPSS Statistical Data Analysis*, Chicago, IL: SPSS Inc.

Obel, C. (1996) Collapsing gender in competitive bodybuilding: researching contradictions and ambiguity in sport, *Review for the Sociology of Sport* 31(2): 185–200.

Penney, D. and Evans, J. (1997) Naming the game: discourse and domination in physical education and sport in England and Wales, *European Physical Education Review* 3(1): 21–32.

Penney, D. and Evans, J. (1999) *Politics, Policy and Practice in Physical Education*, London: E & FN Spon.

Penney, D. and Harris, J. (1997) Extra-curricular physical education: more of the same for the more able?, *Sport, Education and Society* 2(1): 41–54.

Penney, D. and Harris, J. (1998) The National Curriculum for Physical Education: have we got it right?, *British Journal of Physical Education* 29(1): 7–10.

Qualifications and Curriculum Authority (1999) *Terminology in Physical Education,* London: QCA.

School Curriculum and Assessment Authority (SCAA) (1997) Physical education and the health of the nation, in *Conference Proceedings: Full Conference Papers and Discussion Reports*, London: SCAA.

Scraton, S. (1986) Images of femininity and the teaching of girls' physical education, in J. Evans (ed.), *Physical Education, Sport and Schooling: Studies in the Sociology of Physical Education*, London: Falmer Press, pp. 71–94.

Scraton, S. (1987) 'Boys muscle in where angels fear to tread': girls' sub-cultures and physical activities, in J. Horne, D. Jary and A. Tomlinson (eds) *Sport, Leisure and Social Relations*, London: Routledge & Kegan Paul, pp. 160–86.

Sports Council and Health Education Authority (1992) *Allied Dunbar National Fitness Survey: Main Findings*, London: Author.

Stacey, M. (1988) *The Sociology of Health and Healing*, London: Routledge.

Talbot, M. (1993) A gendered physical education: equality and sexism, in J. Evans (ed.) *Equality, Education and Physical Education*, London: Falmer Press, pp. 74–89.

Velert, C.P. and Devis, J.D. (1995) Health-based physical education in Spain: the conception, implementation and evaluation of an innovation, *European Physical Education Review* 1(1): 37–54.

Whitson, D. (1994) The embodiment of gender: discipline, domination and empowerment, in S. Birrell and C. Cole (eds) *Women, Sport and Culture*, Champaign, IL: Human Kinetics.

Williams, A. (1989) Girls and boys come out to play (but mainly boys): gender and physical education, in A. Williams (ed.) *Issues in Physical Education for the Primary Years*, London: Falmer Press, pp. 145–59.

Williams, A. and Bedward, J. (1999) *Games for the Girls: The Impact of Recent Policy on the Provision of Physical Education and Sporting Opportunities for Female Adolescents*, Nuffield Foundation Study.

Wortley, A. (1994) Physical education, in J. Harrison and J. Edwards (eds) *Developing Health Education in the Curriculum*, London: David Fulton Publishers, pp. 110–14.

9 Understanding girls' experience of physical education: relational analysis and situated learning

Anne Williams and Julie Bedward

Introduction

In this chapter we use relational analysis as conceptualised by Apple (1979) and Giddens (1990) in the context of social science, and by Hall (1996) in the context of feminist critique, as a theoretical tool for the exploration of girls' perceptions and experiences of physical education and physical activity in England in the late 1990s. The concept of situated learning, as defined by Lave and Wenger (1991) and Kirk and Macdonald (1998), is also used as an aid to understanding what we conclude is the relative failure, to date, of policies purported to promote curricula which deliver entitlement for all. Our data reveal clear inadequacies in contemporary physical education in relation to the needs and interests of girls.

Relational analysis and situated learning

Kirk (1999) suggests that the value of relational analysis lies in its potential to reveal complexity and to act as an antidote to approaches that over-simplify educational issues through treating them as uni-dimensional. This seems consistent with Hall's (1996) view that relational analysis which acknowledges relationships between categories may be more fruitful than the analysis of categories in isolation. Hall's discussion of relational analysis focuses upon consideration of girls in relation to boys. That is, girls define themselves in relation to boys in different ways with different implications for those seeking to provide relevant physical education programmes for them. Relational analysis is equally useful as a tool for consideration of the experiences of other specific groups within societies, such as different cultural groups. Furthermore, it may provide insights into experiences in school relative to those within the wider community.

As Kirk and Macdonald (1998) have identified, Lave and Wenger's (1991) work on 'situated learning' appears to offer a useful framework for further explorations of this relationship. Although Lave and Wenger (1991) specifically exclude school learning from their discussion of legitimate peripheral participation as a part of situated learning, they nevertheless suggest that learning in the school context could benefit from the application of their thesis. Kirk and Macdonald (1998: 379–80) pursued this potential, explaining that 'Situated learning theories attempt to expand our attention from the learner as an "isolated" individual to include a focus on the social settings that construct and constitute the individual as a learner'. Here we are particularly concerned with inequities in those social settings and the ways in which they are expressed and legitimated via social relationships and within schools. With these interests in mind we pursue the notion (and later, representation in physical education contexts) of 'legitimate peripheral participation' (Lave and Wenger, 1991).

As part of the learning process 'legitimate peripheral participation' implies authentic involvement in the practices of a specific community and acknowledges that progress towards full participation may be affected adversely by denial of access to certain aspects of that community's practice; the social relationships that it promotes, permits and excludes; and who is allowed access to what resources (Kirk and Macdonald, 1998). This prompts us to question the relation of school practices to those of the communities in which schools are located and to investigate the relationship between the world of schooling and the world of adults more generally. While 'legitimate *peripheral* participation' does not preclude learning, an inability to move to '*full* participation', for whatever reason, is certainly relevant in considering the effectiveness of programmes which claim not only to promote learning, but also to interface with the world outside school. Central to the potential move to full participation (and therefore, barriers to realising this potential) are sets of relationships. Participation occurs within the relationships that shape experiences in powerful ways. As we see later, these matters have a particular applicability to our study which specifically sought to further our understanding of how female adolescents conceptualise their participation in physical activity and their participation and learning in physical education. This chapter thus aims to address the need that Kirk (1999) has highlighted, for analyses to go beyond simplistic formulations of participation in various forms of physical culture.

Forms of physical culture and communities of practice

Kirk alludes to the cultural forces within which the construction of identities is located, pointing to the influences of media and advertising as well as social institutions such as school and family. Drawing on Lave and Wenger's (1991) work, Kirk (1999) also proposes the use of the term physical culture to embrace three 'communities of practice' on which physical education draws: sport, physical recreation and exercise. He suggests that currently there is a disjunction between physical education and these associated communities of practice. Here we are concerned to pursue this disjunction in relation to the norms and values that physical educators embrace and then express in their curricula and teaching. Our study has specifically indicated a relative lack of change in physical education practice at a time of rapid and ongoing change in thinking about sport, recreation and exercise.

For Kirk (1999), this relative stability in the cultural practices and norms of the subject and the profession is not only highly problematic but also a critical issue in considering the current state and status of physical education. It may be that teachers insist upon sustaining and privileging the norms and values of their own, school-specific community of practice, rather than seeking to understand and incorporate those of related communities. As Penney and Evans' work has emphasised, it is neither accurate nor appropriate to portray teachers' decisions about these matters as exclusively their own. There are powerful and openly political frames to teachers' thinking and actions, not all of which are easily challenged or deconstructed (see for example, Penney and Evans, 1999). But whatever the collective influences, the situation that we have in many schools in England is that the norms and values of physical education continue to privilege team activities, a highly prescribed uniform chosen by those in authority, and conformity to particular codes of conduct which no longer play any significant part in recreation, exercise or many sports. Thus, disjunction may manifest itself in a variety of ways. Codes of conduct in elite sport may well be very different from those operating within the school context, with the former promoting and the latter dismissing, in some cases, particular behaviours relating for example, to professional fouls and sporting etiquette. The highly prescribed uniform for physical education which is retained by many schools as part of a policy which attempts to protect pupils from the pressures of conforming to transient fashion, not only differs but conflicts with recreational and exercise wear which values individual choice and which promotes such wear as part of the contemporary fashion scene. Individual choice and the scope to express youth, sporting and cultural identities are important issues for physical educationalists to pursue if they are concerned to facilitate engagement in cultures beyond schools. Are physical education and schools failing to provide significant numbers of boys and girls with the skills, knowledge, understanding and experiences that will enable and encourage them to become participants in the communities of practice identified by Kirk? How are they positioning pupils and directing learning in relation to these communities?

The study

The qualitative study from which data for this chapter is drawn aimed to improve understanding of some of the issues which underpin the gender differences which had emerged from earlier work (Williams and Woodhouse, 1996). Further details of the methodological aspects of the research can be found elsewhere (Williams and Bedward, 1999; 2000). Here we provide a brief outline of the focus and design of the study. Specifically, the study sought to pursue:

- the extent to which a 'common curriculum' was available to all pupils and was perceived by them to be equitable;
- the significance of issues such as teaching style, learning context and presentation in relation to these perceptions but also with likely future participation in physical activity and sport in mind;
- relationships between school curriculum experience and out-of-school participation; and
- girls' perceptions of their achievements in physical education.

The study involved the collection of data through interview and lesson observations over a period of half a term (six weeks during 1997 and 1998) in each of three schools, which we have named West Green, North Park and Southside. All three schools are located within a large conurbation. We aimed to achieve a varied sample that would reflect a broad range of experiences in relation to physical education and school sport. Our three schools therefore differed in catchment area, in the quality and quantity of the facilities available for physical education, in specialist staffing levels and staffing deployment. Two of the schools were co-educational, while the third is a single-sex girls' school. This variety was achieved by purposive sampling (Maykut and Morehouse, 1994).

We interviewed 91 students in total, mainly from Year 9 (45) and Year 11 (41). Five students were from Year 10. The student sample was self-selected in that the relevant year group students were invited to participate and volunteered to be interviewed. All students provided written parental consent to participate. Both the students and teachers involved in the research (see below) were given information about the project and about the use that would be made of the data collected. Interviews with the students were held on the school site either before school, during lunchtime and breaks, or after school. Students were given the option of being interviewed individually or in groups. Most (75) were interviewed individually. Group interviews were held with 16 students in seven groups of two or three. The interviews were semi-structured, using hierarchical focusing (Tomlinson, 1989) allowing issues to be explored in depth, and were tape recorded. The ethnic mix of the sample tended to reflect the ethnic mix of the research site. Thirty-three per cent of the students from West Green School and 35 per cent of students from North Park were from minority ethnic groups. At Southside, which served a predominantly white catchment area, just one interviewee was from a minority ethnic group.

Interviews were also held with the physical education teachers who taught the year group samples at each of the schools and again, interviews were conducted on a voluntary basis. Twelve teachers were interviewed all of whom were physical education specialists. All three physical education teachers at West Green were interviewed, one male and two female. Five out of the six physical education staff at North Park were interviewed, all of whom were female; and four out of seven at Southside were interviewed, one male and three female. Most (9) had been in their current posts for some considerable time, that is, between 13 and 24 years. One of the teachers at Southside was in her first year of teaching and two other teachers (one at Southside and one at North Park) were in their second year of teaching. The teacher interviews explored teacher perceptions of the National Curriculum for Physical Education and views on a range of issues relating to physical education provision. All the interview data was analysed using a thematic approach using constant comparative analysis which enabled us both to identify and compare data from different sources within and between schools, and to relate data to the theoretical themes which underpinned the study. Pseudonyms are used throughout our reporting of data.

Activity preferences

In relation to the matter of activity preference students' perceptions seemed largely ability- or context-driven. Our data suggests that we need to be wary of representing girls' attitudes towards different activity areas in over-generalised ways. In 1994 Hargreaves emphasised the gendered notions of sport, with the emphasis on team sports, which have characterised the development and implementation of the national curriculum in England and Wales. She suggested that this has produced a curriculum which stresses activities which girls tend to dislike, that is, team sports, and that diminishes the importance of activities such as dance and gymnastics which appeal more to girls than to boys. We drew similar conclusions from earlier work (Williams and Woodhouse, 1996), reporting that winter team games failed to attract female students. The research reported here leads us to suggest that we cannot make generalisations about girls' physical activity preferences. Specifically, it revealed that while winter team games were anathema to many of our sample, for others they were the highlight of the school week, played with obvious enjoyment and, for these students, their preferred activity choice. Gymnastics, dance and athletics generated equally polarised views. Not surprisingly, students tended to prefer those activities where they felt more competent.

> I'm not really very graceful, I wouldn't say. I'm just not very good at it (gymnastics) so . . . I got laughed at a bit which wasn't very good. I'm just not keen on it.
>
> (Sarah, Year 11 student[1])

> Basically I feel that you have to be good to play against people who actually enjoy them and I just haven't really got much interest in sports. . . . When you have to pick teams and stuff, you feel like, I'm not going to get picked for them and you have to be good.
>
> (Joanne, Year 11 student)

For other some students, these same activities constituted the highlight of their physical education experience.

When we did a performance of gymnastics . . . one person spotted me for this flip thing off the block, and she told everyone else. They were all, 'Watch Ursula in this performance!', and my head swelled. It was good.

(Ursula, Year 11 student)

You're not just relying on yourself, you're relying on other people, you're helping other people. You've got more momentum. You're not just running for yourself, you've got your team and they're shouting for you . . . and you're running a little faster, trying a little harder. And my friends are there.

(Simone, Year 11 student)

The negative view of some activities seemed to be exacerbated by being placed in situations where students felt publicly humiliated, particularly in activities or teaching contexts where individual public performance was demanded.

I did a bit of dance . . . And a couple of times I have had to do it in front of the whole class and it's really embarrassing. So I don't think I like that either.

(Tracey, Year 11 student)

[Gymnastics is Denise's least favourite activity because of] showing it in front of everybody, I suppose, and trying to jump on to those massive boxes that I can't do. It's really embarrassing.

(Denise, Year 9 student)

Nevertheless, it is important to note the gendered division of the curriculum and moreover, students' recognition and criticism of this characteristic. A key issue to emerge with respect to activities offered related to female students' views about the sexist nature of the curriculum offered, resulting from the division of games along traditional lines into boys' and girls' games. In particular most of the girls felt that it was unfair that they were denied the opportunity to play football. Many of the girls had played football at primary school and were critical of the fact that this was not offered to them at secondary school. One student had looked forward to continuing a game begun in primary school.

Well, I don't really like hockey and I enjoy football because I've done football a lot in my primary school. I was going to join a team but then, no. We were going to do a team in Year 7 but then Mr Jacques says you can't.

(Ravinder, Year 9 student)

Another notes the teacher's reaction.

> The teacher says, Oh that's for the boys, you can't play that. I don't think it's really fair because half of us in our year like football, but we don't get the chance to play it.
>
> (Judith, Year 9 student)

At North Park a girls' football club was available at lunchtimes which was extremely popular. However, the girls viewed this as a token gesture and still considered it unfair that football was not taught in physical education lessons.

Students' desire for the inclusion of football in physical education lessons were not limited to those who wished to play it. They saw the situation as a general matter of equal opportunity irrespective of the likely appeal. Similarly they felt that boys should have access to games, such as netball, which were currently restricted to girls. The students' comments may well reflect not merely concerns relating to equal opportunities but also and more specifically, power-relations inherent in physical education and in particular, the scope for them to exercise some power and make some decisions (Laws and Fisher, 1999). One student explained:

> I mean half of the boys probably wouldn't choose netball because they opt for basketball but I think it should be up to the boys, the school shouldn't decide for them and it should be their choice.
>
> (Natalie, Year 9 student)

Teachers appeared to be unaware of the level of interest amongst girls for football outside of school. Robert's belief that 'despite the growth of women's soccer, I still think that there are more girls playing netball when they leave school than are playing football' (Robert, white male head of physical education) is contrary to our evidence. He seemed to be unaware of the level of active interest in football among girls and of the opportunities which now exist for them, outside of school.

> I feel that it is in their interests for us to teach them games that they are actually more likely to be able to follow up after they leave school, so I actually feel that we're better sticking to the traditional range – that we teach rugby to boys and football to boys, basketball to boys, although we have done some mixed basketball, and netball and hockey to girls.
>
> (Robert)

On a reflective note he commented 'I don't think it (football) shouldn't be taught to girls, but I do have a little bit of a mental block about it to be honest, but it's something we may have to think about'.

Preferred teaching contexts

Our data clearly indicated the potential that the context (pedagogical and physical), as much as the activity, has to generate negative views amongst students.

> We have to have it (netball) outside and it's cold. When you've got the ball and you're passing it around it hurts our fingers and if you get caught or anything, the ball's hard and if it hits you it's sore.
>
> (Tracey, Year 9 student)

> I don't like it in the cold because I hate the cold and sometimes we can't wear jogging bottoms when it's really cold she makes us wear a skirt and we don't really like that because of how cold it is.
>
> (Natalie, Year 9 student)

Groupings used in physical education emerged as another critical contextual issue. Much discussion focused on mixed-sex teaching, where students expressed a range of views reflecting significant differences in the way in which they positioned themselves in relation to the boys. This positioning related to playing ability, to concerns about boys' perceptions of the girls' performance and to matters related to appearance. In general, girls who were competent games players welcomed the opportunity to play in mixed-sex teams as they saw playing with and against boys as increasing the competitive element of the game and providing them with more challenges.

> I think I prefer to do it mixed. Especially for tennis. I found that you probably get more competition through boys because of their pride.
>
> (Denise, Year 11 student).

Teachers generally demonstrated an awareness of the potential for other girls' self confidence to be undermined when playing competitive team games against boys, especially after Year 8 when gender differences in relation to physical strength were considered to be more pronounced. As one teacher explained, these differences could result in all but the most able female players being overwhelmed.

> I believe that for the girls who are perhaps not so able, they are disadvantaged mixing with the boys, because the boys are a lot stronger physically and mentally, a lot of the time. . . . I believe that the majority would be held back and they wouldn't want to perform in front of the lads. The lads would take the lead . . . the lads would hog the game, or the practice, or whatever you are doing and the girls would let them. They would stand back and they would rather let them get on with it. . . . Your stronger girls

will be fine; they will cope. Your weaker ones just wouldn't, and they will just cower in the corner somewhere.

(Michael, male head of physical education)

It was notable, however, that while aware of these issues, none of the teachers made any reference to the possibility of intervening to pre-empt such inequities being generated. Instead they appeared to regard particular male–female relationships as inevitable in mixed-sex group settings and as something to be managed rather than changed.

Gymnastics and dance were often identified as activities that students preferred to be offered in single-sex groups, because they considered that the performance aspect of these activities, and the clothing worn, would lead to embarrassment in the presence of the opposite sex. Male–female relationships in which boys were dominant and negative were cited by students as reasons for single-sex teaching and once again, reinforced the important influence of the pedagogical setting on the experiences of pupils.

You have to show the boys your dance and they just laugh. It's really embarrassing. They take the mick out of you. I think it would have been better with just girls in my class, because I would have done it properly, if you know what I mean.

(Teresa, Year 9 student)

A part of the experience of physical education still seems to be inadequately addressed, is that of 'kit' or uniform. Our research revealed significant differences between teacher and student perceptions about the issue of uniform for physical education. At least some of the students' concerns about mixed-sex activities could have been addressed through a different stance in relation to physical education kit. Most of the students accepted the need for a PE kit but felt that this should apply just to the colour of garments worn. They expressed a preference for shorts, jogging bottoms, T-shirts and sweatshirts; namely the type of clothing students would choose to wear for physical activities pursued outside school. The uniform required for physical education was quite different.

The PE skirts are really short, but you have to deal with it because that's the school uniform for PE. And you're not allowed to wear cycling shorts either. I don't think it's fair. . . . We have to wear PE pants. Even though it's not showing your other pants, it's still a bit revealing I think.

(Diane, Year 11 student)

This aspect of uniform rule was in force at all of the research schools. Many students expressed a preference for wearing cycling shorts, and many actually wore these for PE lessons despite being reprimanded.

If, say, you're chubby and you want to wear shorts under your skirt because you get picked on, they (the teachers) don't understand. They always tell you to take them off, but you can't. Like today, we had to stand up whoever didn't have the right PE kit, and I got a warning. . . . I thought it was embarrassing really because I wear shorts every PE lesson, and I get told off for that. I didn't do it. I didn't want to stand up, so I didn't do it.

(Teresa, Year 9 student)

Even where policy was applied consistently to all groups, teachers' arguments against particular choices of clothing seemed to demonstrate more about personal taste and a wish to impose their own definitions of appropriate dress than about sensitivity to adolescents' concerns about decency, and their developing body image. Here the students' preferences were clearly rejected and regarded as incompatible with appropriate dress for physical education.

We did go through a spate of them wanting to wear cycle shorts underneath rather than PE . . . they don't particularly like their PE knickers. It looks absolutely awful. We don't allow that.

(Kim, female head of physical education)

In addition to issues concerning body image, the students also drew attention to more pragmatic matters about what is appropriate and adequate dress for participating in physical activity. It was quite common to find students at one school playing netball during November and December in T-shirts and skirts.

It's just that when it's cold and, like, if you were at home you wouldn't go out in a short skirt and a T-shirt and jumper but for PE we have to. We sometimes can't wear our trousers and . . . It just puts you off totally.

(Helen, Year 9 student)

One of our sample schools had allowed changes to the uniform code that enabled all pupils to wear kit in which they felt comfortable. In another, it appeared that white pupils had to suffer the humiliation of being identified as unacceptably obese before they could access the policy which operated for Asian girls. Both white and Asian students felt that the school policy was unacceptable.

I've had problems this year with a Year 11 young lady who's quite weighty and she had problems trying to get a skirt that fitted her and to be fair to her she tried very hard to get one. And in fact I rang up the stockists for her and tried to get one. But in the end I agreed that she could wear a pair of joggers. That was no problem because as far as I was concerned as long as she was happy and participating I'd rather her be like that then embarrassed and, you know, not wanting to participate.

(Kim, female head of physical education)

Conclusions

In terms of activities within physical education, our findings both confirm the complexity of the issues involved in meeting individual needs (see also Kirk, 1999) and underline the difficulty of finding a common pattern of provision which would meet the needs of all. Our data supports Hargeaves' (1994) advocacy of the pursuit of multiple strategies for the advance of women's and girls' interests in sport and physical education. It has generated issues that are relevant to consider in relation to provision for both boys and girls and perhaps most importantly, has highlighted points of clear disjuncture between the norms and values of school physical education as articulated and reinforced by the teachers, and those of physical activity pursued in other contexts in which many students were involved and to which these students could relate. The disjunction is one that is expressed in various ways and that reflects differential power-relations in schooling. The activity priorities of the school and those of the adolescent girls expected to take part in them are at times openly contradictory, with the girls therefore seeing little relationship between the curriculum offered and their preferred leisure activities. Uniform policy provided one of the clearest examples of disjunction between school-based communities of practice and those related to other physical activity-focused communities. As far as our students were concerned, school expectations within physical education conflicted with out-of-school norms and values and even with school expectations outside the subject. The school concerns appear to prioritise conformity to a mode of dress which is, at best, probably only suitable for those who conform to the stereotypical ideal female body and for participation in a warm indoor environment. Uniform appears to remain as a significant mechanism for social control in many school settings. Students are concerned with warmth, comfort and decency and perceive these as essential prerequisites to enjoyable and meaningful participation in physical activity, regardless of its location.

If we further pursue the responses from the girls, we see that their views of physical education and physical activity are clearly related to ways in which they position themselves relative to boys and to 'male' activities. For some, more equitable provision is about opportunities to 'catch up with the men' (Dyer, 1982), an essentially pragmatic approach, rooted in liberal feminism. These girls want to be able to play 'boys' games' and point to the number of activities available to boys but not to girls, as compared with the single activity, netball, denied to the boys. They see the categorisation of activities along gender lines as anomalous in an education system which has given them equal access to all other areas of the curriculum. For others an inclusive curriculum would involve the opportunity to learn about and participate in more distinctively 'female' activities. These girls appear to locate themselves within a radical feminist paradigm which would support physical education organised by women for women. Such organisation would be on the basis of an equal valuing of activities or approaches which appealed to women and girls, and not on the basis of the assumed biological weaknesses which underpinned separatist developments in physical education earlier this century. It would liberate the girls from domination by boys in co-educational settings or from domination by essentially masculine constructions of activities within single-sex settings. These girls' concerns with their appearance and dress, especially in co-educational settings, and with boys' perceptions of their performance are consistent with radical feminist views about patriarchal power relations (see for example Weiss, 1997).

Our data seems consistent with a view of gender and culture as situated and transient. Our students seemed to position themselves differently, depending upon the context of the conversation. Football within the school context was discussed exclusively in relation to opportunities available to boys but denied to adolescent girls. Out-of-school activity, on the other hand (which included football for many of our sample), was often described in terms which were more culturally specific. That is, students talked of out-of-school opportunities as something which were governed by cultural expectations. These were sometimes related to ethnicity in that requirements to attend the Mosque or assumptions that out-of-school activities were home- and family-based because of a specific cultural affiliation were mentioned. They also relate to female participation more generally. Deem and Gilroy (1998) counsel against the development of strategies to promote sport which neglect the kinds of perceptions women in general have of sport and the negotiations they may need to engage in if they wish to participate in physical activity. They point out that a great deal of women's leisure activity takes place in the home. This is confirmed by the varied experiences of our sample which contrast with much narrower definitions of leisure opportunities suggested by some of the teachers.

Lave and Wenger seem to imply that participation in a particular community of practice beyond the stage of legitimate peripheral participation requires an acceptance of the norms and values of the specific community. Our data leads us to suggest that many girls remain at the peripheral stage for a variety of reasons, which, singly or in combination, serve as barriers to the sorts of full participation that are likely to maximise learning. This is not to say that learning cannot take place as a peripheral participant. Nevertheless, for some students, the activities themselves are associated with values to which they do not subscribe. Others' bodies fail to conform to the norm implied by school expectations of dress and public performance. For others, the context, particularly where activities take place outside in inclement weather, conflicts with their perceptions of physical activity as something to be enjoyed in warmth and comfort. Some of the comments made by our students resonate clearly with the three communities of practice identified by Kirk and indicate that some physical education teachers appear to be sustaining a separate and distinctive community of practice which is not compatible with associated communities. At times this leads to conflict, as girls bring to their physical education experience and expectations which are more consonant with the communities of sport, recreation or exercise. School requirements to exercise outside, in cold weather, dressed in minimal clothing conflict with the norms of exercise-based communities that stress the importance of warmth for effective and safe participation. Compulsory participation in activities which students dislike and for which they feel, rightly or wrongly, that they have no aptitude, conflicts with the values of recreational activity which emphasises choice, both of activity and of the form that participation will take.

We should conclude by noting that, for many of the students we interviewed, physical education is an enjoyable and rewarding experience. In order to extend this positive experience to all, a number of issues relating to inconsistency between school and out-of-school physical culture need to be addressed. Clearly, this inconsistency is not only an issue relevant to girls, but rather, to all young people. It challenges physical education to seek greater engagement with the body-cultures and lifestyles to which students can relate and aspire.

Acknowledgements

The authors would like to acknowledge the support of the Nuffield Foundation who provided funding for this study.

Note

1 The years specified for students refer to years within the National Curriculum framework in England and Wales. Years 9–11 therefore relate to the latter years of secondary schooling, for pupils aged 13–16 years.

References

Adams, N. (1997) Towards a curriculum of resiliency: gender, race, adolescence and schooling, in C. Marshall (ed.) *Feminist Critical Policy Analysis: A Perspective from Primary and Secondary Schooling*, London: Falmer Press.

Apple, M. (1979) *Ideology and the Curriculum*, London: Routledge & Kegan Paul.

Deem, R. and Gilroy, S. (1998) Physical activity, lifelong learning and empowerment: situating sport, *Women's Leisure, Sport Education and Society* 3(1): 89–104.

Dyer, K. (1982) *Catching up the Men: Women in Sport*, London: Junction Books.

Giddens, A. (1990) *The Consequences of Modernity*, Cambridge: Polity Press.

Hargreaves, J. (1994) *Sporting Females*, London: Routledge.

Hall, M.A. (1996) *Feminism and Sporting Bodies: Essays on Theory and Practice*, Champaign, IL: Human Kinetics.

Lave, J. and Wenger, E. (1991) *Situated Learning: Legitimate Peripheral Participation*, New York: Cambridge University Press.

Kirk, D. (1999) Physical culture, physical education and relational analysis, *Sport, Education and Society* 4(1): 63–73.

Kirk, D. and Macdonald, D. (1998) Situated learning in physical education, *Journal of Teaching in Physical Education* 17(3): 376–87.

Laws, C. and Fisher, R. (1999) Pupils' interpretations of physical education, in C. Hardy and M. Mawer (eds) *Learning and Teaching in Physical Education*, London: Falmer Press.

Maykut, P. and Morehouse, R. (1994) *Beginning Qualitative Research*, London: Falmer Press.

Penney, D. and Evans, J. (1999) *Politics, Policy and Practice in Physical Education*, London: E & FN Spon.

Tomlinson, P. (1989) Having it both ways: hierarchical focusing as research interview method, *British Educational Research Journal* 15(2): 155–75.

Weiss, L. (1997) Gender and the Reports, the case of the missing piece, in C. Marshall (ed.) *Feminist Critical Policy Analysis: A Perspective from Primary and Secondary Schooling*, London: Falmer Press.

Williams, E.A. and Bedward, J. (1999) *Games for the Girls: The Impact of Recent Policy on the Provision of Physical Education and Sporting Opportunities for Female Adolescents – a Report of a Study Funded by the Nuffield Foundation*, Winchester: King Alfred's College.

Williams, E.A. and Bedward, J. (2000) An inclusive national curriculum? The experience of adolescent girls, *European Journal of Physical Education* 5(1): 4–18

Williams, A. and Woodhouse, J. (1996) Delivering the discourse: urban adolescents' perceptions of physical education, *Sport, Education and Society* 1(2): 201–13.

Part IV

Extending gender agendas in physical education

10 Gender equity and physical education: a USA perspective

Mary O'Sullivan, Kim Bush and Margaret Gehring

Introduction

The struggles associated with a male-dominated sport curriculum in England (Kirk, 2001, chapter 3; Williams and Bedward, 2001, chapter 9) are also evident in the US (Chepyator-Thomson and Ennis, 1997). From the 1960s to the early 1970s a massive shift occurred in our profession, resulting in the unification of men's and women's physical education pedagogy programs and in boy's and girl's physical education classes. This shift led to the proliferation of a traditionally male model of physical education (Vertinsky, 1992). While curricular initiatives in the last fifteen years have made strides toward providing gender inclusive physical education, the traditional, male-based, multi-activity curriculum is still dominant in the US (Lawson, 1998). One of the biggest barriers to dissemination of new curricula initiatives in American schools is the lack of a national curriculum. The decentralized nature of the education system in the US means that widespread changes to curricula would require intensive, coordinated and sustained efforts with almost unanimous acceptance at the state and local levels.

There have been a plethora of educational reforms in the United States in the last twenty years. Efforts have been made to improve curriculum, bring greater accountability for teaching and learning, improve teacher preparation, provide induction programs for new teachers, and devote more money to support professional development for experienced teachers. In physical education, we have seen the development of national content standards for physical education (NASPE, 1995a) for the curriculum from kindergarten to grade 12[1] and the establishment of teacher preparation standards for beginning physical education teachers that align with the K–12 content standards (NASPE, 1995b). Most recently we have seen a national voluntary certification in physical education for experienced teachers established as one of over twenty such certifications administered by the National Board for Professional Teaching Standards (NBPTS, 1999). This is a system to recognize and reward accomplished teachers. In several states the legislature has agreed to pay enhancements of up to $5000 annually for upwards of ten years upon successful receipt of the Board certification.

There has been little if any attention in these reforms to gender and education (Nilges, 1998). Title IX is the only substantive piece of legislation that deals with gender and education and its most dramatic effect has been in relation to girls' participation rates in sport and physical education in American schools. We therefore begin with a review of some of the key policy documents dealing with sport and physical education and how they have addressed gender equity. We then identify some contemporary curricular trends and specifically consider the degree to which the curricula developed have attempted to address the physical education of *all* students. In the final part of the chapter, we draw some conclusions about gender equity in physical education and make some comparisons between developments in the US and in Great Britain.

Policy initiatives addressing physical education

Title IX

In 1972 the US Congress passed Title IX as part of the Educational Amendments of that year. Specifically, Title IX states 'No person in the US shall, on the basis of sex be excluded from participation in, or denied the benefits of, or be subjected to discrimination under any educational program or activity receiving federal aid' (20 U.S.C. §1681a, 1988).

The purpose of Title IX was to ensure that girls received the same educational opportunities as boys. Title IX applies to all educational institutions receiving federal support, ranging from preschools to post-graduate institutions. Since its inception, Title IX has been responsible for increasing the percentages of women graduating from college and graduating with degrees in mathematics and sciences (USDE, 1997). However, Title IX is perhaps most widely known for the dramatic increases in participation rates among girls and women in sport in the US. For example, in 1971 there were less than 300,000 girls participating in high school sports. This increased to 2.6 million girls by 2000 (NFHS, 2001). Title IX has also been responsible for a four-fold increase in the number of sports offered at the collegiate level since 1971 (Acosta and Carpenter, 2000). Additional benefits of Title IX in the sporting realm include increased funding for female sport programs at the high school and college level, increased numbers of collegiate athletic scholarships for women, and drastic improvements in facilities and equipment used by girls and women.

While the benefits of Title IX have been obvious in the sport arena there is growing concern about the declining physical activity and physical education participation rates, especially among girls. Almost half of the young people in the US aged 12–21 years are not active on a regular basis (USDHHS, 1996). Furthermore, adolescent girls are twice as likely to be inactive compared to adolescent boys (USDHHS, 1996), and African American girls have the lowest participation rates among all groups of US adolescents (USDHHS,

2000). Add to this the fact that in physical education classes girls have fewer opportunities to respond and lower participation rates in comparison to boys (Griffin, 1984) and one begins to wonder who is benefiting from Title IX. These findings suggest that while Title IX has afforded girls and women numerous formal sporting opportunities, the same is not true regarding physical activity and physical education opportunities. This quandary has prompted many teachers and scholars to examine the differential impact of Title IX on the physical education curriculum for boys and girls.

Coeducational ('coed') physical education

Prior to the passage of Title IX, most physical education classes were sex segregated. The largest influence of Title IX has been the mandate that physical education classes, like other disciplines, be offered on a coeducational basis. There are some exceptions to mandatory coeducational classes in physical education as Title IX does not prohibit sex-segregated classes when the purpose of the activity involves bodily contact (i.e. wrestling, boxing, rugby, ice hockey, football, basketball). However in sports not involving such contact (i.e. tennis, volleyball, track and field), classes must be coeducational. Students may also be grouped according to ability for instruction if objective standards of individual performance are applied without regard to sex and do not adversely effect members of one sex. An example would be if students were divided for archery instruction by their pre-test scores. In such cases, it is possible that classes could be comprised entirely of one sex. Finally, if students' religious beliefs prohibit them from participating in coeducational physical education, they may be excused from such classes or offered sex-segregated physical education (34CFR106.34). A rationale for such legislation was that boys and girls would have equitable opportunity for instruction and practice (Griffin, 1984). However, as other chapters in this collection have also noted, scholarly analyses of typical practices acknowledge a need for more careful distinctions between access and equity. Indeed access has not ensured gender equity. While coeducational physical education was originally mandated to ameliorate the conditions and quality of physical education for girls, researchers have found differential participation patterns and percep-tions when comparing boys and girls in coeducational environments, and when comparing coed PE to single-sex PE.

In studying participation patterns of girls in a coed middle school physical education unit, Griffin (1984) found that the majority of girls exhibited one of four nonassertive behavior types: giving up, giving away, hanging back, and acquiescing. Lirgg (1993) found that in comparison to single-sex classes, coed physical education classes can benefit boys more than girls. In a study comparing both class formats, Lirgg found that boys in single-sex classes had decreased self-confidence, while boys in the coeducational classes had increased self-confidence over the course of a ten-week basketball unit. Meanwhile girls in single-sex classes showed increased confidence levels but decreased levels in the coed classes. Lirgg (1993) maintained that boys' self-confidence may be influenced by social comparison and that their comparison reference group is likely to include more lower-skilled performers in coeducational classes than in single-sex settings. However, other data indicates that we need to be cautious in making connections between these effects on self-confidence and students' grouping preferences. In a study of 466 middle school students, Treanor, Graber, Housner and Wiegand (1998) found that 60 per cent of boys and 67 per cent of girls preferred single-sex to coed physical education. Both genders perceived that they had greater practice opportunities, performed skills and team sports better, and were less fearful of getting injured in single-sex classes. In addition, boys perceived that they competed harder, learned more, and behaved better in single-sex classes. The only significant preference for coeducation classes was that girls perceived that they competed harder in coed classes. The authors did not recommend single-sexed physical education but suggested that pre-service and in-service teacher education programs must acknowledge the challenges associated with administering coeducational physical education (Treanor *et al.*, 1998).

Other researchers have engaged with these challenges and gender equity debates more broadly in relation to physical education in the US. Siedentop (2001) asserted that grouping students according to interest and ability will make lessons more profitable for students. Vertinsky (1992) argued that coeducational physical education has led to the adoption of a male model of physical education. Coed programs 'implied that male standards would be the ones to emulate, reifying the values of competitive sport and further reinforcing masculine hegemony' (Vertinsky, 1992: 378). This is similar to gender equity concerns expressed by Talbot (1993) in the British context. Nilges (2000) contends that physical education curricula structured to focus primarily on team sports are likely to promote the traditional male model of movement. Meanwhile, some researchers believe the problems in physical education go beyond the content and relate to gender biases in how we evaluate students. Along these lines, Smeal, Carpenter and Tait (1994) argue that characteristics such as power, speed, strength, competitiveness, and aggression that are typically male dominated, are overemphasized in the content of physical education.

Vertinsky (1992) maintained that the major concern for most physical education teachers is to provide equal access for girls as opposed to questioning the relevance and consequences of a male dominated curriculum for all students. Referring to Title IX, the Holmes Report, and the Women's Educational Equity Act (Lock, Minarik and Omata, 1999: 403) stated, 'noticeably absent from the language of diversity is any reference to an educational system's moral and legal obligation to provide equality of opportunity, much less the equality of outcomes'. Recently researchers have challenged educators to move beyond 'equal opportunity' and focus on the power structures of the classroom. In studying a 4th grade (for students aged

9) physical education class over a 14-week period, Nilges (1998) found the physical education environment laden with 'patriarchal ideologies and patterns of gender differentiation' (ibid.: 189). This was evident in the trivialization of the physical performances of girls, and in the 'we–they dichotomy' that depicted boys as the privileged class members. Nilges (1998) called for physical educators to challenge gender-equitable teaching beyond the liberal definition of Title IX and move towards a feminist pedagogy. In Nilges' view physical educators and teacher educators should challenge the traditional norms of feminine and masculine movements and promote an atmosphere with which students can openly explore and understand all movement patterns (Nilges, 2000).

Although substantial research regarding participation rates in different physical education settings is lacking, many physical education teachers believe that participation rates for girls are higher when classes are single sex (Griffin, 1985; Lynn, 1999). They provide various reasons for the decline in mixed settings, including suggestions that sports and games are geared more toward boys' interests since physical education became coeducational; that girls are overly concerned about how they are perceived by boys; and that the physical, mental, emotional and social challenges of puberty are too overpowering in a coeducational setting to provide an environment conducive for optimal learning (Lynn, 1999). In response to these challenges and perhaps further complicating the issue, is that many physical education teachers 'get around' the coeducation stipulation by separating boys and girls for sport or fitness activities.

It is clear that Title IX has had differential effects on the experiences, opportunities and participation rates of girls and women in sport as compared to girls and women in physical education classes. Due to the lack of research and the multiple variables involved it is difficult to ascertain reasons for the differential effects between girls' and boys' participation rates in physical education, and between girls' sport opportunities and girls' physical education opportunities. Although Title IX is the only federal policy directly addressing gender in education, there are other federal policies that potentially impact the physical education and physical activity opportunities available to girls. Some might suggest that Title IX has unintentionally reinforced dichotomous images of gender and presented a shaky foundation from which to address the diverse educational needs of both boys and girls. In considering other policy developments since Title IX, we discuss the degree to which they have better addressed these complexities and the structural dimensions of inequity.

Healthy People 2010

Healthy People 2010 is a ten-year federal public health plan that was submitted by the United States to the World Health Organization (WHO) as part of a 'Health For All' strategy. The authors of the report presented two goals for the American public: to increase the quality and years of healthy life and to eliminate health disparities 'regardless of their age, race, ethnicity, gender, sexual orientation, disability status, income, educational level or geographic location' (USDHHS, 1996: 4). One of the twenty-eight areas of the report was devoted to physical activity and physical fitness among children and adults.

With the goals of Healthy People 2010 in mind, the US has devoted much time to collecting data relating to healthy lifestyles and physical activity levels of our society, to reset standards to improve the overall health and well-being of our country. One example of a massive data collection effort is The Youth Risk Behavior Surveillance (USDHHS, 1999). It concluded that only one half of young people aged 12–21 years and about one third of high school students participated in vigorous physical activity (activity that makes you sweat and breathe hard such as running) on at least three of the seven days preceding the survey. It also reported that male students were more likely than female students to report both vigorous and moderate physical activity, to participate in strength exercises, to play on sports teams and to exercise for longer than twenty minutes in an average physical education class. Several barriers to physical activity were identified: lack of time, lack of access to convenient facilities, lack of safe environments. Despite these barriers, the present goal is to have 85 per cent of adolescents and 30 per cent of adults participate in the recommended amounts of physical activity by 2010. Specifically, the goal is to increase the proportion of adolescents who engage in vigorous physical activity that promotes cardio-respiratory fitness three or more days per week for twenty or more minutes per occasion. Specific types of physical activity and exercise that young people might participate include 'walking, bicycling, playing actively (unstructured physical activity), participating in organized sports, dancing, doing active household chores, and working at a job that has physical demands' (Center for Disease Control and Prevention (CDC), 1997: 3).

Healthy People 2010 established seven objectives for physical activity among children and adolescents, of those, three are directly related to physical education in schools:

- Increase the proportion of the nation's public and private schools that require daily physical education for all students. The goal is a 47 per cent improvement for middle and junior high schools, and a 150 per cent improvement for high schools.
- Increase the proportion of adolescents who participate in daily school physical education. The suggested improvement is from 27 per cent to 50 per cent.
- Increase the proportion of adolescents who spend at least 50 per cent of school physical education class time being physically active from 32 per cent to 50 per cent.

(USDHHS, 1996)

These recommendations indicate goals for our country, but what is not addressed is how we may accomplish these goals or where gender fits into these goals.

The Center for Disease Control and Prevention (CDC) has responded to these recommendations by outlining ten strategies to promote health through lifelong participation in enjoyable and safe physical activity and sports. These guidelines address: Policy; Environment; Physical Education Curricula and Instruction; Extracurricular Activities; Family Involvement; Training; Health Services; Community Programs; and Evaluation. A specific example of one of the above guidelines would be the efforts that are being made to encourage communities to offer activities before and after school for our youth. The Prevention Institute provided a list of guidelines to promote physical activity in schools that require daily physical education for students in grades K–12. They indicated a need to provide a diverse range of age, developmentally and culturally appropriate activities that young people can enjoy throughout their lives, such as walking, running, swimming, cycling and dancing; and provide time and space during the day for unstructured physical activity (before or after school, and during break or lunch times). In addition the institute stated that adults should emphasize activity enjoyment more than competition for youth and form partnerships with businesses, community organizations, and parks and recreation, to provide diverse and quality programs in schools and neighborhoods. Although these recommendations appear to be reaching out to the needs of a diverse population, there was an absence of any objectives directly related to gender. Once again, we find ourselves with limited information; most notably about 'how' to implement policy recommendations. There seems to be a gap in policies that presents others, be they teacher educators, state departments officials, or state and local agencies, with a key role to play in advancing gender equitable practices.

On the state level, The Prevention Institute has developed a handbook titled 'Promoting Physical Activity Among Youth: It's Everyone's Business' (2001). This document explores 'why children, who appear to be in a state of perpetual motion from the day they are born, decrease or abandon physical activity as they progress through adolescence' (The Prevention Institute, 2001: 5). In addition to leading to overweight and obesity, physical inactivity can cause high blood pressure, poor self-concept, increased anxiety, stress, and depression (CDC, 1997). Long-term consequences often include 'chronic disease and conditions such as cardiovascular disease, diabetes, and colon cancer that affect quality of life and/or cause premature death' (The Prevention Institute, 2001: 6). Again, although a variety of topics such as why children are inactive and consequences of inactivity are addressed, the notion of how to get youth to be active is neglected.

It appears that although there are not direct strategies or recommendations as to *how* to promote and provide gender equitable physical activity programs, there is encouragement. The policy recommendations from the President's Council Report emphasized the fact that girls need safe and healthy environments within physical activity and sport that support them to excel and grow (USDHHS, 1997). In addition, this document stated that 'policies need to tap the power and potential of physical activity and sport to advance girls' health, physical and emotional development, social well-being and educational aspirations and achievements. Efforts must be directed towards increasing girls' participation in physical activity and sport' (USDHHS, 1997:1). This document provided three general realms of concern: the first was related to increasing participation among girls in physical activity and sport, the second related to better utilizing physical activity and sport as vehicles to promote girls' physical and mental health; and the third area focused on enhancing the contributions of physical activity and sport to girls' educational achievements and social development. It is vital to note that these recommendations are important for both sexes and could also enrich the experiences of boys as well.

National content standards for physical education (K–12)

Unlike most countries worldwide, education in America is mostly a state, not a federal, responsibility. The effect for any subject area is that adoption of a nationally deliberated set of standards or curriculum framework is voted on by each state level board of education (sometimes in conjunction with the state legislature) and often then by each school district. Thus there is little possibility for a national curriculum that would be similar to the National Curriculum for Physical Education in England and Wales. While such a decentralized system has some advantages, a key disadvantage is the difficulty of disseminating curricular innovations in any timely manner.

In the early 1990s, the National Association for Sport and Physical Education (NASPE) published a document that defined what it means to be a physically educated person following completion of a K–12 program of physical education (NASPE, 1992). This stated that a physically educated person is someone who:

- has learned skills necessary to perform a variety of physical activities;
- is physically fit;
- does participate regularly in physical activity;
- knows the implications of and the benefits from involvement in physical activities; and
- values physical activities and their contribution to a healthy lifestyle.

In 1995 NASPE (1995a) expanded the 'outcomes project' and developed a set of national content standards for physical education. The seven content standards established what a student should know and be able to do as a result of a quality physical education program and highlighted benchmarks for each standard for kindergarten, 2nd, 4th, 6th, 8th, 10th, and 12th grades. The content standards indicated that a physically educated person:

- demonstrates competency in many movement forms and proficiency in a few forms;
- applies movement concepts and principles to the learning and development of motor skills;
- exhibits a physically active lifestyle;
- achieves and maintains a health enhancing level of physical fitness;
- demonstrates responsible personal and social behavior in physical activity settings;
- demonstrates understandings and respect for differences among people in physical activity settings;
- understands that physical activity provides opportunities for enjoyment, challenge, self-expression, and social interaction.

From an equity perspective the content standards are a significant and positive development in that they attend to several components of physical education beyond psychomotor skill development and psychomotor skill competency. Only four of the seven content standards focus on fitness and psychomotor skill development. Two standards focus on personal responsibility for, and personal benefits of, physical activity and a seventh standard focuses on students respecting others and appreciating how their preferences and needs for physical activity may differ from others. The latter three standards clearly present the opportunity to engage with gender equity issues in the physical education curriculum. We would particularly anticipate that the assessments for Standard 6 (i.e. has respect for differences among people in physical activity settings) would address gender. In tenth grade, students are expected to complete an assignment that addresses the role of women in sport. In twelfth grade they might review offensive mascots from gender, ethnicity and cultural perspectives (see table 10.1).

The assessment of content has been presented to physical education teachers as an enhancement of learning. The assessment model is formative in nature and used to support instruction of physical education and student learning for all. Theoretically this approach encourages teachers to move away from a focus on psychomotor skill development and knowledge of the rules of the game/activity to a more diverse set of assessments that allow students to demonstrate the variety of ways they can be physically educated. Yet, of the examples provided to assess student learning, only four of 106 assessment examples focus directly on gender issues and the relationships between gender and sport. Despite their potential there is little in the sample assessments presented the NASPE Task Force that encourages discussion of differential access to physical activities and how gender (or race, sexual orientation, or class) might impact upon the ways in which sport is organized, structured and controlled in the students' school and community (NASPE, 1995a).

The national standards do encourage more student choice within the physical education curriculum but actual choice is still a local issue (i.e. school

Table 10.1 Selected physical education assessments by grade and standard*

Standard	6th grade	8th grade	10th grade	12th grade
1 Competency in many and proficiency in few movement forms	Design performance Routine	AAHPERD skill test	Skills test (Red Cross level 4)	Portfolio on three areas of personal skill competence
2 Applies concepts and principles to learning motor skill	Analyze HRF of physical activity	Develop training plan for a sport of interest	Self analysis of skill from video	Select PA for post graduation and res. Psychological factors of PA
3 Physically active lifestyle	Survey school and community physical activities	Join in a physical activity and journal the experience	*Survey community physical activity opportunities and develop plan to increase accessibility*	*Interviews of men/women in different age groups. *Engagement in PA (age/gender effects)*
4 Achieves and maintains health fitness levels	Log PA across weeks Design fitness plan	Record HR in different PAs and write of physiological responses	Assess fitness and plan program	Predict PA 10 years out and barriers to engagement Assess fitness levels
5 Demonstrate personal and social behavior in PA	Design a game with others	Reflect on engagement in PA and comment to improve for all	*Discuss influences on achieving personal PA goals*	Observe a peer mediation and comment on it
6 Has respect for differences among people in PA settings	Participate in a game with a 'disability', e.g. blindfolded	*Observe class for exclusionary behavior and suggest ways to improve*	*Role of women in sport*	*Factors that impact PA engagement across the life-span (gender, age, class)* *Review offensive mascots (gender, ethnicity, culture)*

Table 10.1 (continued)

Standard	6th grade	8th grade	10th grade	12th grade
7 Understands PA provides oppor- tunities for enjoyment, challenge, self- expression	Feelings from adventure education experience	*Positive and negative feelings from sport involvement*	Write a dialogue to get a friend active Journal feelings on physical activity plan	Design camp experience for urban children

Source: Adapted from NASPE (1995a). *Moving into the Future: National Physical Education, Standards*. New York: Mosby.

Note The italicized assessments by standard and grade level indicate assessments that have direct or indirect potential to focus students' attention on the role of gender in developing and sustaining a physically active lifestyle.

by school more than state by state). Once again we see that policy guidance can be interpreted in several ways. Physical education is still required of students in most elementary and middle school and for two of eight semesters in high school. However, requirements and provision vary greatly nationwide and with curriculum overload there are fewer students opting for elective physical education if offered this beyond the 10th grade.

Curricular initiatives in physical education

There is a predominantly sport/games oriented curriculum in American middle and high school levels (Lawson, 1998). At the elementary grades physical education is focused on developing fundamental motor skills and movement, with some concern for a developmental approach to movement tasks and the integration of physical education with other content areas. In recent years there has been a growing interest in fitness and wellness programs with a move away from team sports especially at the high school level. Most physical education programs reflect a multi-activity program focus especially at the middle and secondary school. There is also some evidence that teachers are beginning to narrow their focus rather than trying to be all things to all students with limited time allocation. The major curricular initiatives that have gained the attention of physical education teachers in recent years are sport education (Siedentop, 1994 and below), teaching for responsibility (Hellison, 1995), and Fitness for Life curriculum (Corbin and Lindsey, 1997). Corbin's curriculum is quite prescriptive on content coverage while Hellison's model is prescriptive in terms of instructional goals and processes. Adventure education has also attracted attention, particularly in its focus upon conflict resolution and social skills content (Siedentop and Tannehill, 2000). Unlike in Britain (in examination program contexts) and in Australia and New Zealand, there has been little attention given to physical education as a 'content space' to study the theoretical aspects of physical education. The cultural studies approach (Kinchin and O'Sullivan, 1999) is one effort to develop students as literate and critical consumers of sport and has borrowed and adapted curricular ideas for classroom physical education in Australia and England for the American high school.

Focus on health-related physical activity: CATCH, SPARK and Fitness for Life

There are two nationally recognized school-based curricula found to be effective with regards to promoting physical activity: the *Child and Adolescent Trial For Cardiovascular Health* (*CATCH*) and *Sports, Play, and Active Recreation for Kids* (*SPARK*). CATCH was the first school-based multicenter randomized trial ever conducted, and was a national trial to educate elementary school children to develop healthy habits to prevent heart disease. The study involved more than 5000 ethnically diverse students in grades 3–8 from nearly 100 schools across four states. The goal of the study was to determine if health promotion efforts targeting the school environment and children's behaviors would reduce cardiovascular disease risk factors later in life. Significant increases in out-of-school moderate–vigorous physical activity were found and a three-year follow-up study indicated that students who participated in CATCH continued to pursue more vigorous physical activity levels than students in control groups. The data from CATCH were dis-aggregated by gender and it was found that boys were more active than girls. CATCH has since been replicated in other communities throughout the United States as a model of a comprehensive school-based approach to increasing physical activity. SPARK is an elementary (K–6) physical education curriculum and staff development program that offers materials and services to 'schools, university grants, recreation departments, after-school programs, hospital community outreach and health organizations on a non-profit basis, through San Diego State University Foundation' (The Prevention Institute, 2001: 16). Positive program effects have been found on variables such as physical activity, lesson context, teacher behavior, motor skill development, and long-term effects. SPARK indicated that trained classroom teachers improved children's physical activity levels compared to untrained teachers, but that physical education specialists produced even greater results (Sallis and Owen, 1999). The results of SPARK were also dis-aggregated by gender, but no suggestions were made as to how to address these gender differences.

At the secondary level Corbin's Fitness for Life curriculum focuses on important national health objectives from Healthy People 2000 and teaches students concepts of personal health and fitness. The purpose of the Fitness for Life program is to assist students in achieving three objectives: acquire knowledge about the benefits of physical activity, health and wellness and about the principles of fitness; become physically active while pursuing goals to become physically fit; and become an independent decision maker who can plan his or her own personal fitness program (Corbin and Lindsey, 1997). The program focuses on different aspects of health and fitness including: cardio-vascular fitness, strength, muscular endurance, flexibility, fat control and health-related/skill-related fitness. Although we did not read about any particular discussion on gender, gender concerns or gender differences in the Fitness for Life material, we did notice the following: there were pictures of both boys and girls throughout the sources, and there were occasional references to both girls and boys such as 'to better him or herself' but no explicit effort to discuss differential access to physical activity for girls was presented.

After reviewing health-related materials such as: CATCH, SPARK and Fitness for Life; and after reflecting back on statistics regarding the activity levels of boys versus the activity levels of girls, it is evident that our country has dis-aggregated data on boys and girls. However, there appears to be an aspect that is missing: what can we do to meet the varying needs of boys and girls to promote physical activity?

Trial of Activity for Adolescent Girls (TAAG)

As a consequence of the differential effects of physical activity programs on boys and girls, a multi-center study called a *Trial of Activity for Adolescent Girls (TAAG)* has begun in six centers around the country. These centers are responsible for designing, implementing, and monitoring a comprehensive, school-based, community-linked intervention to promote physical activity and physical fitness among middle-school girls. This is a six-year study with a 30 million dollar budget from the National Institute of Health (NIH) supporting six multi-trial sites with a goal of better understanding of how to prevent declines in physical activity levels among adolescent girls. The good news about this nationally funded project is that it is one of the few to focus directly on girls' physical activity levels. The intent is to design integrated in-school and after-school programs that are meaningful to young females lives. The sad news is that only a single pedagogy scholar is involved on the six research teams that will be studying these issues. There is not space in this chapter to discuss the politics of physical activity funding in the United States but we would argue that the absence of sport pedagogy faculty in these curricular innovations should be of serious concern to all interested in physical education experiences in schools for girls.

Restructuring games teaching in physical education: sport education

In the mid-1980s Daryl Siedentop introduced the sport education curriculum model in the United States. This model evolved from Siedentop's 'play education' theory which was premised on the notion that play, in the physical education sense, is 'central to a full and meaningful existence' (Siedentop, 1980: 266). Siedentop believed that by incorporating the most attractive features of institutionalized sport to a physical education context students would be more enthused about the subject matter, take greater ownership in their efforts and experiences and become well-rounded sports people.

The three main goals of sport education are to develop students who are competent, literate, and enthusiastic sports persons (Siedentop, 1995). These goals are achieved through incorporating characteristics traditionally associated with sport into the physical education context. For instance, rather than dividing the physical education curriculum into units, activities are presented within seasons, comparable to that of institutionalized sport. Seasons last longer than typical units, thereby providing students with a greater depth of experience within the sport and ultimately enhancing students' competence in the sport. Students are affiliated with teams and maintain their team membership throughout the season, thus promoting enthusiasm and teamwork among students. In addition to being affiliated with a team, each student has a role on the team (such as captain, referee, statistician, trainer). Team roles are intended to promote individual responsibility and engage students in all aspects of the sport. Teams are designed as equitably as possible to foster close competitions. Similar to traditional sporting settings, formal competitions take the form of dual competitions, round-robin tournaments, etc. Each season ends with a culminating event in which a championship team is determined. Finally, records specific to the sport are kept throughout the season and maintained over the years.

Siedentop (2001) contends that good competition engages students and is educationally useful. He maintains that sport education differs from institutionalized sport in three distinct ways. First, all students are involved in the planning, participation, and competition at all times. Second, games are modified to allow for developmentally appropriate competition. Finally, in addition to being performers, students have a wide variety of roles such as referees, record keepers, trainers, coaches, and managers. While the sport education model has an inherent competitive focus, if implemented properly it should promote cooperation; as team success is dependent upon maximizing the contribution of all team members. For example, it would behove the higher skilled students to assist and support their lower skilled teammates. A key issue here is the teachers' ability to provide such contingencies and to support captains and student leaders in their efforts to provide meaningful and plentiful opportunities for all students (D. Siedentop, personal communication, April 27, 2001).

While Siedentop (1995) maintains that long-term purpose of sport education is for sport involvement to benefit all participants regardless of gender, race, disability, or socioeconomic status, most of the research and literature on the sport education curriculum model does not address gender equity or girls' participation rates. Furthermore, traditionally male dominated sports are typically cited in the limited research examining sport education programs. The value of the sport education model as a means of promoting participation for all students needs further study. This is particularly important in light of research indicating that a major reason why girls opt not to participate in physical education is due to the excessively competitive environment (Browne, 1992; Carlson, 1995).

To date, few studies have compared the impact of the sport education model on both genders. Hastie (1998) examined the participation patterns and perceptions of middle school students participating in a twenty-lesson floor hockey season utilizing a sport education model. Results showed that boys had significantly more responses per minute and higher success levels than girls during the formal competition phase. No differences were found in participation patterns during the skill practice sessions or in the early season scrimmages. Girls preferred the sport education unit to previous experiences in physical education, indicating that it allowed them more opportunities to play. Girls preferred playing on mixed-sex teams rather than single-sex teams, with many indicating that they played harder on the mixed-sex teams. The finding that girls perceived they played harder on coed teams is consistent with Treanor *et al.* (1998).

In Hastie's (2000) study, positions of leadership (captains and referees) were overwhelmingly held by boys. Girls often commented that the boys were bossy and tended to dominate team decisions. These results suggest that the sport education model may not provide similar benefits to all participants. In particular, while girls enjoyed this experience more so that non-sport education experiences, they still had less opportunity to respond in a competitive setting or to engage in leadership roles when compared to boys, irrespective of skill level. Hastie (2000) suggests some problems with implementing the sport education model relate to the level of expertise of captains and student leaders. For instance, captains may be highly skilled players, however they may not have the skills to provide quality practices for all skill levels. Furthermore, it seems that practices are geared toward the higher skilled students. It would appear that girls might be at greater risk of not receiving beneficial practice opportunities. These research findings suggest that greater teacher involvement is needed in choosing leaders and in guiding leaders in their quest to administer effective practices.

The findings that were most encouraging from Hastie's (2000) study are that girls enjoyed their experiences more and perceived that they tried harder on coed teams as compared to single-sex teams. Yet, having studied a teacher implementing sport education for the first time Curnow and Macdonald (1995) questioned whether sport education could be inclusive of girls. It is clear that more research needs to be done to determine if the sport education is effective in promoting meaningful and active experiences for all girls. Some questions to consider in such inquiry are:

- How are teams chosen to ensure proper representation of both genders and all skill levels?

- How are captains and other student leaders chosen? And how do the genders of the captains or other leaders impact the experiences of all team members?
- How are games modified to promote active and meaningful participation among all team members regardless of skill level or gender?
- How does the type of sport impact upon the experiences of all students?
- What role should the teacher play in ensuring active and meaningful participation among all students?

A cultural studies approach to physical education

Physical education curricula that encourage students to question taken-for-granted assumptions about sport and physical education in today's society have received significant attention internationally (Kirk *et al.*, 1998; Kirk and Tinning, 1990; Macdonald and Tinning, 1995), but comparatively little attention in the United States (Kinchin and O'Sullivan, 1999; O'Sullivan *et al.*, 1996). Yet such curricula offer a potentially exciting complement to the practice of physical education in American high schools and furthermore, enhanced potential for addressing gender equity within and beyond physical education. Sport and physical activity play a central role in adolescents' lives (more boys than girls), yet all too many students (more girls than boys) are disenfranchised from the joys and benefits of physical activity. The cultural studies (CS) approach to high school physical education has been an attempt to help students appreciate and critique the role of physical activity and sport in their school, their community, and their own lives. The curriculum attempts to make meaningful connections between physical education in school and sport and physical activity, or lack thereof, in students' lives, and encourages intellectual engagement with what physical activity and sport experiences mean to young people. Time is allocated for discussions on the role and meanings of sport and physical activity in students' lives and in the wider community. Two key goals of the model are to assist students to develop as literate and critical sports persons who are cognizant of the 'structural and social inequities in their local, regional, and national sport culture' (Siedentop, 1994: 23).

Addressing issues of gender

Classroom experiences are designed to help students discuss factors that support or inhibit their own and others' opportunities for physical activity and sport. Gender equity in sport is one of several themes addressed in the curriculum. The historical and geographical roots of a sport are presented and students have opportunities to consider the role of sport (e.g. volleyball) in their lives and those of their family and friends. A key goal is the development of students as critical consumers. Students research the possibilities for sport and physical activity in their school and community and consider factors that influence access and interest in sport for themselves, their friends, and neighbors. Journal writing, student presentations and discussions are used to explore the role of gender, media, and body image in sport and society in relation to these issues. This approach to physical education has been tried in a number of urban high schools in Ohio (O'Sullivan *et al.*, 1996), with teachers and university staff working collaboratively to design the cultural studies curriculum. Following two pilot studies and subsequent revisions to the curriculum, we studied the curriculum and 9th and 10th grade students' reactions to it at a third high school.

Students were very positive about lessons on sport and the media, sport and gender, and gender and body image and they enjoyed the opportunities to debate and critique contemporary sports issues (Kinchin, 1997). One class session on body image began with students responding to a picture of a female beach volleyball player and a five-minute video segment of men's beach volleyball. Several students contributed to a lively and lengthy debate on the issue of clothing in sport. The following fieldnote provides an example of the issues that such activities can provoke among students:

> 'What do you notice about the picture and video you have just seen?' says the teacher.
> 'The guys have tank-tops on' says Ray.
> 'The women have sport bras' adds Donnelle.
> 'They [women] need to get their shorts on' says Myshona.
> Tim says, 'Nobody would watch if they did not wear skimpy stuff' . . .
> 'Are you saying that women have to take their clothes off for us to watch?' asks Genevieve.
> 'No that is not what I am saying' replies Tim. . . .
> 'What does this say about our society?' asks the teacher.
> 'Athletes knew when they decided to become pro-beach volleyball players that they would wear this stuff,' says Jae.
> Tim adds, 'It is not them that is making that choice, the endorsers may make those and determine what they wear.'
> 'Society views women as sex objects' Donnelle says.
>
> (Fieldnote, 9th grade lesson #9)

Other students spoke favorably of a lesson in which they investigated sport coverage in a local newspaper. Each student recorded the coverage of different sports, the types of advertisement, and differences amongst pictures of athletes in terms of race and gender. The teacher began the lesson distributing a journal page with an advertisement from a local university and community newspaper. The advertisement asked for male basketball players with prior high school varsity experiences to practice with a Women's Division 1 collegiate program. The advertisement was deemed sexist and discriminatory by some of the female students. Michelle referred to a heated discussion that took place with Jason during the class, on the issue of skill differences among men and women. She noted 'me and Jason got into it and he got into it with somebody else . . . that made us better people though' (Int. #3).

The unit also enabled students to make meaningful connections with each other. A highly skilled student, who initially was reluctant to help peers during practice sessions and was intent on winning volleyball games, learned to be more helpful to his classmates as the unit progressed. A low skilled female student wrote about the experience:

> I think I have learned something new about people. I mean that you can go up to a person and tell them that you are doing this wrong but you are doing a good job . . . you know just make it clear to them. I have a lot of people on my team who care about me . . . and you know I care about them. I have learned that people really do care about you.
>
> (Jnl. #15)

Addressing the interests of all students

While some students did not appreciate time taken from physical activity for discussions on sport, others favored this approach. The mixed reactions can be seen as reflecting the diversity of students in the two classes studied. A curricular approach that takes time from physical activity is problematic for many teachers given the continuing demise of mandated time for physical education in public high schools in the United States, and clearly, these are international concerns. However, given the central role that sport plays in our society, we need to provide opportunities to engage students not just in activity but as critical consumers of physical activity and sporting practices in their schools and communities. From this perspective the cultural studies approach was of particular interest to girls and to low skilled boys, and deserves further examination by teachers and by teacher educators who prepare teachers to teach a physical education for a contemporary time.

A more positive future?

Despite the dismal statistics regarding physical education and physical activity there is optimism in the United States with the approval of the Physical Education for Progress (PEP) Act on December 15, 2000 by the US Congress. This bill is a piece of legislation introduced by Senator Ted Stevens (Republican Senator from Alaska) that authorizes 400 million dollars to be spent over the next five years, with 5 million dollars being appropriated for the 2001 fiscal year. This program authorizes the Secretary of Education to award grants to help initiate, expand and improve physical education programs for grades kindergarten through to 12. Funds may be used for equipment

Table 10.2 National standards for beginning and experienced physical education teachers

Beginning teacher standards	National Board for Professional Teaching Standards
1 Content knowledge	Knowledge of subject matter
2 Growth and development	Knowledge of students
3 Diverse learners	Equity, fairness, and diversity
4 Management and motivation	Curricular choices
5 Communication	High expectations for learners
6 Planning and instruction	Sound teaching practice
7 Learner assessment	Assessment
8 Reflection	Reflective practice and professional growth
9 Collaboration	Collaboration with colleagues
	Family and community partnerships
	Learning environment
	Promoting an active lifestyle
	Engagement

Source: Adapted from NASPE (1995b) and NBPTS (1999).

purchases, to develop curriculum, hire and train physical education staff, and support other initiatives designed to help students participate in physical education activities. In addition, this legislation will require schools to provide 150 minutes of physical education by trained physical education teachers (NASPE, 2001). At the time of writing a section of the Elementary and Secondary School Act had been repealed by President Bush that includes the funding for the PEP Act. Passage of federal legislation could be a significant catalyst to focus attention and support on school physical education and appropriate distribution of the funding might encourage and support quality programs for children and youth. Increasing efforts to link federal spending on education to stricter accountability for students and teachers has been reflected in recent policy initiatives by the American Alliance for Health, Physical Education, Recreation and Dance.

Performance standards for novices and accomplished teachers

In the early 1990s NASPE established a task force of seven teacher educators to develop a set of standards for what beginning teachers should know and be able to do. The nine standards (see table 10.2) that were established represent teachers as 'reflective, inquiry oriented, professionals who are cognizant of equity and diversity issues, competent in their subject matter, and able to select instructional strategies best suited to the varying needs of their students' (NASPE, 1995b: 4). Each standard addresses what are considered central and specific dispositions, knowledge, and performance for beginning physical education teachers. They were designed with input from teachers and aligned with the content standards developed earlier for K–12 physical education curricula.

The standards represent what the profession believes is important for beginning teachers to know and learn. The task force argued that 'standards for beginning physical education teachers be congruent with those of teachers in other subjects' (NASPE, 1995b: 2) and so modeled the standards on the work of the Interstate New Teacher Assessment and Support Consortium (INTASC) (a collaboration of key stakeholders in teacher education).

One of the nine standards focuses specifically on diversity and how a beginning teacher must 'understand how individuals learn and develop, and can provide opportunities that support their physical, cognitive, and emotional development' (ibid.: 10). A number of the other standards address the importance of attending to all students' needs more indirectly (see standards 2, 4, 5, and 8 in particular). We found it quite interesting that in a thorough analysis of the document, gender equity was *never* mentioned. Indeed only one standard (Communication) suggests that the teacher be knowledgeable and communicate in ways that demonstrate sensitivity to gender. We would contend that much more direct, explicit, and frequent statements about gender equity in the curriculum, instruction, and assessment of physical education programs are critical if we are to design teacher education programs that prepare teachers to physically educate *all* students.

The National Board for Professional Teaching Standards does a somewhat better job of directly addressing gender equity (NBPTS, 1999). The standard on equity, fairness, and diversity indicates that accomplished physical education teachers must strive 'to eliminate gender-specific units or activities' (ibid.: 28) and teach content that transcend stereotypes with males teaching dance and females teaching wrestling units. Clearly there is much still to be done, as it is a long way from policy documents to the implementation of gender equity curriculum and instructional practices in US physical education programs. Encouragingly, there is a growing trend in larger high schools that support several physical education teachers to provide curricular choice within the program (Durante, 1997). In some cases, this allows girls to pursue activities that are of more interest and relevance to them. Student choice within units of work offer students options of cooperative and competitive practices, provide for greater student ownership of learning experiences and enable students to pursue various roles in physical education and sport settings. Instructional models such as Sport Education are making their way into physical education programs nationally as a consequence of better teacher preparation programs and in our view have the potential to provide more relevant and enjoyable physical activity experiences for all students, especially girls and less skilled boys. However, we are also aware that there are many programs that are overly teacher centered, lack student choice, and pay little attention to the needs/interests of students.

Where to go from here?

Policy perspectives

In the United States we have witnessed a tremendous amount of national attention on public health policy. We have gathered data to evaluate the health, fitness and physical activity levels of young and old alike, such as The Youth Risk Behavior Survey (YRBS). Federal agencies such as the National Institute for Health have supported clinical trials of in-school activity programs such as CATCH and SPARK. The data on the effectiveness of these programs when dis-aggregated by gender indicate that boys are more active than girls and in particular, African-American adolescent females are the least active of youth (CDC, 1997). Although our physical educators are being trained based on a set of national standards, it appears that a significant number of physical educators in our country are not familiar with the policy initiatives of our country. In addition, if we examine these policy documents closely, we observe an almost universal silence of gender, with the exception of the TAAG grant. There is a silence with regards to how to appropriately address the disparities that exist between genders within physical activity and physical education. We have had much policy in the United States, but what we are realizing is that policy is not driven by research. It is instead, driven by power. One of the two goals of Healthy People 2010 focuses on eliminating health disparities 'regardless of their age, race, ethnicity, gender, sexual orientation, disability status, income, educational level or geographic location' (USDHHS, 1996: 4). What is evident is that there have been great efforts to examine the activity levels of the American youth, but there continues to be a shortage of materials and policies that surround the specifics of this goal which address age, race, ethnicity, gender and sexual orientation, disability status, income, educational level or geographic location. In order for notice-able changes to be made regarding the activity levels of our youth, we need to begin to address boys and girls differently and meet their specific needs and not conglomerate our goals and methods into a patriarchal realm. With the great advances our society has made in developing programs and methods of collecting data, there is optimism that we can now incorporate this informa-tion into a game plan that will ensure success for all.

Instructional perspectives

Echoing the comments made by Penney in chapter 7, we conclude that the gender inequities in school physical education in the USA have as much to do with silences in state and national policy documents as with attitudes and practices of physical education teachers and teacher education training programs. There are still too many stereotypical unreconstructed PE programs. Perhaps one of the most significant differences between US and

Britain is that physical education programs in the USA are for the most part not sex differentiated. However, we still have a long way to go to convince some conservative physical educators of the value of alternative teaching strategies and curricular initiatives. In a recent opinion piece in the *Journal of Physical Education, Recreation and Dance* on the place of dodgeball[2] in physical education, the author noted that 'In this time of political correctness, adventure education, and cooperative games, dodgeball stands tall among them all' (Swartz, 2001: 55).

There have been some significant and meaningful efforts at gender equity in physical education in the United States when compared to some of the accounts presented in other chapters in this collection. There are now far fewer single-sexed classes, with more physical education classes being taught as legitimate co-educational classes than are not. While this is not in and of itself any guarantee of greater equity we do feel that significant and substantive progress has been made. Student choice in clothing for physical education is also commonplace and much less an issue than it seems to be in England. When uniforms are used teachers include policies that recognize various body types and gender. The physical education policies are likely to allow shorts and sweat pants while covering one's hair is a typical adjustment to religious customs. Showering is for the most part a non-issue in American physical education programs as physical education teachers no longer require that students shower following classes. Some critics might suggest that students don't work hard enough in PE to need a shower and the expectation was a moot one from a health and safety perspective. Many more teachers now group students on ability and not gender. While this too is problematic, it has focused teachers' attention on designing tasks that allow all to be successful. There has been a curricular shift from a dominance on psycho-motor skill development to other orientations that teachers, parents, and students value: taking responsibility for their learning, contributing to the sport in ways other than elite performance, and social interaction and peer support in physical activity settings (Ennis and Chen, 1993).

Federal rules and school policies have also established an agenda of social inclusion and equity in schools. In some instances physical education is one of the front line subjects in the implementation of this policy for children and youth with special needs. Most physical education teachers and teacher education programs have taken this task seriously. There are several studies that have looked at students' perceptions of inclusive classrooms from the perspectives of children with and without special needs (Murata *et al.*, 2000; Slininger *et al.*, 2000; Webb, 2000). The focus on teacher certification in adapted physical education may be a model for many other parts of the world.

While wanting to celebrate progress we are also aware of what is yet to be done and the areas of neglect in developments to date. We have not paid the same kind of attention to the inclusion of the physical cultures of the many different ethnic groups that populate our schools. There is a silence in our pedagogical research on these issues. Indeed there is much to be learned on this issue by American pedagogy scholars from a number of chapters in this book. We have a long way to go before we can refute the concern expressed by Penney (chapter 7 in this text) that all too often boys and girls will leave schools with their conceptions of femininity and masculinity and applications in contexts of physical activity and sport essentially intact and unchallenged.

Curricular perspectives

Recently there has been a concerted effort to respond to the needs and desires of all students through development and diversification of curricular perspectives in physical education. This is especially true for fitness activity models (TAAG, SPARK, CATCH). The cultural studies approach and recent adventure education/outdoor education initiatives appear promising in the quest to provide beneficial, meaningful and substantial opportunities for girls. The Sport Education model may have been founded on participation for all principles, but participation is not an automatic outcome of the model. Providing meaningful and plentiful opportunities for all is dependent upon teachers' cognizance of and ability to promote an appropriate environment for all to respond and achieve. Before implementing a curriculum, teachers must critically examine the impact such a curriculum is likely to have on all students, and then adapt as necessary to benefit all students in their classes. This may entail paying particular attention to girls and/or lower skilled students. Additionally, teachers need to extend the sporting and game opportunities beyond the traditionally male dominated sports; as gender and skill differences are diminished with novel sports and games. Some teachers have experimented with adopting the sport education model in a dance curriculum (Graves and Townsend, 2000). We need more teachers to not only experiment with different curricular models, but to also research the processes and outcomes associated with such initiatives.

Many students in the US have similar perceptions regarding physical education to those in England (Williams and Bedward, 2001, chapter 9). More girls than boys view themselves as marginalized in PE and girls seem to have fewer opportunities to participate in school sports (though their access to interscholastic activities seem to be significantly better than in Britain). However, moving forward on a gender equity agenda must not be done in isolation. The role of class, race and sexual orientation must be part of the conversations that shape new policies and practices to allow all boys and girls to gain the benefits of involvement in physical activity and sport in ways that are meaningful and relevant to their lives. We have much to learn from each other as we attempt to highlight and inform these agendas for physical education in our respective countries.

Notes

1 K–12 represents children aged 5–19 years.
2 Dodgeball is an elimination game (there are a variety of ways to play) where students are divided into teams. The objective of the game is to get points for your team. Points are accumulated by hitting players on the opposing team by kicking or throwing a ball at them. Most rules specify that hitting above the waist is a rule violation. See the issue section of *JOPERD* (April, 2001) for a discussion on the place for the game in PE. What has been amazing to watch in recent months is the interest of the media (with national editorials) on this game as an educational experience in contrast to what has been hyped as the New PE (student-centered, less sport-oriented, physical education programming).

References

Acosta, R.V. and Carpenter, L.J. (2000) Women in intercollegiate sport: A longitudinal study – twenty-three year update (1977–2000), unpublished manuscript, Brooklyn College, Brooklyn, NY.

Browne, J. (1992) Reasons for the selection or nonselection of physical education studies by year 12 girls, *Journal of Teaching in Physical Education* 11: 402–10.

Canadian Association for Health, Physical Education, Recreation and Dance (1995) *Gender Equity Through Physical Education and Sport*, Reston, VA: CAHPERD.

Carlson, T.B. (1995) We hate gym: student alienation from physical education, *Journal of Teaching in Physical Education* 14: 467–77.

Center for Disease Control and Prevention (CDC) (1997) *Guidelines for School and Community Programs to Promote Lifelong Physical Activity Among Young People, 1997*, 46, pp. 1–36.

Center for Disease Control and Prevention (CDC) (2000) Youth risk behavior surveillance: United States, 1999, *Morbidity and Mortality Weekly Report*, 49, SS–5.

34CFR106.34 (1999) Code of Federal Regulations. Title 34, Volume 1, Parts 1 to 299. Revised as of July 1, 1999 From the US Government Printing Office via GPO Access.

Chepyator-Thomson, J.R. and Ennis, C. (1997) Reproduction and resistance to the culture of femininity and masculinity in secondary school physical education, *Research Quarterly for Exercise and Sport* 68: 89–99.

Corbin, C.D. and Lindsey, R. (1997) *Fitness for Life*, Glenview, IL: Scott Foresman-Addison Wesley.

Curnow, J. and Macdonald, D. (1995) Can sport education be gender inclusive?: A case study in an upper primary school, *The ACHPER Healthy Lifestyles Journal* 42(4): 9–11.

Durante, F. (1997) Let your students choose! The PCAB method, *Runner Journal* 35: 3.

Ennis, C.D. and Chen, C. (1993). Domain specifications and content representativeness of the revised Value Orientation Inventory, *Research Quarterly for Exercise and Sport* 64: 436–46.

Graves, M.A. and Townsend, J.S. (2000). Applying the sport education curriculum model to dance, *The Journal of Physical Education, Recreation and Dance* 71(8): 50–4.

Griffin, L. (1984) Girls' participation patterns in a middle school team sports unit, *Journal of Teaching in Physical Education* 4: 30–8.

Griffin, P. (1985) Boys' participation styles in a middle school physical education team sports unit, *Journal of Teaching in Physical Education* 4(2): 100–10.

Hastie, P.A. (1998) The participation and perceptions of girls within a unit of sport education, *Journal of Teaching in Physical Education* 17(2): 157–71.

Hastie, P. (2000) An ecological analysis of a sport education season, *Journal of Teaching in Physical Education* 19(3): 355–73.

Hellison, D. (1995) *Teaching Responsibility Through Physical Activity*, Champaign, IL: Human Kinetics.

Henry, F.M. (1964) Physical education: an academic discipline, *Journal of Health, Physical Education and Recreation* 35: 32, 33, 69.

Kinchin, G.D. (1997) High school students' perceptions of and responses to curriculum change in physical education, unpublished doctoral dissertation, The Ohio State University.

Kinchin, G. and O'Sullivan, M. (1999) Making physical education meaningful for high school students, *Journal of Physical Education, Recreation and Dance* 70(5): 40–4, 54.

Kirk, D. (2001) Physical education: a gendered history, in D. Penney (ed.) *Gender and Physical Education: Contemporary Issues and Future Directions*, London: Routledge.

Kirk, D. and Tinning, R. (1990) *Physical Education, Curriculum and Culture: Critical Issues in Contemporary Crisis*, London: Falmer Press.

Kirk, D., Burgess-Limerick, R., Kiss, M., Lahey, J. and Penney, D. (1998) *Senior Physical Education: An Integrated Approach*, Champaign, IL: Human Kinetics.

Lawson, H. (1998) Rejuvenating, and transforming physical education to meet the needs of vulnerable children, youth, and families, *Journal of Teaching in Physical Education* 18: 2–25.

Lirgg, D.D. (1993) Effects of same-sex versus coeducational physical education on the self-perceptions of middle and high school students, *Research Quarterly for Exercise and Sport* 64(3): 324–34.

Lock, R.S., Minarik, L.T. and Omata, J. (1999) Gender and the problem of diversity: Action research in physical education, *Quest* 51: 393–407.

Lynn, S. (1999) *Should Physical Education Classes Return to Teaching Males and Females Separately?*, retrieved March 20, 2001 from the World Wide Web: http://mailer.fsu.edu/~slynn/issues1999.html

Macdonald, D. and Tinning, R. (1995) Physical education teacher education and the trend to proletarianization: a case study, *Journal of Teaching in Physical Education* 15(1): 98–118.

Murata, N.M., Hodge, S.R. and Little, J.R. (2000) Students' attitudes, experiences, and perspectives on their peers with disabilities, *Clinical Kinesiology* 54(3): 59–66.

National Association for Sport and Physical Education (NASPE) (1992) *Outcomes of Quality Physical Education Programs*, Reston, VA: NASPE.

National Association for Sport and Physical Education (NASPE) (1995a) *Moving into the Future. National Physical Education Standards: A Guide to Content and Assessment*, New York: Mosby.

National Association for Sport and Physical Education (NASPE) (1995b) *National Standards for Beginning Physical Education Teachers*. Reston, VA: NASPE.

National Association for Sport and Physical Education (NASPE) (2001) *Physical Education for Progress Bill Update*, retrieved May 4, 2001, from the World Wide Web: http://www.aahperd.org/naspe/whatsnew-pep.html

National Board for Professional Teaching Standards (NBPTS) (1999) *Physical Education Standards*, Arlington, VA: NBPTS.

National Federation of High Schools (NFHS) (2001) *National Federation of State High School Associations 1999–2000 Athletic Participation Summary*, retrieved March 20, 2001 from the World Wide Web: http://www.nfhs.org/part_survey99-00.htm

Nilges, L.M. (1998) I thought only fairy tales had supernatural power: a radical feminist analysis of Title IX in physical education, *Journal of Teaching in Physical Education* 17(2): 172–94.

Nilges, L.M. (2000) A nonverbal discourse analysis of gender in undergraduate educational gymnastics sequences using Laban effort analysis, *Journal of Teaching in Physical Education* 19(3): 287–310.

O'Sullivan, M., Kinchin, G., Dunaway, S., Kellum, S. and Dixon, S. (1996) High School physical education comes alive at your school: a unit on the culture of sport for your students, presented at *AAHPERD National Convention*, Atlanta, GA.

Sallis, J.F. and Owen, N. (1999) *Physical Activity and Behavioral Medicine*, Thousand Oaks, CA: Sage.

Siedentop, D. (1980) *Physical Education: Introductory Analysis*, Dubuque, IA: Wm. C. Brown.

Siedentop, D. (1994) *Sport Education: Quality PE Through Positive Sport Experiences*, Champaign, IL: Human Kinetics.

Siedentop, D. (1995) Improving sport education, *The ACHPER Healthy Lifestyles Journal* 42(4): 22–4.

Siedentop, D. (2001) *Introduction to Physical Education, Sport and Fitness* (4th edition), Mountain View, CA: Mayfield Publishing.

Siedentop, D. and Tannehill, D. (2000) *Developing Teaching Skills in Physical Education* (4th edition), Mountain View, CA: Mayfield Publishing.

Slininger, D., Sherrill C. and Jankowski, C.M. (2000) Children's attitudes toward classmates with severe disabilities: Revisiting contact theory, *Adapted Physical Activity Quarterly* 17: 176–96.

Slobogir, K. (2001) *New Physical Education Favors Fitness Over Sports*, retrieved May 18, 2001, from the World Wide Web: http://fyi.cnn.com/2001/fyi/teachers.ednews/o5/17/new.pe/index.html

Smeal, B., Carpetner, B. and Tait, G. (1994) Ideals and realities: articulating feminist perspectives in physical education, *Quest* 46: 410–24.

Swartz, M.J. (2001) Issues, *Journal of Physical Education, Recreation and Dance* 72(4): 54.

Talbot, M. (1993) Gender and physical education, in J. Evans (ed.) *Equality, Education and Physical Education*, London: Falmer Press.

The Prevention Institute (2001) *Promoting Physical Activity Among Youth: It's Everyone's Business*, Columbus, OH.

20 U.S.C. §1681a (1988) *Title IX, Education Amendments of 1972*, Public Law 92–318, 1972.

Treanor, L., Graber, K., Housner, L. and Wiegand, R. (1998) Middle school students' perceptions of coeducational and same-sex physical education classes, *Journal of Teaching in Physical Education* 18(1): 43–56.

US Department of Education (USDE) (1997) *Title IX: 25 Years of Progress*, Washington, DC.

US Department of Health and Human Services (USDHHS) (1996) *Physical Activity and Health: A Report of the Surgeon General*, Atlanta, GA: US Department of Health and Human Services, Centers for Disease Control and Prevention, National Center for Chronic Disease Prevention and Health Promotion.

US Department of Health and Human Services (USDHHS) (1997) President's Council on Physical Fitness and Sports Report *Physical Activity and Sport in the Lives of Girls: Physical and Mental Dimensions from an Interdisciplinary Approach*, Washington, DC.

US Department of Health and Human Services (USDHHS) (1999) Youth risk behavior surveillance, *Morbidity and Mortality Weekly Report*, 47, SS–3, Washington, DC.

US Department of Health and Human Services (USDHHS) (2000) *Healthy People 2010: Understanding and Improving Health*, Washington, DC: US Department of Health and Human Services, Governing Printing Office.

Vertinsky, P.A. (1992) Reclaiming space, revisioning the body: the quest for gender-sensitive physical education *Quest* 44: 373–96.

Webb, D. (2000) *An Attitudinal Analysis of Students with Orthopedic Disabilities Toward General Physical Education: A Pilot Study*, unpublished doctoral dissertation, The Ohio State University, Columbus, OH.

Williams, A. and Bedward, J. (2001) Understanding girls' experience of physical education: relational analysis and situated learning, in D. Penney (ed.) *Gender and Physical Education: Contemporary Issues and Future Directions*, London: Routledge.

11 Physical education teacher education: sites of progress or resistance

Jan Wright

Introduction

In chapter 6, Brown and Rich draw attention to the relative dearth of research in physical education teacher education which looks specifically at gender issues when compared to that addressing school-based physical education. They focus specifically on 'gendered student teacher identity', how this is constituted, and how it impacts on teaching practice. In this chapter I want to draw attention to the 'gender agendas' that have informed physical education teacher education (PETE) in Australia and the active role that research and researchers have played in this process. In the second part of the chapter I discuss how these agendas have been taken up and/or been resisted in contexts of initial physical education teacher education (IPETE) and teacher professional development. This chapter enables a comparison with the situation in England and Wales, which as Penney and Evans suggested in chapter 2, points to silences and absences in policy and practice in both contexts.

Ways of thinking and doing gender in PETE: a discursive history

Social practices are always embedded in the discourses circulating at a particular point in time. Some of these discourses will be more powerful in their effects than others. Earlier chapters in this book have pointed to the ways in which power has worked in the UK to shape policy and practice in relation to gender at all levels of education and schooling. Given the focus in this chapter on PETE in Australia, a useful starting point is to ask what ways of thinking about gender have been available to inform PETE curriculum, policy and practice.[1] In response to this question I will begin with a brief narrative of my own thirty years of experience in physical education secondary and tertiary institutions. My story is suggestive of the insularity that physical education has had for many years from feminist and social theory.

As a student at Sydney University in the late 1960s, I, together with the other students in my course, were oblivious to the feminist activity and writing around us. In my year there were ten women and one man. Our university education foundation subjects certainly never dealt with social issues or gender, except as a variable in education psychology. I attended single-sex classes in dance, gymnastics and games and I completed my practicum in a private girls' school. As far as I understood my own history at this stage, I had no personal experience of discrimination, nor had I much opportunity to witness it in my university or secondary practicum experiences. There was very little to draw gender issues to my attention until I began to teach, and even then in the 1970s, I mostly taught single-sex physical education classes. It was only when I took postgraduate courses at university, studied the sociology of education and met some 'radical women' in my subjects that feminism and gender issues began to be something that I read and thought about.

As a tertiary educator in physical education, my feminist position served for many years to marginalise me as a staff member, and my interpretation of physical education and sporting practices. However, national and state policies relating to gender equity eventually permeated to IPETE and teacher professional development, and gender issues are now much more widely researched and discussed in IPETE and to a certain extent, promoted as part of a teacher's professional development. While it would now be rare for an IPETE course coordinator not to be able to point to places in the course where gender issues are discussed, this does not necessarily mean that all is resolved. As so many point out (Dewar, 1990; Fernandez-Balboa, 1997; Flintoff, 1993; Kirk *et al.*, 1997), physical education teacher education and school-based physical education are still far from exemplary sites of gender practice (whatever these might look like), and to expect them to be so ignores the very complex interplay of institutional investments in particular forms of physical education practice, the discursive resources available to think differently about physical education, lecturer, student teacher and student identities, and the very structure and organization of IPETE programmes.

To understand why this might be so, I want to explore the discursive and institutional resources that have been available from the 1970s to the current day to inform the thinking about, and the doing of, gender reform in schools and tertiary institutions in Australia. What research, researchers, legislation and policy has been available to inform discussion and practice in relation to gender in physical education? In answering this question I do not intend to survey general and education-based feminist research and writing that would have been widely available during this period. As suggested above the insularity of physical education generally from feminist theory and activism suggests that for resources to have been drawn upon, they would need to be readily available and immediately relevant to teachers and academics. One of the main academic resources available to physical educators from the 1960s has been the *Australian Council for Health, Physical Education and Recreation (ACHPER) National Journal*. The national professional association ACHPER has provided the major forum for discussion and dissemination of information important to physical education policy and practice, through its state and national conferences and its journal. The journal, now called *The ACHPER Healthy Lifestyles Journal*, is the national professional and academic journal for physical educators in Australia. An analysis of articles in the journal provides a good indication of the interest or lack of it in gender issues.

Prior to the 1970s, there were no articles in the national journal which dealt with gender issues. A survey of the *ACHPER National Journal* in the 1970s and 1980s suggests that there was little written in the 1970s except for two notable exceptions: articles in 1975 by Geoffrey Watson and by Ponch Hawkes and her colleagues. These two exceptions were in their different ways informed by a liberal feminist approach which drew attention to the ways in which the practices associated with contemporary physical education and sport disadvantaged girls. Whereas Watson's (1975) article reported empirical research informed by psychological notions of sex role and sex role socialis-ation, the Hawkes *et al.* (1975) article documented inequalities in physical education and sport opportunities, resources and facilities for girls as compared to boys in Victorian and New South Wales schools. Watson (1975) was interested in asking how the dependent variable of measurable sex type attributes correlated with children's evaluation of Little Athletics. His prediction, which was confirmed by the study, was that girls would reveal a preference for 'more expressive activities such as the jumping events' and boys for 'the more challenging and aggressive activities such as throwing, hurdles and distance events' (p. 11). For Watson, writing in the context of social psychology, the issue was not so much about providing girls with the same opportunities as boys but about providing opportunities for girls and women to achieve and enjoy their participation in ways which fitted essential feminine characteristics. In contrast, for others like Hawkes *et al.*, the issue was more how particular sex role expectations led to assumptions about girls' lack of interest and ability in physical activity and how this argument in turn led to justifying inequalities in opportunities. Hawkes' and her colleagues' study demonstrated how girls were offered fewer sports and activity choices than the boys, and the boys had generally access to more and better facilities than the girls.

From the prevailing liberal feminist point of view, discriminatory practices based on sex stereotyping was the main issue. *The Girls' School and Society Report* (Schools Commission, 1975), for instance, was concerned to advise teachers that through the ways that they interacted with students, and particu-larly through their different expectations, they were at risk of socialising students into stereotypical sex roles which would disadvantage girls. This document recommended that teacher education should ensure that their students were 'at least correctly informed about the social basis of sex differences: we see these questions as being so fundamental as to warrant their inclusion in the main body of teacher education courses' (p. 97). On the basis of reports of discrimination the Report argues that:

The sex role socialisation in sport and physical education is particularly damaging for girls since it merely results in the self-fulfilling prophecy of weak and physically dependent females.

(p. 69)

In comparison to the two articles found in the ACHPER journal in the 1970s, the 1980s were characterised by considerable discussion and activitism beginning with the New South Wales (NSW) government sponsored 'Fit to Play' Conference in January 1980. This conference brought together leading British, North American and Australian feminist researchers from the human movement sciences, sociology of sport and physical education, to speak specifically on women and sport and physical education. At the time, the conference was a major source of inspiration to women working in sport, physical education and recreation. It was a catalyst for numerous actions to improve opportunities for women and to promote the recognition that the athlete and physical education student are not generically male. As part of its contribution to the conference, the Social Development Unit of the NSW Ministry of Education provided a 'discussion paper on the interrelationship between social attitudes and participation of girls in school sport' (Coles, 1980: 3). This paper and the conference sought to dispel the prevailing myths about women's participation in sport and the discussion paper in particular is clear that girls are discriminated against in school sport. Coles argues that '[o]nly by providing extra opportunities will the school be able to provide these students with "equal opportunities"' (p. 42).

Given the importance attributed to the teacher as a role model and an agent of socialisation, Coles (1980) is very critical of the professional preparation programmes for physical education specialists of the time. She attributes physical education teachers' failure to impact on their students' quality of life to the recruitment of a particular kind of person to physical education, and to professional preparation which does nothing to sensitise student teachers to the needs of their students, especially students who are not like themselves. She is also critical of professional preparation that does nothing to develop an understanding of physical education and sport beyond the most technical details of teaching practical skills and games. She attributes the poor performance of girls in high school to the lack of skills and enthusiasm of their primary school (that is, female) teachers. This is a line of argument which has continued to receive considerable coverage to the present day (Senate Standing Committee on Environment, Recreation and the Arts, 1992).

Despite the growing coverage of gender issues, little attention seems to have been paid to issues of equity in the selection of keynote and plenary speakers for the ACHPER Commonwealth and International Conference associated with the Commonwealth Games in Brisbane in 1982. There were few female speakers and those who were invited presented mostly on dance and health. It was one of the men however, Richard Gruneau, the Canadian sociologist, who was the only speaker to directly address the topic of women in sport. In a radical move (for the time), in his abstract for the conference, he argued that:

> much of the literature on women in sport, while extremely provocative, is limited by its focus on women's involvement as an independent object of study rather than as a mediated set of practices constitutive of a whole social and material process. Related to this, I suggest (in my paper) how the focus which has developed in this literature on unequal opportunities in sport for women has tended to divert attention away from the more important questions about the role of sport as a contributor to the reproduction of patriarchal social relations.
>
> (Gruneau, 1982: 22)

In 1982 a Women in Sport and Recreation ACHPER Special Interest Group was established, but at the 1984 National Conference none of the abstracts in the Conference Issue of the journal (including my own) dealt with gender issues.

In 1984 the Anti Discrimination Act galvanised attention and action in education. It had very practical implications particularly for physical education where most schools had single-sex physical education classes except for social dance. In her paper in the *ACHPER National Journal*, Jennifer Browne interpreted the Act and its implications for the physical education and sport community, providing a detailed checklist of questions for teachers of physical education, as a means of determining whether they were implementing the intent as well as the letter of the law. The following extract provides a sense of the kinds of questions asked and some insights into the ways in which the Act was being interpreted:

> Are physical education requirements the same for boys and girls?
> Are all physical education and interschool sporting activities offered to both boys and girls?
> Are all facilities and equipment available equally to both sexes during breaks?
> Are the same events in track and field athletics championships offered to both boys and girls?
>
> (Browne, 1985: 7)

With gender issues clearly on the education agenda, funding followed policy, including funding for physical education projects. In 1984 a national project (Girls Achievement and Self-Esteem – the Contribution of Physical Education and Sport, also known as the GAPA project) was funded by a Commonwealth Schools Commission Grant for three years to address inequalities of opportunity for girls in physical education and sport (Oldenhove, 1989). Specifically, the project engaged schools across all states in action research projects designed to increase girls' involvement in physical activity – not so much for their 'fitness' as would be the case today but to improve their self-esteem, self-confidence and body image. The project tapped into the prevailing discourses and motivated considerable activity, particularly in South Australia where the project team was located. The project produced a number of resources that were distributed to schools and tertiary institutions around Australia, including a regular newsletter, a video and kits for classroom observations and for teaching about women in sport. The extent to which these were used is uncertain. The focus on girls meant that if used in tertiary settings it was likely to be by female physical educators who were still a small minority in colleges and universities. As I explain below, it is a question of what spaces were available in IPETE to discuss gender issues, by whom and with whom.

By the early 1990s, the other main sources of information on gender issues were North American (and some Australian) textbooks on the sociology of sport (e.g. Coakley, 1990; Leonard, 1993; and from Australia: Lawrence and Rowe, 1986; McKay, 1991; Stoddard, 1986) and an increasing collection of feminist texts on gender and sport (Birrell and Cole, 1994; Boutelier and San Giovanni, 1991; Messner and Sabo, 1990). The extent to which these were used as resources beyond undergraduate sociology of sport subjects is doubtful. However, with the growth of postgraduate courses, and particularly those informed by a critical pedagogy model such as the Master of Education programme at Deakin University, these resources were more likely to be taken up. As one notable example, the British feminist academic Sheila Scraton (1990) was invited to write and edit a Deakin distance education monograph which brought readily accessible ideas about gender to teacher education for both pre-service students and teachers undertaking professional development.

Until the 1990s the writing on gender which filtered through into PETE was primarily informed by liberal and radical feminist analyses of gender issues, although Tinning's (1985) paper on 'The cult of slenderness' looked forward to one of the main agenda items for the 1990s. In the 1990s, following trends in social and cultural theory which had gained prominence elsewhere in the decade before, the gender agenda shifted to engage with the notion of gender as socially constructed. This raised questions about the ways in which the practices associated with sport and physical education influenced gender construction, including the ways in which language in physical education lessons (Evans and Clarke, 1988; Evans, Davies and Penney, 1996; Wright and King, 1991; 1997) and in the media (Creedon, 1994; Lenskyj, 1998) promoted particular notions of femininity. This move away from discrimination to 'social construction' also provided a space in which researchers and educators could talk about the social construction of masculinity (Connell, 2000; Whitson, 1994).

There is now a wealth of accessible research drawing on social theories of the body and on the social constructions of femininity and masculinity to inform discussion of gender issues in physical education teacher education.

Again the impact that these are likely to have depends on the spaces available in IPETE programmes for their use. As will be discussed below there are organisational and curricula features of IPETE which continue to marginalise the discussion of social issues, including those concerning gender, and in this respect there are important similarities between training programmes in Australia and the UK. On the other hand, there are now national and state policies in Australia which are explicitly informed by the notion of gender as socially constructed. For instance the following statements are included in the 'Principles for Action' in the national document, *Gender Equity: A Framework for Australian Schools* (Gender Equity Taskforce for the Ministerial Council on Employment Education Training and Youth Affairs):

> Schools should acknowledge their active role in the construction of gender, and their responsibility to ensure that all organisational and man-agement practices reflect [a] commitment to gender equity.
>
> (Gender Equity Taskforce, 1997: 9)

And in defining gender in the New South Wales Gender Equity Strategy, *Girls and Boys in Schools, 1996–2001* (Specific Focus Directorate, 1996) the following statement is included:

> A complex range of historical and social factors influence the ways in which girls and women, boys and men experience and express their femininity and masculinity. Current beliefs about feminine and masculine behaviours shape differences in educational and social outcomes for girls and boys.
>
> (Specific Focus Directorate 1996: 2)

As will be demonstrated below these policies have been important in motivating strategies for gender reform at the level of state Departments of Education. In addition, gender and sexuality have been more explicitly written into physical and health education syllabuses, particularly at the senior level of schooling. While this does not necessarily bring about changes in practices – in IPETE or in schools – it does provide a context within which it is possible to argue for some attention to gender issues and for changes to practices which bring more socially just outcomes for female and male students.

The potential of PETE programmes as institutional sites for gender reform

The first section of this chapter provided some indication of the discursive context in which IPETE programmes have been organised and taught. From the 1970s it is obvious that there was information, research, government policies and strategies to draw on for IPETE curricula. The question is to what extent have these resources been taken up and with what likely impact? What is there about IPETE programmes, the contexts in which they are produced, the lecturers who teach in them and the students who attend them which facilitate or work against a gender equity agenda?

Unlike England and Wales I would suggest that in Australia government policy specifically concerning curricula in physical education has far less impact on what is taught in IPETE, when compared to the traditional understandings within IPETE programmes of what constitutes content knowledge in physical education. This has in turn been shaped by strong university traditions of what constitutes valued knowledge (that is scientific knowledge) and the long-standing dominance of sport and games in the Australian practice of physical education. To a great extent this is because universities are nationally funded, while government education systems are state based. University programmes are not directly accountable to state-based departments of education. However, as employers of university trained teachers and through their development of school syllabi, state education systems indirectly affect what is taught as content. Yet at the time of writing, no state had produced explicit criteria for the characteristics necessary for teachers of physical education, beyond holding a degree with some physical education content knowledge (rarely made explicit) and a teacher education component with a specified amount of practical experience in schools. In most states it is also now a requirement that teachers of physical education have some content knowledge in health. This has had one of the more radical impacts on IPETE programmes in the recent past, as universities have adapted their syllabuses to meet this requirement. Subjects taken in the context of health range from broad public health issues to subjects such as 'drugs', 'nutrition', 'personal health' and 'community health', designed specifically to assist the teaching of health in schools. Thus the inclusion of Health provides a space to examine 'health discourses' such as those around exercise and fitness, sexuality and gender and other forms of difference. The resources and spaces to do this are now widely available. Whether they are utilised in this way depends on teachers' and students' choices of subjects and topics.

It follows that there is little accountability (and considerable flexibility) in what university programmes can do in producing physical education teachers. The constraints and the reshaping of programmes that have occurred in many universities in recent years are more an outcome of university economic and political decisions than choices made in the context of changing government policy about physical activity and sport. In this context it is competing interests within university IPETE programmes, budgetary constraints and teachers' and students' own investments that are likely to provide or shut down opportunities to address gender issues in the IPETE curriculum.

Although it is difficult to make many generalisations, there is enough evidence in Australia and elsewhere to suggest that physical education teacher education has not been one of the most responsive sites for the promotion of discussion and change in relation to gender issues. Indeed studies in the

UK (Flintoff, 1993, 1997), North America (Dewar, 1990) and Australia (Macdonald, 1993; Swan, 1995) suggest that PETE programmes have typically been underpinned by patriarchal discourses and practices which are recognisable in staff hierarchies, course organisation, the curriculum, the relationships between staff and students and in students' relationships with each other.

As Kirk points out in chapter 3 and elsewhere (Kirk, 1992), one of the most compelling explanations for this is the dominance within physical education since the 1950s of masculinist ways of thinking and doing movement. Despite their original pre-eminence, forms of physical activity and physical education pedagogy associated with a female tradition have been marginalised in UK, Australia and the US (Dewar, 1990; Kirk, 1992 and chapter 3; Wright 1996). Shifts to coeducational physical education and physical education teacher education have ensured that games and sports hold a privileged position over gymnastics and dance, and more recently aerobics, despite high levels of participation in these areas of physical activity outside of school (Australian Bureau of Statistics 1997; Williams and Woodhouse, 1996). As Kirk, Macdonald and Tinning (1997) argue, physical education teacher education in Australia is currently regulated by outmoded cultural imperatives which emerged in the 1940s and 1950s – that is, physical education centred on multi-activity sports based programmes. They go on to argue that:

> physical education teacher education regulated in part by a post-war form of physical culture is likely to be working within functionalist assumptions about gender, race and social class, if these are acknowledged at all, that may be culturally obsolete and certainly dangerously misleading.
>
> (p. 291)

In this context it becomes almost impossible to think and know physical education teacher education differently – to imagine other forms of pedagogy and knowledge. Change to the status quo becomes very difficult to argue, particularly when the social identity of some members of staff rests on the maintenance of a strong 'practical studies' component based on traditional sports and games. As I discuss below, challenging the place of team games also becomes difficult when students' pleasures and identities are bound up with sport.

The domination of PETE by a sports and games model of physical education has been complemented by the pre-eminence of the biophysical sciences in PETE curricula and a technocratic approach to the teaching of physical education (Tinning, 1991). The organisation of IPETE courses in Australia has helped to confirm the place of the biophysical sciences as the fundamental and essential basis for physical education teaching. In some cases an undergraduate education in human movement science and a background in sport, plus one year of professional preparation are taken as sufficient preparation for teaching physical (and sometimes health) education. With teacher shortages this form of preparation is likely to have more and more acceptance.

In Australia there are three broad models of professional preparation: integrated or concurrent degrees, e.g. Bachelor of Education (Physical and Health Education); parallel or double degrees, e.g. Bachelor of Teaching/ Bachelor of Applied Science; and an end-on model, with three years of an undergraduate degree plus one or two years of teacher education. In each of these models, if gender issues are to be discussed, it is in the context of educational foundation subject(s) and/or a specialist sociology subject on leisure, sport and/or physical education. Traditionally the most common programme has been the concurrent degree that usually involves a cohort of students studying a highly structured syllabus with few options. For some degrees a greater part of studies are shared with exercise science students preparing for work in areas other than teaching. Increasingly, numbers of students are completing end-on programmes with the professional component available through on-campus and distance modes. The first degree for most of these students is an exercise science/applied science degree.

There are few spaces in any of these courses for subjects which deal with social issues; and social issues are rarely integrated into science or pedagogy subjects. IPETE subjects tend to fall into strongly bounded or classified categories: biophysical sciences, pedagogy subjects tied to practicums which usually have a strong technical emphasis, practical studies (when these exist at all), educational foundations and one or two social science subjects. The inclusion of health education in state syllabuses in the last decade has led to the addition of health and health pedagogy subjects in most concurrent, parallel and the professional component of end-on degrees.

While it can be said that IPETE courses in Australia in general share a core curriculum of the human movement sciences, the degree to which broader education and sociocultural studies are included varies but only around a small range – that is, from none at all to one or two subjects in the core/mandatory component. The opportunities to study social or gender issues may be extended through elective subjects, though these often have to compete with practical and/or scientific subjects which many students may see as having more relevance to their future careers. Research in the UK, US and Australia on the concurrent model suggests that subjects that cover social issues including gender issues are not only marginalised in the programme – i.e. they receive little space, time and few resources – but are also regarded by students as irrelevant, soft options and where possible to be avoided, particularly when compared to the 'hard' sciences (Dewar, 1990; Macdonald, 1993; Swan, 1995). As Swan and others (Dewar, 1990) point out, the sociology subjects are often designed to challenge the taken-for-granted and thereby challenge the values and beliefs that are central at this stage to students' sense of identity as athletes and future physical educators who will encourage students to be more like themselves.

While it is in the education foundation subjects and in the sociocultural subjects that gender issues are most likely to be taken up, the other site with increasing potential for addressing these issues in IPETE is health/health education. Again health can be taught primarily from a bio-medical position and/or a position which emphasises individual responsibility for health outcomes. There is thus no guarantee that gender will become any more than a variable to be correlated with specific health dispositions. However, the expectation that senior (post-16) physical and health education will be taught from a sociocultural perspective has the potential to impact on IPETE curricula as well as school-based health and physical education and thereby provide a space for the discussion of issues concerning gender and sexuality.

At the time of writing, state and federal governments and professional teacher organisations in Australia had little control over what a physical and health education teacher might be expected to know in terms of content and pedagogical knowledge. Discussions are currently in progress to introduce a form of teacher registration which will recognise a wide range of attributes including those related to teaching diverse groups of students. However, until these deliberations produce results, the organisation and curriculum of IPETE in Australia continues to privilege the human movement sciences and sports performance, and thereby provide minimal spaces for the discussion of gender issues.

IPETE students

Swan (1995) and Macdonald (1993) in Australia and Hargreaves (1986) in the UK all describe a powerful 'normalising' process which both attracts students to, and then privileges certain kinds of students in physical education teacher education. As a profession physical education tends to attract students who themselves enjoy, are good at and identify with the values associated with sport and physical activity. As Hargreaves (1986) and others (Swan, 1995) point out, PETE students (and PETE lecturers) share a common interest, perhaps passion for recreational physical activity and/or sport. In addition or perhaps partly because of this, as many studies have suggested, PETE students as a group tend to be conservative. The IPETE student body is also not notable for its cultural diversity. In Australia this means students are primarily from a British heritage, with increasing numbers from second generation or later European families. There are very few Asian or Middle Eastern heritage students in physical and health education, despite the increasing proportion of these cultural minorities in Australia. Aboriginal students are underrepresented in Australia universities generally, but some students do take up scholarships in physical education teacher education. As a group, however, PETE students seem to have little experience of marginality or discrimination; students who do not identify within the majority cultural groups often bear an unrealistic burden to represent and articulate the experience of difference or else remain silent (and often extremely angry) as difference is either ignored, treated tokenistically or even pejoratively.

This is not a fruitful environment for radical change nor for the ready acceptance of values which are fundamental to gender reform in IPETE and in schools. The dominance of the human movement sciences, technocratic ways of working and thinking, the privileging of competitive games and sports all compound ways of thinking and being which have already been profoundly shaped by an immersion in a masculinist sports culture. In addition, for many students what will be important during their initial teacher education is survival – passing subjects and surviving their practicum, as well as enjoying their time at university or college and the companionship of their fellow students. What students value is the usefulness of knowledge, how it can be applied in, for example, a teaching, coaching or outdoor education context; that is, knowledge that can be applied to performance (Dewar, 1987). Such imperatives allow little room for critical reflection, particularly in the context of the teaching practicum unless explicitly required, which seems rare. As Luca, a very thoughtful mature age student, said on reading one of Juan-Miguel Fernandez-Balboa's papers challenging traditional practices in physical education:

> Reading Balboa, the impression that I have, and it is an excellent paper in terms of the way he mentions that as teachers we not only have to teach the PE content but be able to challenge the issues and bring that into our teaching and making that something that we are trying to get across – the Schulman categories. It is important that as teachers we are aware of the social issues, it is not easy, there are too much stigmas in society about what issues a teacher should not do and even the ways of talking, the ways of behaving, that, as a teacher – I am aware of those issues and it's interesting reading. In terms of thinking about that as a teacher, I am not at that stage. I am not at that stage of thinking about how my messages affect the boys or the girls. It's interesting reading and I enjoyed doing all those assignments and thinking about those issues but in terms of bringing that to my teaching it's going to take a while. I think it's probably easier to think than act and that's why research is probably so interesting in that area.
>
> (Interview with exiting student)

Not all students feel this way. However, experience suggests that these students are already identified in the programme as 'different', not necessarily in a pejorative way but as more academic, more likely to take a provocative position in relation to their peers and in some cases self-identified as different in terms of cultural background or sexual identity. For these students the opportunity to engage in questioning of the taken-for-granted is welcome. However, at times they seem to make up a very small minority of students and can be marginalised because of their different positioning.

Dealing with gender in the curriculum

At this point the outlook for influencing gender reform from physical education teacher education in Australia looks rather grim. However, there is room for optimism and spaces for change. In the first instance although they may often identify with conservative discourses associated with sport and/or fitness, like the students in Brown and Rich's study, most IPETE students are concerned to increase the participation and enjoyment of students in their classes. They often recognise the resistance of many girls and some boys to traditional physical education lessons and are ready to examine the reasons for this. But like many teachers (Wright, 1999) and the students interviewed by Brown and Rich, the kind of 'useful knowledge' that they wish to acquire is often a set of strategies which will increase participation in the forms of activity that they value.

I would want to argue that the kinds of resources that are needed are not a 'kit' of strategies which will have universal effectiveness. Indeed I would argue that no such strategies exist. Instead, an understanding of how the social practices associated with sport and physical education work to construct limiting notions of masculinity and femininity is required to assist teachers and students to interrogate their practice and to think about and practice physical education teaching differently. As Flintoff (1997: 164) suggests on the basis of her own ethnographic work in IPETE, 'without an understanding of gender relations and how they may be transmitted through schooling and PE, students will be unable to adopt strategies to challenge these in their own teaching'.

IPETE is clearly an important site to begin the process of gender reform through raising students' awareness, introducing the issues, current policy and the research on gender and physical education. Ideally such a process should be integrated throughout an IPETE course; it should become an important aspect of the way prospective teachers think about and evaluate their practice and the practices of others in physical education lessons. It should become part of what Tinning (1991) described as 'problematising practice' in physical education. In addition, gender issues need to be dealt with explicitly in a range of contexts. Given the structure of physical education teacher education this is most likely to be in educational foundation courses, sociology of sport and leisure subjects, and in physical education pedagogy subjects. In Australia and New Zealand gender and sexuality topics are also likely to be covered in the context of health education subjects. As indicated above, health as a 'content area' provides a space in which to examine 'health discourses' such as those relating to health and fitness and to examine problematic constructions of bodies. The spaces and resources to do this are usually available (students can take subjects as electives if they are not available as core subjects) but whether academic staff or students have the desire to do so depends very much on the kinds of identifications that they make with physical education as discussed above. Encouragingly there are increasing numbers of academics in IPETE interested in addressing gender issues explicitly in their teaching. However, most do not always find it an easy task. An informal survey of PETE practitioners working with gender issues in Australia and my own experience suggests that teaching through case studies, stories and media analysis provides a way of asking questions and of avoiding pronouncements. A hermeneutic approach – problematising practice during in-school observations, microteaching and practicum experiences through the use of video or critical friends – also provides ways of raising questions and seeking information from research and the practices of others (Wright, 1998).

How the knowledge and values produced in ITPETE programmes is taken up will vary considerably across programmes – depending on how important gender issues are across subjects and strands – and from one student to another. It will depend on the biographies of students and their investments in maintaining or discarding beliefs and practices which subscribe to dominant gender discourses. In the last few years the emergence of feminist informed masculinity studies in the area of sport has provided an important space to look more broadly at gender issues from a perspective which understand femininity and masculinity as constructed in ways which are limiting to both women and men. It helps to address the position so often taken by many male and quite a few female students that their female lecturers are all feminist extremists who hate men (Wright, 1998). A social construction position allows for a more nuanced understanding of traditional physical education practices as being potentially limiting and inappropriate not only for many girls but also for the many boys who do not conform or wish to conform to dominant notions of masculinity. It follows that if gender issues are dealt with across IPETE courses and/or in depth in some subjects in PETE courses most students will not leave the preservice education untouched whether they choose to reject, accept it, or simply put ideas about gender 'on file' until later.

Given the constraints that preservice education poses, it becomes obvious that educating about gender issues needs to go beyond initial teacher education to working with practising teachers. Postgraduate programmes such as those conducted at Deakin University, which promoted critical reflection through teacher engagement in action research in their own classrooms, provide another way in which practising teachers can become more aware of gender issues and work to address these. A promising approach, but one reliant on elusive government funding, has been taken in NSW. Prompted by the restitution of a 'gender agenda', derived in part by a focus on gender equity which included the 'education of boys', funding has followed State policy once again. In physical education this has taken the form of a professional development project for teachers and consultants. Following the national and state guidelines, this project was informed by an understanding that gender was socially constructed and that the social practices that are part of everyday school life have the potential to (re)produce narrow and limiting forms of femininity and masculinity or to challenge them. The Gender

Issues in Physical Activity (GIPA) Project initially involved Personal Development Health and Physical Education (PDHPE) teachers and consultants representing all Department of Education and Training districts in NSW in workshops and school-based initiatives (see Wright 1999, for a more detailed description).

Most recently the project has focused on involving and supporting the PDHPE faculties from four schools in contracted programmes of work addressing gender issues in the context of physical and health education. What has been important about this aspect of the project is the ways in which, through whole faculty involvement, it has raised awareness and promoted change in the practices of female and male teachers for whom gender was formerly not on their personal agendas. In addition most of the faculties have been involved in the planning and teaching of units of work which in their different ways take up the notion of the 'social construction' of gender. In undertaking this work the teachers have needed to clarify their own understanding and develop ways of communicating these to others.

What is particularly interesting about the GIPA initiative from a policy point of view is how strategic action was taken at a particular juncture when several government concerns intersected to provide an opportunity to apply for funding to work with teachers on gender reform in schools. To a very large extent this was also about the specific interest of key departmental officers in gender reform, their perceptions of the issues and their vision for change. Using the motivations provided by a government funded survey confirming (once again) the lower skill and fitness levels of girls and a renewed impetus in gender issues arising out of the 'boys education' push, the Department officials developed a notion of a project based on the current preferred model of professional development in the Department – one focused on whole school change to successfully attract funding in a context of economic constraint.

Conclusion

A reading of this chapter against others in this book suggests that in Australia, the constraints on gender reform do not come so much from national policy imperatives but through the discursive construction of IPETE programmes and the investments of those who teach and study in them. Indeed state government policies such as the integration of a broad notion of health with physical education in state syllabuses, and the move to a sociocultural perspective on physical activity and health in senior school physical and health education syllabuses provides opportunities to explicitly address gender issues in schools. This in turn provides an incentive to give more space to health and sociocultural perspectives in the IPETE curriculum. In addition, at least in NSW, government initiatives have promoted intensive professional development programmes addressing gender reform in physical education. The long-term potential of such initiatives will always depend on how their effects are promoted more widely, the lessons learned disseminated, and how this information finds its way into initial physical education teacher education.

Note

1 Following Penney and Evans (1999) policy is understood as a complex sociocultural and political process. Similarly curriculum is taken to be more than the content of specific syllabus documents; instead it is understood as a process of interaction between teacher, (IPETE) students and the content of their courses in the context of a particular social and cultural milieu. In this sense the boundaries between policy and curriculum are not fixed. Practice is the process by which policy and curriculum are constituted and enacted in time and space. Practice takes into account the specific biographies of participants, their investments and the social and cultural context which acts to constrain and make possible particular choices of action.

References

Australian Bureau of Statistics (1997) *Participation in Sport and Physical Activities 1995/96*, Canberra: ABS.

Birrell, S. and Cole, C. (1994) *Women, Sport and Culture*, Champaign, IL: Human Kinetics.

Boutelier, A. and San Giovanni, B. (1991) *The Sporting Woman*, Champaign, IL: Human Kinetics.

Browne, J. (1985) Equal opportunity in physical education and sport, *Australian Journal for Health Physical Education and Recreation* 110: 6–8.

Coakley, J. (1990) *Sport in Society: Issues and Controversies*, St Louis: Times/Mosby.

Coles, E. (1980) *Sport in Schools: The Participation of Girls*, Social Development Unit, Ministry of Education, NSW Government Printer.

Connell, R.W. (2000) *Men and Boys*, Sydney: Allen & Unwin.

Creedon, P.J. (ed.) (1994) *Women, Media and Sport: Challenging Gender Values*, Thousand Oaks, CA: Sage.

Dewar, A. (1990) Oppression and privilege in physical education: struggles in the negotiation of gender in a university programme, in D. Kirk and R. Tinning (eds) *Physical Education, Curriculum and Culture: Critical Issues in the Contemporary Crisis*, Basingstoke: Falmer Press, pp. 67–100.

Evans, J. and Clarke, G. (1988) Changing the face of physical education, in J. Evans (ed.) *Teachers, Teaching and Control in Physical Education*, Lewes: Falmer Press, pp. 125–43.

Evans, J., Davies, B. and Penney, D. (1996) Teachers, teaching and the social construction of gender relations, *Sport, Education and Society* 1(2): 165–84.

Fernandez-Balboa, J.-M. (1997) Knowledge base in physical education teacher education: a proposal for a new era, *Quest* 49(7): 161–81.

Flintoff, A. (1997) Gender relations in physical education initial teacher education, in G. Clarke and B. Humberstone (eds) *Researching Women and Sport*, Basingstoke: Macmillan.

Flintoff, A. (1993) Gender, physical education and initial teacher education, in J. Evans (ed.) *Equality, Education and Physical Education*, London: Falmer Press, pp. 184–204.

Gender Equity Taskforce (1997) *Gender Equity: A Framework for Australian Schools*, Canberra: Ministerial Council on Employment Education Training and Youth Affairs.

Gruneau, R. (1982) Class sport and patriarchy (an abstract), *Australian Journal for Health, Physical Education and Recreation* 96: 22.

Hargreaves, J. (1986) *Sport, Power and Culture*, Cambridge: Polity Press.

Hawkes, P., Dryen, R., Torsch, D. and Hannan, L. (1975) Sex roles in school sport and physical education – the state of play, *Australian Journal for Health Physical Education and Recreation*, March: 8–17.

Kirk, D. (1992) *Defining Physical Education: The Social Construction of a Subject in Postwar Britain*, Basingstoke: Falmer Press.

Kirk, D., Macdonald, D. and Tinning, R. (1997) The social construction of pedagogic discourse in physical education teacher education, *The Curriculum Journal* 8(2): 271–98.

Lawrence, G. and Rowe, D. (1986) *Powerplay*, Sydney: Hall & Iremonger.

Leonard, W.M. (1993) *A Sociological Perspective of Sport* (4th edition), New York: Macmillan.

Lenskyj, H.J. (1998) 'Inside sport' or 'On the margins'?: Australian women and the sport media, *International Review for the Sociology of Sport* 33(1): 19–32.

Macdonald, D. (1993) Knowledge, gender and power in physical education teacher education, *Australian Journal of Education* 37(3): 259–78.

McKay, J. (1991) *No Pain, No Gain*, Sydney: Prentice Hall.

Messner, M. and Sabo, D. (eds) (1990) *Sport, Men and the Gender Order*, Champaign, IL: Human Kinetics.

Oldenhove, H. (1989) Girls' PE and sports, in G. Leder and S. Sampson (eds) *Educating Girls: Practice and Research*, Sydney: Allen & Unwin, pp. 39–48.

Penney, D. and Evans, J. (1999) *Politics, Policy and Practice in Physical Education*, London, E & FN Spon.

Schools Commission (1975) *Girls, School and Society: Report by a Study Group to the Schools Commission*, Canberra: Schools Commission.

Scraton, S. (1990) *Gender and Physical Education*, Geelong: Deakin University Press.

Senate Standing Committee on Environment, Recreation and the Arts (1992) *Physical and Sport Education*, Canberra: AGPS.

Specific Focus Directorate (1996) *Girls and Boys in Schools, 1996–2001*, Sydney: NSW Department of School Education.

Stoddard, B. (1986) *Saturday Afternoon Fever: Sport in Australian Culture*, Sydney: Angus & Robertson.

Swan, P.A. (1995) *Studentship and Oppositional Behaviour within Physical Education Teacher Education: A Case Study*, unpublished Doctor of Education Thesis, Deakin University, Geelong, Australia.

Tinning, R. (1985) Physical education and the cult of slenderness, *The ACHPER National Journal* 107: 10–13.

Tinning, R. (1991) Teacher education pedagogy: dominant, discourses and the process of problem setting, *Journal of Teaching in Physical Education* 11(1): 1–20.

Watson, G. (1975) Sex role socialisation and the competitive process in Little Athletics, *Australian Journal for Health Physical Education and Recreation* 50: 10–22.

Whitson, D. (1994) The embodiment of gender: discipline, domination and empowerment, in S. Birrell and C.L. Cole (eds) *Women, Sport and Culture*, Champaign, IL: Human Kinetics, pp. 353–71.

Williams, A. and Woodhouse, J. (1996) Delivering the discourse: urban adolescents' perceptions of physical education, *Sport Education and Society* 1(2): 210–13.

Wright, J. (1996) Mapping the discourses in physical education, *Journal of Curriculum Studies* 28(3): 331–51.

Wright, J. (1997) The construction of gendered contexts in single sex and coeducational physical education lessons, *Sport, Education and Society* 2(1): 55–72.

Wright, J. (1998) Reconstructing gender in sport and physical education, in C. Hickey, L. Fitzclarence and R. Matthews (eds) *Where the Boys Are: Masculinity, Sport and Education*, Geelong: Deakin Centre for Education and Change, pp. 13–26.

Wright, J. (1999) Changing gendered practices in physical education: working with teachers, *European Physical Education Review* 5(3) 181–97.

Wright, J. and King, R.C. (1991). 'I say what I mean,' said Alice: an analysis of gendered discourse in physical education, *Journal of Teaching in Physical Education* 10(2) 210–25.

12 Extending agendas: physical culture research for the twenty-first century

Doune Macdonald

Introduction

The outcomes of gender research in physical education give us little cause for celebration. Despite many years of gender being on educators' agendas, practices in physical education lessons, school staff-rooms, community sport, and teacher education programmes, continue to be sexist. Meanwhile, gender research has become increasingly sophisticated, posing complex questions and drawing on contemporary feminist and poststructuralist theories. This chapter argues that there is a gulf between research and practice and provides some signposts for future gender research agendas that may attempt to address this gulf. These include moving beyond narrow conceptions of what is physical education, who are our partners, where learning occurs, narrow research paradigms, and the school/university divide.

Growing divides?

Recently I had the opportunity to teach physical education to years 8 and 9 students in a co-educational secondary school. In the twenty years since I last donned a tracksuit and whistle and agonised over lesson planning, I had developed my understanding of the gendering of physical education through academic reading and research. In doing so I also had become familiar with the wide-ranging strategies available to teachers and schools to promote equity. I therefore entered the school environment as a physical education teacher, curious to see how 'things had changed since my day'.

What did I find? In a student-led year 8 games-making unit the boys seized upon foam swords and devised a game with the aim of beating the opposition into submission. The girls crafted games with intricate rules using netballs, cones and ropes. When organising an associated mini-Olympics, the girls prepared the letters, posters and advertising materials while the boys chose to organise the equipment and prepare draws and score sheets on the computers. One girl wanted to help with the equipment but she was shunned by the boys and ostracised by the girls. Meanwhile, the year 9 unit focusing on physically active lifestyles revealed different student choices and interactions. Most boys and girls agreed that they would like to try indoor rock-climbing, judo, karate, and aerobics as part of their formal programme and participated enthusiastically. For their own fitness programmes, mixed-sex groups opted to play ball games, go walking or jogging, or do basic strengthening exercises together, appreciating the opportunity to engage in physical activities with which they felt most comfortable.

Why am I recounting these informal observations in this concluding chapter? They help remind me that many students' and teachers' experiences of physical education have not become more gender inclusive despite widespread awareness of equity issues and strategies. Indeed, Evans and Penney in the Introduction to this text ask 'Why has there been so little surface level, let alone deep structural, change?' (p. 3). This has been exemplified in previous chapters that have drawn our attention to continued exclusions and silences with respect to equity and social justice in contexts of physical education. Importantly, my school observations also remind me that many young people, and those who teach them, are looking for new versions of physical education where gender, body shape, sexuality, ethnicity, and physical ability do not limit individual involvement. Further, my experiences highlight that there is frequently a disjunction between research discourses and physical education practice. While the equity research that I was familiar with was concerned with bodies, subjectivities, sexualities, masculinities, policy analyses, and the like, it helped little in a school that was coping with an increasingly conservative and competitive marketplace, and the day to day stresses of students who felt alienated, harassed and bored. My intention here is not to blame teachers or researchers, or indeed reinforce any false dichotomy, but rather to highlight how the agendas have often grown apart.

A focus of this chapter is therefore this drift between the respective interests, questions, and language of those who practice physical education in universities and schools, typically researchers and teachers. I suggest that this has not always been so. In the 1970s and 1980s when gender equity was an explicit priority across various sites of physical education, research was largely concerned with questions such as student–teacher interaction and inclusive language, class organisation, and selection of activities (see for example Bischoff, 1982; Evans, Rosen and O'Brien, 1986; Griffin, 1985; Scraton, 1986; Vertinsky, 1984). Drawing on liberal, and less radical, feminist perspectives, this research conducted in university–school partnerships generated strategies in schools including inclusive language policies, single-sex classes, girl-friendly content, and girls' only spaces and facility usage. School communities themselves also initiated projects based upon this heightened consciousness and, using action research methodologies, addressed local questions such as the appropriateness of the physical education uniform and interventions for sex-based bullying and harassment. Since that time researchers have asked other questions, while in important respects the institution of schools and the above mentioned problems have remained the same. As modernist institutions, schools are still shaped by timetables, space allocation, bounded subject communities, industrial models of teachers' work, and frequently traditional syllabuses. Further, the physical education profession still attracts those who are middle class, heterosexual, able-bodied, and committed to sport and performance discourses (e.g. Armour and Jones, 1998; Macdonald and Tinning, 1995). While there have been some initiatives to shift curricula to more socially critical outcomes (e.g. Kirk and Macdonald, 1999; Wright, 1997), many position sporting performance as central (e.g. Penney and Evans, 1999). As what counts as research increasingly borrows from poststructuralist perspectives, it seems to have disengaged from the modernist and conservative institution of schooling which is still looking for strategies and practices that promote equity and justice.

The notion of a 'gender agenda for the twenty-first century' begs the question of 'for whom should agendas be'? All boys and girls? Schools? Teachers? Researchers? Policy-makers? Who, then, is this gender agenda for? It speaks to all those who might undertake physical education research – teachers, academics, students, professional associations, and policy-makers, wherever they might be located. Here, research is considered to be the systematic and empirical search for truth or truths. The following four signposts may be helpful across the spaces and places where gender equity is an issue. They may, it is to be hoped, play a part in reviving the gender debate, which in 1994, Ball argued was largely 'off the agenda' (p. 125).

Signposts for future gender agendas: moving beyond

Underpinning the research/practice disjunction have been dualistic discourses. For reasons such as interest, context, language and tradition, past and current physical education discourses have taken a dualistic position: female/ male; boys/girls; masculine/feminine; social structure/subjectivity; modern/ postmodern; homosexual/heterosexual; individual/societal; curricula/extra-curricula; Anglo-Saxon/Asian; curriculum/pedagogy; theory/practice; schools /universities – the list goes on (e.g. Layder, 1997). These binaries have been used differently depending upon the physical education context. For example, in schools, binaries have been used as a way of focusing 'problems', programmes and strategies, while in universities they have served to focus research perspectives and projects, academic territory and communities. Yet, as has been illustrated in earlier chapters, binaries, polarities and boundaries obscure differences within, and reproduce narrow and overly simplistic ways of thinking, talking and behaving. It is time to *move beyond* binaries and to establish some shared principles for how gender equity can be promoted across sites and by a variety of stakeholders who are concerned with physical education.

To move from overly narrow and singular/dualistic foci of research and account for complexity and interdependency of social practices, I am also arguing for the widespread use of relational analyses (Brown and Rich, chapter 6 in this text; Hall, 1996). Kirk (1999: 64) suggests the value of relational analysis lies in its potential to reveal complexity. It can:

> provide an important corrective to simplistic, one-dimensional analyses of education by revealing the interdependency of social practices across sites and . . . the complexities revealed by relational analysis may allow individuals and groups to transform unjust, inequitable and oppressive practices by providing powerful and sophisticated explanation of the practices constituting physical education that inform interventions for change.

Within this text, relational analysis has been associated with extending agendas (Chapter 2) and appreciating ripple effects (Chapter 6). The message for research is that it should frame questions of gender equity as complex, contextually-embedded, and potentially far reaching.

1 Beyond physical education

School and tertiary knowledge has tended to exist within highly bounded systems that we typically call subjects (e.g. physical education) and disciplines (e.g. sports science, human movement studies). The preceding chapters suggest that this arrangement of knowledge has not always served society well in terms of offering contexts that are inclusive, engaging, safe, or innovative. They have indicated that in schools, narrowly conceived, masculinized versions of physical education dominate, while PETE continues to alienate those who do not conform. The first signpost for all physical educators, whether they be located in schools, clubs or universities, is to think beyond physical education's boundaries in order to share, learn, dilute, and shift what have been discriminatory and sedimented discourses. Thinking beyond physical education may involve school curricula viewing physical education more broadly and establishing alliances that enrich the questions that are asked and the knowledge that is brought to bear on equity issues.

One way of viewing physical education more broadly and understanding the complexity of contextual influences shaping young people's involvement in physical activity is to work with the concept of physical culture. Kirk (1993: 340) uses the term physical culture to refer to:

> a range of practices concerned with the maintenance, representation and regulation of the body centred on three highly codified, institutionalised forms of physical activity: sport, physical recreation and exercise. Physical culture may be thought of, in turn, as one source of the production and reproduction of corporeal discourse, of a whole array of interconnecting symbol systems concerned with the meaning-making centred on the human body.

Preliminary work by Wright and Macdonald (in press) reveals that exploring not only students' perceptions of physical education but also the significance of symbol systems associated with clothes, friendship groups, music, and the media as they relate to physical culture, provides a richer understanding of inequity in physical education than would a focus upon the subject itself. Physical culture encourages a broader lens that helps to locate physical activity within the totality of young people's lives and thereby generate more impactful strategies for change.

Another way of moving beyond physical education is to recognise shifts in disciplinary knowledge and its representations in school subjects. The structure of the disciplines in universities and their translation into school subjects triumphed in the 1960s. Recently, in line with rapid growth in new and varied applications of knowledge (Bernstein, 1996), reconfigurations of disciplinary knowledge have occurred. Contemporary curriculum documents are not necessarily stories of 'the translation of an academic discipline, devised by "dominant" groups of scholars in universities, into a pedagogic version to be used as a school subject' (Goodson, 1988: 177). Particularly in the Australian context, middle schooling literature exploring the needs of 9 to 15 year olds has challenged the extent to which disciplinary and/or strongly collected knowledge meets the needs of young people. This knowledge has been shown to limit the possibilities for freedom or autonomy in learning and the opportunities for students to make meaningful connections across schooling (see for example Hargreaves and Earl, 1994). It is therefore argued that teachers should recognise and support new configurations of knowledge that encourage connectivity across subject matter, in order to produce well-rounded learners with economic, political, cultural and sociological understandings (Connell, 2000; Young, 1998). In response, in some contexts we are seeing the clustering of subject matter into learning *areas* that extend beyond subjects. In Australia and New Zealand this clustering has been reflected in the creation of 'key learning areas', with physical education re-positioned to sit with health education, outdoor education, home economics and religious education under the umbrella of Health and Physical Education (e.g. Glover and Macdonald, 1997; Macdonald *et al.*, 2000).

However, like Penney's observations in the UK context (chapter 7), my recent teaching experiences indicate that new curriculum documents may provide a platform for more equitable practices but do not necessarily ensure shifts in practices and relationships. What might this mean for research both within and beyond school? One possible response is to trial and monitor how best educators can work beyond their disciplines. More specifically, it generates questions concerning how teams of teachers can become 'cross-departmental' in their knowledge bases and justifications, traditions and practices, behavioural norms and priorities, and thereby possibly destabilize inequitable practices and promote new approaches to the study of physical activity. Accordingly, in universities, tertiary physical educators should be working with health professionals, social scientists, home economists, and academics in gender, cultural and leisure studies (Macdonald *et al.*, in press) to gain a fuller understanding of the complexities of inequity. The chapters by Benn, Brown and Rich, and Wright in this text suggest that tertiary physical education or human movement studies/science is still not adequately challenging gender inequity, extending understandings of gender equity, or providing clear insights into ways in which gender equity can be advanced in and via teaching and learning in physical education. Talbot (2000) argued that programmes have been gender blind and that critical issues and subjective experiences have been sidelined. It is important that researchers acknowledge that to continue to work within a bounded discipline is not helpful and that physical education would be well-advised to position itself with multi-disciplinary partners or teams. No one discipline has the intellectual resources to deal with the complexities of inequities. If physical educators considered themselves as part of a public health team alongside epidemiologists, nutritionists, psychologists, sociologists, health promotion professionals, school nurses, and social workers, the issues raised would take them (and their research) beyond their curriculum and pedagogical concerns to broader questions of access and opportunity to become physically educated.

Certainly, to research with partners beyond physical education is not easy. Bringing together professionals with different interests, priorities, knowledge and experience to set the parameters of equity issues, let alone address the issues, may be fraught. However, there are examples of positive progress in these respects. When physical educators have drawn upon feminist cultural studies they have been prompted to engage with a field in which different disciplines intersect in the analysis of culture defined as the 'social forms though which human beings live, become conscious, and sustain themselves subjectively' (Hall, 1996: 34). Feminist cultural studies draws upon sociology, political science, philosophy, semiotics, history, literature, and feminism to examine culture (or physical culture) in action. Work that stems from physical education with a feminist cultural studies perspective would thus include historically grounded studies, applications of feminist theory to the study of men, sport and masculinity, and deconstructs of the significance of the body. For some there may be a fear that with such approaches the theoretical and applied contributions of physical education may become lost in others' agendas. Yet, without broadening our focus beyond physical education to physical culture, key learning areas, and other sociocultural and biophysical sciences, we are likely to be asking questions and seeking solutions that are impotent.

2 Beyond school

Following the encouragement for equity research to move beyond physical education is the signpost for this research to account for factors or discourses both within and beyond school to more closely reflect young people's lives and learning. While several of the chapters in this text have addressed important questions relating to school curriculum and policy in terms of privileged discourses, I would argue that with the school as a bounded sphere of learning failing so many children, we need to recruit, recognise and understand new spaces and places for learning that are effective, inclusive and engaging, but are beyond formal school programmes (Tinning and Fitzclarence, 1992). We are increasingly aware that in any one space, such as a school system or school, there are multiple cultural identities (Ross, 2000). This has profound implications when we are asked to select a set of cultural attributes, knowledge bases, meanings, values, skills etc. for conscious transmission through the planned physical education curriculum. Increasingly, to make a selection and shape it into a physical education curriculum that suits the heterogeneity of young people is highly contentious if not impossible. Yet curriculum-makers continue to make selections, with assumptions and particular interests in mind (see Penney in Chapter 7). Therefore, the second signpost encourages researchers to recognise, trial, monitor, and analyse engagement in physical education or physical culture that is beyond the school. Work that seeks to understand people's multiple identities is already taking us beyond class-rooms, gymnasia, playgrounds, staffrooms, and school perimeters (see for example Benn, and Clarke, in this text). Meanwhile policy developments in England particularly are directly addressing the relationship between opportunities within physical education and those provided beyond it, in arenas of school, club and community sport (DCMS, 2000). Furthermore, young people are also actively extending the contexts of their learning. Many now have the motivation, lifestyle and resources to learn outside formal schooling given shifts in their access to money, the media, technology, and transport (Eisner, 2000; Young, 1998). What it means to be a school student is being reinvented through the interests of corporate capital. 'As culture becomes increasingly commercialised, the only type of citizenship that adult society offers to children is that of consumerism' (Giroux, 2000: 19). Young people's approach to learning is arguably now far more closely aligned to that of a consumer and a product. They may engage in physical education at school or, indeed, prefer options available through their families or communities. Further, the information revolution and the public pedagogies that it entails frees many learners to haphazardly explore as they wish, without boundaries and prescribed direction. 'Materials and means to construct personal projects of education and communication will be available . . . to us all' (Reid, 1998: 501) although we are warned that many girls are not engaging with information technology as readily as boys (Gilbert, 2001).

Wright and Macdonald's (in press) work with young people echoes other research (see, for example, Flintoff and Scraton, 2001) that has indicated that for girls particularly, activity out of school may have a far greater appeal than that within the curriculum and that for young people, there is often a lack of clear linkages between activity within and beyond schools. The indication is that for many girls and boys, their preferred engagement with physical activity outside school is at odds with what the formal school curriculum offers. As they become increasingly intolerant of curricula that are deemed irrelevant or inappropriate, and aware of alternative places and pathways for learning, as critical consumers they can bypass pre-selected, given, and inert curriculum and seek other products. In doing so, the learning/leisure binary conflates. Yet most of our equity research continues to focus narrowly upon the school as *the* site of meaningful learning for young people. In order to address inequity, research needs to include sites of learning outside schools and in particular, the meanings students make of 'on-line discourses' about lifestyle, diet, the body etc. This behoves researchers to account for the contemporary physical culture of different groups of young people and to explore these cultural spaces in terms of equity, access and responsible citizenship.

As all educators, physical educators need to recognise and work alongside not only the new spaces, places and technologies that now play a part in the physical education of young people, but also new people.

> If the school curriculum is to become an emancipatory experience for a much larger section of each cohort of students, this is going to require much greater involvement of many people who currently have no direct links with school, including parents and employers, and many activities by teachers and pupils which are not confined to the school nor, in conventional terms, are usually defined as 'educational' at all.
>
> (Young, 1998: 32).

This sentiment has also been expressed in much of the recent work of Hal Lawson (1998) who is arguing for attention to shift beyond the formal curriculum delivered by specialist physical education teachers to how coalitions of professionals and community members can become available to young people to enhance their learning.

Again, this signpost returns us to the question of what and how new spaces and places for equitable practices might be created and who might constitute partners in trialing and monitoring these. Also again, the new challenges bring potential hazards. The school environment can offer a relatively safe and supportive learning environment for the student-as-consumer compared to many options beyond school. Further, school–community links may not always see educational (and specifically equity) agendas remaining intact. For example, sporting organisations seeking to boost numbers could conceivably initiate a school–community programme with the aim of recruitment and not necessarily provide inclusive educational experiences for all students. If we are genuinely concerned with promoting greater equity in sport and in society it is arguably essential that more efforts are made to extend beyond binary relations. For researchers this demands the evaluation of the nature of engagements and transitions as young people move across sites of learning and physical activity.

3 *Beyond structuralism or poststructuralism*

The first two signposts are intended to encourage all those involved with researching gender questions related to physical education to set 'problems' in a broader, and I would argue, more contemporary framework, beyond the confines of the physical education subject, the school and its teachers. The second two signposts shift in their focus to questions of theoretical perspectives and approaches to gender equity research. More specifically, the third signpost gives some direction to the theoretical tension between structuralism and poststructuralism.

If the role of education systems is to assist all students to reach their individual potentials, then they have patently failed, as evidenced in this text and elsewhere (e.g. Apple, 1999; Morris, 2000; Young, 1998). We have seen ways in which equity policies and programmes have failed to override the influences of hegemonic masculinities, homophobia, and sportist discourses that are underpinned by power structures framed by gender, class and race and that social institutions such as schooling are generally *reproductive*; active in reproducing economic and cultural imbalances upon which a society is built (e.g. Bowles and Gintis, 1976). Bourdieu (1974) analysed cultural reproduction and the ways in which particular cultural capitals based upon language and values 'combine to create differential experiences for children of different social classes' (Bourdieu, 1974: 36). The point here is that structures relating to, for example, sex and class appear to still strongly shape students' experiences of schooling, and physical education within it, and therefore structuralism as a theoretical perspective has credence (Gilbert, 2001). Indeed, as Kirk *et al.* (1997) found in their studies of junior sport in Australia, socio-economic status had a strong bearing on the opportunities that children had to pursue club and representative sport. In the Introduction to this book, Evans and Penney also share my support for retaining a focus upon class, alongside other structural factors, to guide the research that we undertake. We agree that whether researching school physical education, club sport, recreational spaces, PETE, or physical culture, the intersection of structures such as gender, class and race remain significant but all too often are inadequately embraced.

However, there is a contrasting theoretical perspective, poststructuralism, that rejects the explanatory power of social structures as oversimplifying the complexity of social relationships and change. Rather, it focuses upon difference and diversity and views the self as socially and historically constructed and constantly changing with shifting contexts (Leistyna *et al.*, 1996). As reflected in several chapters in this text, this perspective shifts questions of gender equity from the experiences of all men, or all women, to differences within these categories. But as with any theoretical perspective, we should be circumspect in engaging in it wholeheartedly or exclusively. In a compelling paper, McLaren and Farahmandpur (2000) argue that poststructuralist positions are 'hyperindividualistic' with an overemphasis on identity politics, consumerism, pluralism and choice, and have lost sight of the reproductive structures. They do, however, acknowledge that post-structuralisms have drawn our attention to the complexity of circuits of power, the globalisation of knowledge and culture, shifts in time, space and boundaries, and how individuals may be active in constructing their life choices. Indeed, the first two signposts that I have outlined, draw on post-structuralist thinking with their encouragement to ask new questions that are beyond modernist curricular and institutional boundaries.

So where does this leave us in terms of gender agendas and theoretical perspectives that might shape our future research programmes? Here, we should return to the rejection of yet another dualism; structuralism versus poststructuralism. In the words of Apple (1999), we should retain our structuralist memory and when researching, trespass across structuralist and poststructuralist positions. Such a question might be, 'How does the socio-economic status of young people shape their engagement in physical culture? Furthermore, how does this class status articulate with gender, race, ethnicity and sexuality?' As Stanley (1997: 11) argues:

> The person missing is one who is complex and rounded, who is 'raced' and classed and gendered, who has a body and emotions and engages in sensible thought, and who inhabits space and place and time, and a person who may be a man but can be pathetic and weak, or who may be a woman but can be confidently powerful.

Connell's (2000) work with men and masculinity provides a good example of this type of research. In order to understand gender regimes, he encourages foci on globalization (e.g. technology, markets), bodies (e.g. sport, violence, health), symbolism (e.g. language, dress, sports), and power relations alongside their interface with practical issues and social problems that stem from differences within males and their widespread subordination of women. This call for plurality in theoretical perspectives brings us to the final signpost.

4 Beyond theory or practice

Signpost four returns to the opening of this chapter and the concern for the slippage between school/practitioner and university/theorist discourses together with questions of how policy-makers are positioned in the curriculum construction process. It directly aims to challenge the theory/practice binary. Physical education needs theory, policy and research that is grounded in practice or as Hall (1996: 30–1) wrote, research becomes 'prescriptive, exclusive and elitist'. Indeed, Connell (2000: 150) reflected that, 'Researchers have not done a great deal to help schools', predicated on the assumption that researchers are academics divorced from schools. It has also been claimed that schools and their teachers have become preoccupied with management and accountability issues and have not engaged with the intellectual dimension of their work (Smyth and Shacklock, 1998). We can reflect that in recent years, the imperatives of academics', policy-makers' and teachers' workplaces have undermined opportunities for educators across sites to engage with each others' perspectives and concerns. The slippage in the questions and language of research, policy and school practice is not unique to physical education gender research. In response to the 'crisis' in schooling, recent debates surrounding curriculum studies, theorizing and reform have been highly critical of the field with the use of descriptors such as 'disarray', 'blind', 'floundering' and 'schism' based upon the fragmentation of interests and the separation of concerns into theory and practice (e.g. McGinn, 1999; Morris, 2000; Reid, 1998). Might the same be said of gender research in physical education?

A way forward is to more closely link theorizing to action, to engage in praxis. Frequently the principle of praxis is best exemplified in research projects that entail partnerships that extend across the boundaries of schools, universities, clubs, teachers, parents and students (Fullan, 1999). For example, Ennis and her colleagues in the USA (1999) have worked with students, teachers, school administrators, and community leaders in a programme to increase physical activity participation amongst urban, African–American girls. In England, the Youth Sport Trust has brought together a multi-disciplinary team to work with a number of schools, their students and communities, to develop girl-friendly physical education (Kirk *et al.*, 2000). A strength of these examples of praxis is the breadth of voices which have had input. As both projects acknowledge, a weakness is school administrators' and teachers' difficulty in moving outside institutional constraints (e.g. showering policies, uniform) and conventional content (e.g. health-related fitness, sport, physical skill development). A number of curriculum projects in Australia would suggest that praxis is enriched when policy-makers and policy-making are integral to the change process preferably through all partners having a voice in policy creation (Kirk and Macdonald, 2001; Macdonald and Brooker, 1997).

The principle of praxis requires all potential stakeholders to also be involved in problem-setting. Transdisciplinary approaches to research take this further and suggest that problems are best defined by a community/group who 'lives' with the problem and that they recruit academics and other relevant professionals to come together with them, address the issue at hand, and move on (Johnston, 1998). Such an approach to knowledge production and problem-solving in equity research would be dynamic, share power and ownership, allow for a breadth of input, and be weakly institutionalised and bounded. Nevertheless, as with signpost two, there is a caution with this approach in the current climate. What the communities/groups 'set' as the problem might be framed within the discourses of the feminist backlash (e.g. Lingard and Douglas, 1999) and the pro-sport lobbies and thereby have a minimal or negative impact upon new ways of seeing gender equity in physical education.

Conclusion: what are we concerned about?

Why are we concerned about gender equity and physical education? Are we concerned that as a result of inequitable practices and programmes, fewer students are likely to lead a physically active lifestyle with health budget consequences? Or are we concerned about the emotional wellbeing of pupils and teachers who are oppressed, marginalised and harassed for their skills, interests, appearances, cultural practices or sexualities, that lie outside hegemonic discourses? Or are we concerned that unless physical education shifts to become more inclusive, that it will be considered anachronistic in schools, education systems, and universities? Or are we concerned that without drawing upon the skills and interests of all young people across a breadth of physical activities, the quality and success of elite sport performances will decline? The possibilities are many yet such positions shape academics', policy-makers', teachers', parents', community groups', and students' engagement with questions of gender equity.

Each reader will have her/his own position with respect to why gender equity in physical education may be important. With our own unique subjectivities, we identify with different politics, policies, imperatives, and strategies. However, as highlighted in the Introduction of this book and borne out in several chapters, while most physical educators claim a commitment to equity, there has been little surface level, let alone deep, change. It is hoped that the above-mentioned signposts may inform and strengthen your gender agendas as a physical educator in a school, bureaucracy, or university. Further, you might be encouraged to extend your networks to form partnerships with health professionals, 'classroom' teachers, youth workers, recreation officers, policy-makers, community organisations, parents, and, especially, students. It is important to remember that any strategies for change are frequently met with a mixture of resentment, anger, comfort, contempt, strength or relief (Fullan, 1999). Yet, taken alone or together, the signposts might generate new ways to add depth, breadth or relevance to the gender problem, challenge or task at hand.

While the literature in gender equity and physical education recognises the difficulty in creating meaningful change within current educational structures, the majority of analyses and innovations overlook the broader and more significant questions. Who are our young people, and what, where and how do they learn? For as long as gender reform focuses upon subjects, teachers, school-based lessons, and other modernist structures of schools that obfuscate difference, meaningful learning and the impact of technology, gender equity initiatives will fail to produce significant advances. Also, while physical education academics and teachers talk past each other, their gender agendas will be fractured and physical education will become more alienating for more students.

References

Apple, M. (1999) *Power, Meaning and Identity*, New York: Peter Lang.

Armour, K. and Jones, R. (1998) *Physical Education Teachers' Lives and Careers*, London: Falmer Press.

Ball, S. (1994) *Education Reform: A Critical and Post-structural Approach*, Buckingham: Open University Press.

Benn, T. (2001) Muslim women in teacher training: issues of gender, 'race' and religion, in D. Penney (ed.) *Gender and Physical Education: Contemporary Issues and Future Directions*, London: Routledge.

Bernstein, B. (1996) *Pedagogy, Symbolic Control and Identity: Theory, Research, Critique*, London: Taylor & Francis.

Bischoff, J. (1982) Equal opportunity, satisfaction and success: an exploratory study on co-educational volleyball, *Journal of Teaching in Physical Education* Fall: 3–12.

Bourdieu, P. (1974) The school as a conservative force: scholastic and cultural inequalities (trans. J. Whitehouse), in J. Eggleston (ed.) *Research in the Sociology of Education*, London: Methuen, pp. 32–46.

Bowles, S. and Gintis, H. (1976) *Schooling in Capitalist America: Educational Reform and the Contradictions of Economic Life*, London: Routledge.

Brown, D. and Rich, E. (2001) Gender positioning as pedagogical practice in teaching physical education, in D. Penney (ed.) *Gender and Physical Education. Contemporary Issues and Future Directions*, London: Routledge.

Clarke, G. (2001) Difference matters: sexuality and physical education, in D. Penney (ed.) *Gender and Physical Education: Contemporary Issues and Future Directions*, London: Routledge.

Connell, R. (2000) *The Men and the Boys*, Sydney: Allen & Unwin.

Department for Culture, Media and Sport (DCMS) (2000) *A Sporting Future for All*, London: DCMS.

Eisner, E. (2000) Those who ignore the past . . . : 12 'easy' lessons for the next millennium, *Journal of Curriculum Studies* 32(2): 343–57.

Ennis, C. (1999) Communicating the value of active, healthy lifestyles to urban students, *Quest* 51: 164–9.

Evans, J. and Penney, D. (2001) Introduction, in D. Penney (ed.) *Gender and Physical Education: Contemporary Issues and Future Directions*, London: Routledge.

Evans, M., Rosen, D. and O'Brien, D. (1986) Three teachers share their views on the teaching of mixed physical education, *British Journal of Physical Education* 17(4): 152 and 154.

Flintoff, A. and Scraton, S. (2001) Stepping into active leisure? Young women's perceptions of active lifestyles and their experiences of school physical education, *Sport, Education and Society* 6(1): 5–21.

Fullan, M. (1999) *Change Forces: The Sequel*, Lewes: Falmer Press.

Gilbert, P. (2001) Redefining gender issues for the twenty-first century: putting girls' education back on the agenda, *Curriculum Perspectives* 21(1): 1–8.

Giroux, H. (2000) *Stealing Innocence*, New York: St Martin's Press.

Glover, S. and Macdonald, D. (1997) Working with the health and physical education statement and profile in physical education teacher education, *The ACHPER Healthy Lifestyles Journal* 44(2): 21–5.

Goodson, I. (1988) *The Making of Curriculum*, London: Falmer Press.

Griffin, P. (1985) Teachers' perception of and responses to sex equity problems in a middle school physical education program, *Research Quarterly for Exercise and Sport* 56(2): 103–11.

Hall, M.A. (1996) *Feminism and Sporting Bodies*, Champaign, IL: Human Kinetics.

Hargreaves, A. and Earl, L. (1994) Triple transitions: educating early adolescents in the changing Canadian context, *Curriculum Perspectives* 14(3): 1–9.

Johnston, R. (1998) *The Changing Nature and Forms of Knowledge: A Review*, Canberra: Department of Employment, Education, Training and Youth Affairs.

Kirk, D. (1993) *The Body, Schooling and Culture*, Geelong, Vic: Deakin University Press.

Kirk, D. (1999) Physical culture, physical education and relational analysis, *Sport, Education and Society* 4(1): 63–73.

Kirk, D., Carlson, T., O'Connor, A., Burke, P., Davis, K. and Glover, S. (1997) The economic impact on families of children's participation in junior sport, *The Australian Journal of Science and Medicine in Sport* 29(2): 27–33.

Kirk, D., Fitzgerald, H., Wang, J., Biddle, S. and Claxton, C. (2000) Towards girl friendly physical education? A report on a large-scale, school-based intervention. Paper presented at the Pre-Olympic Congress, Brisbane, September.

Kirk, D. and Macdonald, D. (1999) Imagining beyond the present, *Teaching Elementary Physical Education*, November: 25–8.

Kirk, D. and Macdonald, D. (2001) Teacher voice and ownership of curriculum change, *Journal of Curriculum Studies* 33(5): 000–00.

Lawson, H. (1998) Here today, gone tomorrow? A framework for analyzing the development, transformation, and disappearance of helping fields, *Quest* 50: 225–37.

Layder, D. (1997) *Modern Social Theory*, London: UCL Press.

Leistyna, P., Woodrum, A. and Sherblom, S. (1996) *Breaking Free: The Transformative Power of Critical Pedagogy*, Cambridge: Harvard Educational Review.

Lingard, R. and Douglas, P. (1999) *Men Engaging Feminisms: Pro-feminism, Back-lashes and Schooling*, Buckingham: Open University Press.

Macdonald, D. and Brooker, R. (1997) Moving beyond the crisis in secondary physical education: an Australian initiative, *Journal of Teaching in Physical Education* 16: 155–75.

Macdonald, D. and Tinning, R. (1995) Physical education teacher education and the trend to proletarianization: a case study, *Journal of Teaching in Physical Education* 15(1): 98–118.

Macdonald, D., Glasby, P. and Carlson, T. (2000) The health and physical education profile Queensland style, *The ACHPER Healthy Lifestyles Journal* 47(1): 5–8.

Macdonald, D., Penney, P., Hunter, L. and Carlson, T. (in press). Teacher knowledge and the disjunction between school curricula and teacher education, *Asia-Pacific Journal of Teacher Education*.

McGinn, N. (1999) What is required for successful education reform? Learning from errors, *Education Practice and Theory* 21(1): 7–21.

McLaren, P. and Farahmandpur, R. (2000) Reconsidering Marx in post-marxist times: a requiem for postmodernism, *Educational Researcher* 29(3): 25–33.

Morris, M. (2000) The pit and the pendulum: taking risks talking about the future of the curriculum, *Journal of Curriculum Theorizing* 16(3): 3–6.

O'Sullivan, M., Bush, K. and Gehring, M. (2001) Gender equity and physical education: a USA perspective, in D. Penney (ed.) *Gender and Physical Education: Contemporary Issues and Future Directions*, London: Routledge.

Penney, D. (2001) Gendered policies, in D. Penney (ed.) *Gender and Physical Education: Contemporary Issues and Future Directions*, London: Routledge.

Penney, D. and Evans, J. (1999) *Politics, Policy and Practice in Physical Education*, London: E & FN Spon.

Reid, W. (1998) Erasmus, gates, and the end of curriculum, *Journal of Curriculum Studies* 30(5): 499–501.

Ross, A. (2000) *Curriculum: Construction and Critique*, London: Falmer Press.

Scraton, S. (1986) Gender and girls' physical education, *British Journal of Physical Education* 17(4): 145–7.

Smyth, J. and Shacklock, G. (1998) *Re-making Teaching*, London: Routledge.

Stanley, E. (1997) *Knowing Feminisms*, London: Sage.

Talbot, M. (2000) Deconstruction – reconstruction of physical education: gender perspectives. Pre-Olympic Scientific Congress, Brisbane, September.

Tinning, R. and Fitzclarence, L. (1992) Postmodern youth culture and the crisis in Australian secondary school physical education, *Quest* 44: 287–303.

Vertinsky, P. (1984) In search of a gender dimension: an empirical investigation of teacher preferences for teaching strategies in physical education, *Journal of Curriculum Studies* 16(4): 425–30.

Wright, J. (1997) Fundamental motor skills testing as problematic practice: a feminist analysis, *The ACHPER Healthy Lifestyles Journal* 44(4): 18–20.

Wright, J. (2001) Physical education teacher education: sites of progress or resistance, in D. Penney (ed.) *Gender and Physical Education: Contemporary Issues and Future Directions*, London: Routledge.

Wright, J. and Macdonald, D. (in press) Young people and physical culture, *Leisure Studies*.

Young, M. (1998) *The Curriculum of the Future*, London: Falmer Press.

Index